Picture Piecing

Traditional Quilts

Cynthia England

Acknowledgements

Special thanks to the quilt artists who made the quilts in this book so beautiful; Denise Green, Richard Larson, Rhonda Gabriel and Ronda Stockton. A big thank you to my editors, Jerryann Corbin and Sherry McConnell whose suggestions and attention to detail were greatly appreciated.

My sincere gratitude to the supporting staff whose constant encouragement made this book possible: Lynn Berna, Linda Bannan, Ivy Croft, Patty Dillon, Sharon Dinsmore, Donna Dockall, David Gabriel, Christine Jahnke, Phyllis Hall, Julie Moser, Dorothy Owens, and Virginia Spiers. Thanks to my husband, Warren, and children, Monica, Travis and Stephen for putting up with a flaky artist who is a workaholic.

I am grateful to my enthusiastic students who over the years have taught me so much!

Dedication

For Mr. Loopner whose wit and twisted sense of humor make life worth living.

Rather than use the Trademark (™) and the Registered Trademark (®) symbols on products referenced throughout this book we have credited them in the Resource Listing. There is no intention of infringement. The product names are used in an editorial context.

Printed in the United States of America

Picture Piecing Traditional Quilts

LCCN 2013948150
ISBN 978-0-9720963-1-7

1. Patchwork. 2. Quilting - Patterns. 3. Picture Piecing.

Credits

Editor-in-Chief........................Sherry McConnell
Managing Editor......................Jerryann Corbin
Cover Design....................................Peri Poloni
Book Design / Illustration........Cynthia England
Quilt Photography............Michael McCormick
Photography...........................Cynthia England
Hand Model............................Monica England

Front Cover Quilt:
Wanda's Violets by Cynthia England
Inside Cover Quilting: Richard Larson
Back Inside Cover Quilting: Denise Green
Back Cover Quilts: top - right to left):
Indigo Lights by Cynthia England
Autumn Leaves by Cynthia England
Sweetheart Roses by Cynthia England
Field of Violets by Cynthia England
Center, down
African Violets by Cynthia England
Falling Leaves by Rhonda Gabriel
Christine's Rose Garden by Cynthia England

Quilts designed and pieced by Cynthia England unless otherwise noted.

England Design
1201 Sunset Drive
Dickinson, TX 77539
(281) 534-1858
fax (281) 534-1623

www.englanddesign.com

Contents

Picture Pieced Designs

Traditional Pieced Designs

Introduction

Inside you will find designs for all levels.
Each design gives you several options.
Choose a quick project, like a table runner,
a medium sized project, such as a wall hanging,
or a more challenging full-size quilt.

Picture Pieced design blocks are based on a 6″ finished block and will fit into a multitude of traditional quilts.

The quilt designs will stand by themselves as well.
You can leave out the Picture Pieced designs
to make your own traditional quilt.
Let your imagination run wild!

The Picture Piecing technique is VERY forgiving with options for a lot of cheating.... read on!

Traditional Basics

As a quilter who has been sewing for over 40 years, take some advice....*If you are a new quilter, either take a beginner class or purchase a beginning quilting book. You will not regret it!*

Even after all this time, I still find time saving tips and techniques. Quilters are known for coming up with innovative techniques to make things easier. If there is a technique you don't understand, look it up on the internet. There are videos that will explain the process.

Use high quality 100% cotton fabric. It is best to buy different types of prints. Mix it up; batiks, plaids, calicos. Variety makes the quilt more interesting. Test colorfastness beforehand to avoid surprises later.

Before beginning a large project I would recommend making one block so you can see how the blocks go together before rotary cutting the entire quilt.

Tools

Gather the tools that you will be using.

- Use a good quality sewing machine. Use scant 1/4″ seam allowances with 12 stitches per inch for the stitch length. It is helpful to use a single hole needle plate in the machine. Most machines come with a wide hole that allows the needle to go back and forth to produce a zig-zag. This plate can be replaced with a single-hole needle plate which only allows the needle to go straight up and down. The advantage is that small pieces of fabric do not slip down into that larger zig-zag hole, making intricate piecing easier.

- Rotary cutter, ruler and mat. It is important to be familiar with rotary cutting methods. This is a *must have* tool. There are many different size projects and blocks in this book. But, all of the Picture Pieced blocks finish at 6″. It is very helpful to have a $6^{1/2}$″ X $6^{1/2}$″ square for final trimming.

- A good hot iron; one that does NOT have the auto-shut-off feature. Press every seam.

- A Strip Stick. This is a pressing stick that was designed by Anne Babb for ironing seams when strip quilting. Similar to a sewer's ham, only crafted with the quilter in mind. When several sewn strips are next to each other, seams get in each other's way. This curved stick elevates the seam and allows you to iron each seam separately. Seams come out so flat that you don't have the little "folds" on the other side of the seam. So, you just have to iron one side of the seam, rather than both sides. This cuts your ironing time in half!

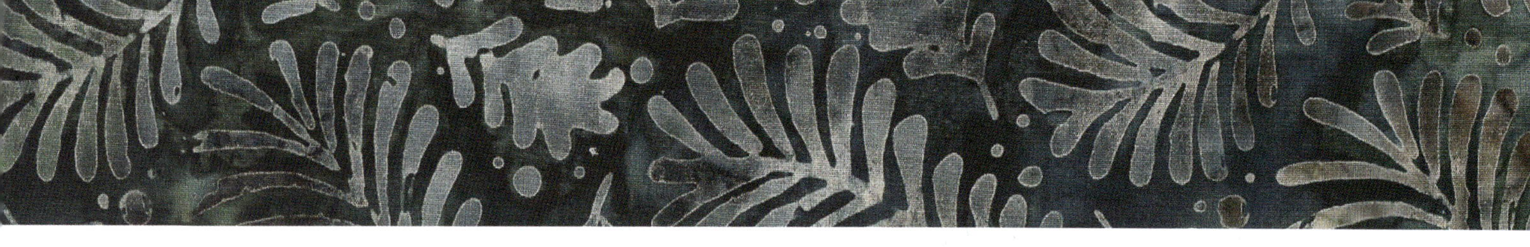

Triangle Piecing Techniques

One of the great things about quilting is that there is more than one technique to get the same result. Following are three options for half square triangles. Check the internet for videos on both of the speed demon methods.

Many, many designs call for half square triangles. I decide on the technique by the quantity I have to make. For instance, if 12 half square triangles are needed, I would take 6 squares and cut them diagonally, but if I need 120 half square triangles it is much faster to choose one of the quick paper techniques.

Half Square Triangles

Start with a square and cut it in half diagonally to yield two triangles. To account for the diagonal seam allowance add 7/8" to the finished size of the half square triangle to determine the cut size of the square.

Triangles on a Roll

This is a very popular technique. Use purchased triangle paper that is printed on a roll of thin paper. These rolls come in many different sizes. Place fabrics right side together, place the triangle paper on top and sew a small stitch along the dotted lines. No need to add the 7/8" here. All of the math has been calculated for you. Trim with a rotary cutter along the solid lines. On the plus side this is *very* accurate. The only down side is purchasing the triangle rolls for every project.

Half Square Grid Papers

My favorite way of piecing mass quantities of half squares is the Triangulations method developed by Brenda Henning. In this technique, you purchase a disc for your computer. In addition to half square triangle grid papers there are quarter square triangles and flying geese units.

Working with Stripes

Striped fabrics add interest to any quilt. But, working with stripes and rotary cutting shapes can be tricky.

For instance, when a square is cut diagonally to yield two triangles, the stripe looks like this when cut apart:

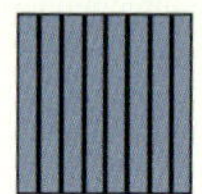

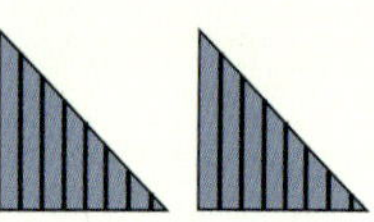

No difference here. The stripes run up and down.

But, take that same square and quarter cut it to yield four triangles.

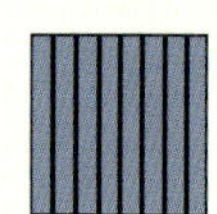

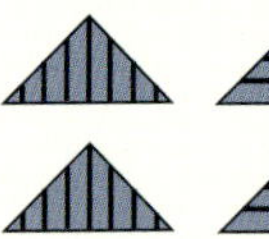
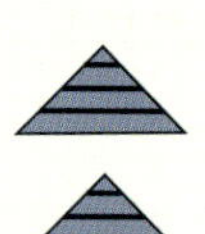

This time there will be four triangles; two with stripes running up and down, and two with stripes running side ways.

When rotary cutting squares, be *very* careful when laying the striped patches out in the block. If necessary, individual patches can be rotary cut using templates. You can always buy more fabric. Stripes are worth the trouble!

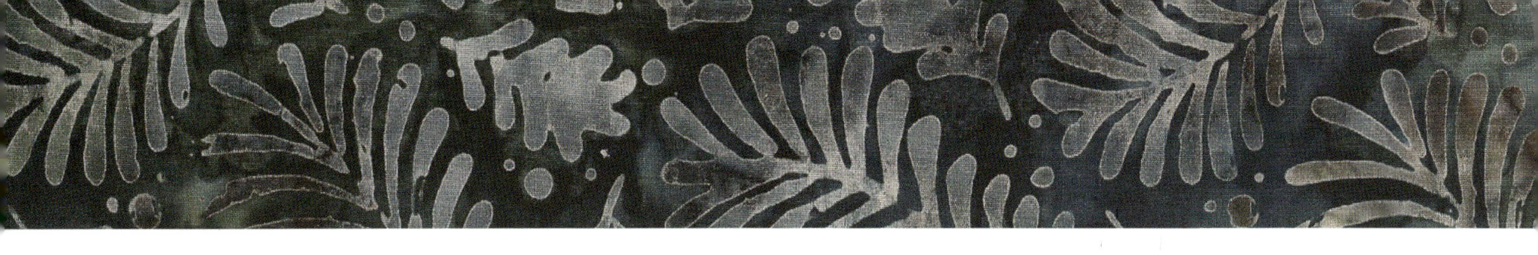

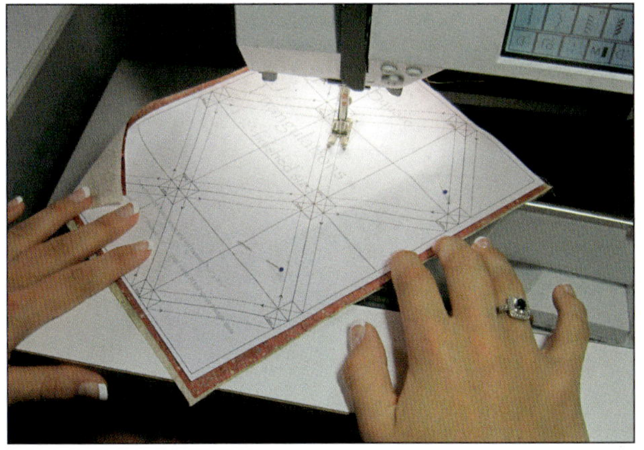

Select the size of finished triangle you want and print off that page from your computer. *Make sure there is no page scaling selected on your computer. It needs to be printed at 100%.* When the page is printed, compare the measurement of the printed Triangulation grid to the dimensions stated on the grid. It is important that the size is accurate.

I copy this sheet on my copy machine for the number of half square triangles needed. Some quilters are concerned that the copy machine may slightly change the size. In my experience, this has not been an issue. Sewing is the same as for triangle rolls. Fabrics are cut about the same size as computer paper ($8^{1/2}$" X 11") and faced right sides together. Place printed grid paper on top, and sew along dotted lines with a small stitch. Cut on solid lines. The best thing about the Triangulations disc is that there are *all kinds* of sizes for future projects, and you don't have to keep buying the papers. In addition to half square triangle grid papers, there are quarter square triangles and flying geese units. Save the planet! Recycle those messed up letter-sized sheets of paper.

Detailed Finishing

Picture Pieced blocks in this book have embroidery details for stems in each design. They are indicated by squiggly lines on their corresponding Trim Guides.

Use 2 strands of matching DMC embroidery thread and stem stitch the lines. These lines can also be stitched using the sewing machine, if you prefer.

Stem Stitch
Work from left to right, take even slightly slanted stitches along the line. The needle comes out on the left side of the previous stitch.

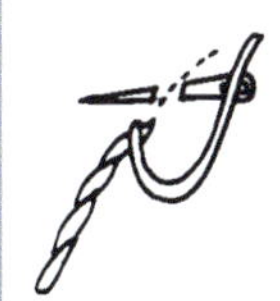

Assembling the Top

After making the blocks, square to the size indicated, and follow the setting directions for each of the designs. In this book there are three types of block sets used: Straight Set, Strip Set and my favorite, the Diagonal Set.

Straight Set

Blocks are joined horizontally by rows. Rows are then sewn together. Match seams when joining. Autumn Leaves on Page 49 is an example of a straight set quilt.

Strip Set

Falling Leaves on Page 43 is a Strip Set quilt. Blocks are joined in long strips and then sewn together, vertically. Match seams when joining rows.

Diagonal Set

Blocks are placed on point. Construction is by rows with side triangles and corners incorporated into those rows. If you choose a stripe fabric for the setting triangles, beware! See the "Working with Stripes" box on Page 6.

The reason this set is my favorite is because the diagonal lines move your eye around the quilt and frequently creates secondary patterns. Take the same blocks and set them with a straight set, they will have a totally different look. A diagonal set also makes a larger quilt.

Side triangles and corners are generally larger than needed, and after sewing, the edges are trimmed straight. The Field of Violets quilt on Page 101 is a diagonal set quilt as well as Corbin Gold Rush on Page 109.

Border Treatments

Sometimes before you begin, you know what the border will be. Frequently, I find a focus fabric and pull fabrics for my quilt around this favorite fabric; but, not all of the time. Sometimes the blocks come first, and the border later. The border should repeat the colors that are in the quilt top. Hang your quilt top on the design wall, and try different fabrics to see which is the best fit.

After your finished quilt top is squared with a ruler, rotary mat and cutter, it is time to add the borders. Press the quilt top carefully. Do not stretch it out of shape. I prefer to cut on the straight of grain for borders. If strips need to be joined to obtain length, join at a 45 degree angle. Press the seam open. It is less noticeable than a straight seam across. If borders will be seamed, add extra fabric to account for diagonal seaming.

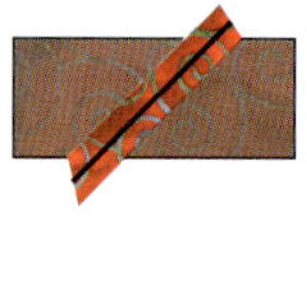

There are three basic border techniques commonly used to finish a quilt: square cut corners, pieced corners, and mitered corners.

Square Cut Corners

The square cut corner border is the fastest and easiest of the three. Side borders are joined to the quilt top first, then the top and bottom borders are attached. To make a square cut corner border, begin by measuring your quilt. See illustration below.

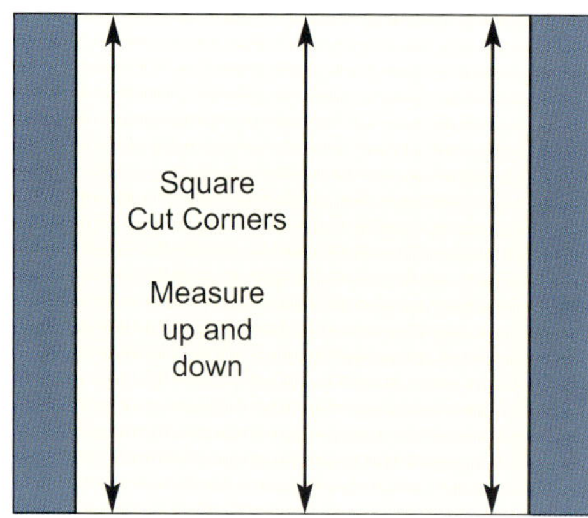

- Measure the length of the quilt top vertically. Measure from both sides, and again, down the center. Take the average of the three for the final measurement. No matter how careful you were when the quilt

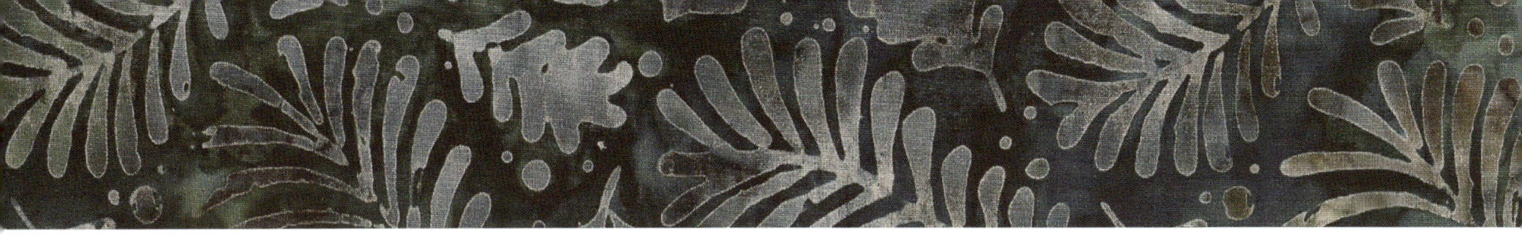

top was constructed there will probably be some variance in these measurements

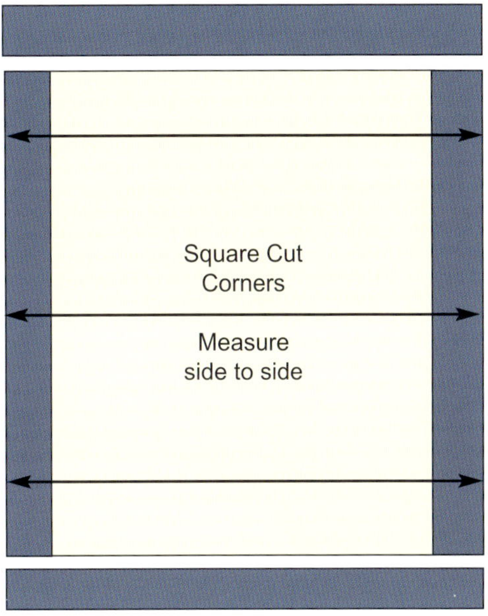

- Cut border strips the width of the border desired, and seam to the correct length.
- Sew a border strip to each side of the quilt top. Press the seam toward the border.
- Repeat the process this time measuring the quilt horizontally.
- Cut border strips the desired width, and seam to the horizontal measurement. Sew to the top and bottom of the quilt top. Press.

Southern Cross is an example of a quilt with a Square Cut Corner. See Page 123.

Pieced Corners

This type of border allows you to add that little bit of pizazz in the corners. It is best to repeat some of the same units from the quilt top; sometimes extending out of the quilt top design. The width of the pieced block determines the width of the border.

- Measure the quilt top vertically in three places. Average these measurements and cut your two side borders.
- Measure your quilt top horizontally in three places. Average these measurements and cut your top and bottom borders.
- Sew on side borders. Press towards border.
- Sew a corner block to each end of the top and bottom borders. Press towards border.
- Sew the top and bottom borders to the quilt top. Press seam toward border.

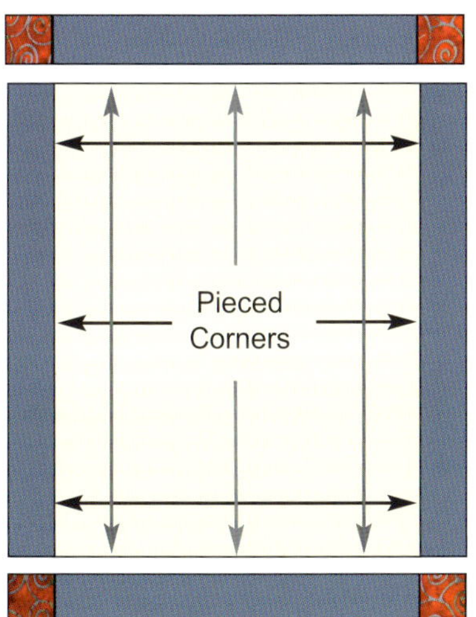

Mitered Corners

Mitered corners resemble a picture frame. If you have more than one border, sew them together before mitering. Sweetheart Roses (Page 75) and Indigo Lights (Page 115) both have mitered corners.

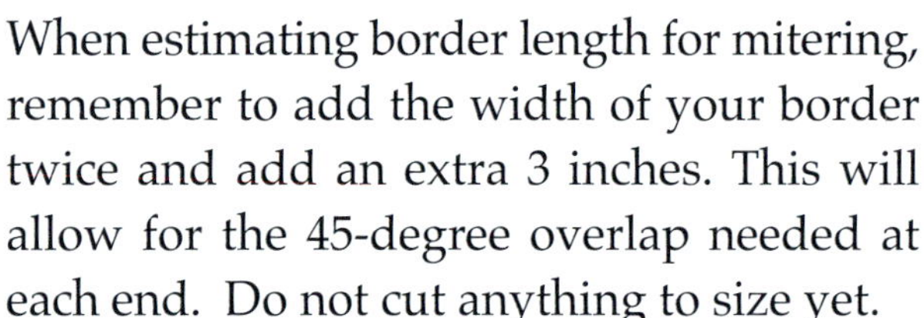

When estimating border length for mitering, remember to add the width of your border twice and add an extra 3 inches. This will allow for the 45-degree overlap needed at each end. Do not cut anything to size yet.

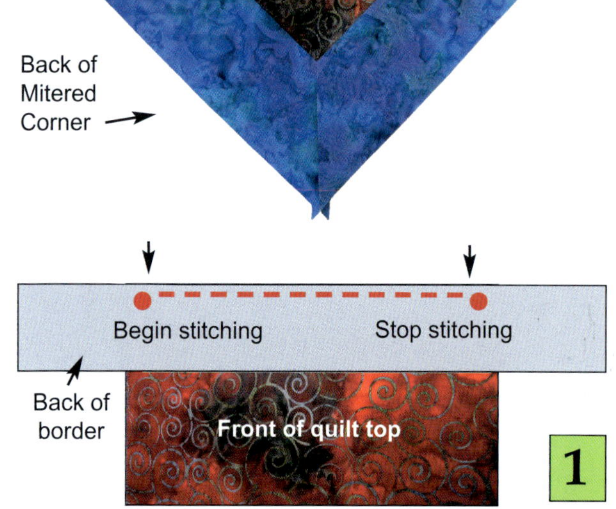

Center the border strip on the quilt top edge, and begin stitching 1/4″ from the left quilt top edge, to 1/4″ from the right quilt top edge. Backstitch to secure (Photo 1). Press toward the border. Do the same on the other sides.

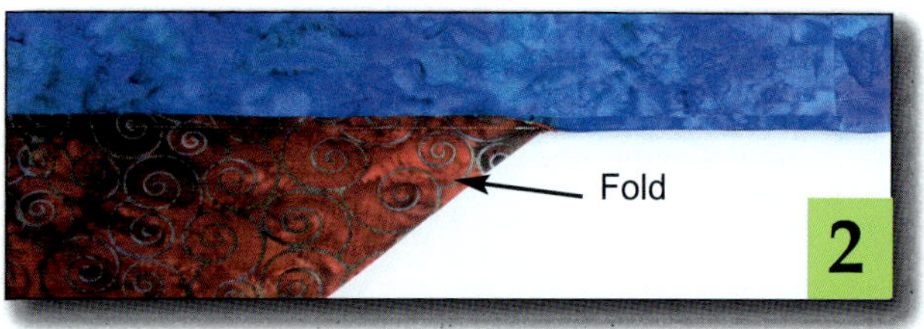

Face the quilt top, right side up, on a flat surface. Bring the right side up at a 45-degree angle and align the border edges. Check to make sure that the seams line up on both borders (Photo 2).

Place a quilter's ruler along the fold, and use a pencil to mark a line (Photo 3).

Pin the borders together and stitch this line (Photo 4). Backstitch to secure. Do not cut anything at this point. *Before trimming,* open up the top, and check to see that seams align (especially if you have more than one border to miter). If they do not, make adjustments to the seam.

Use the quilter's ruler and cut 1/4″ beyond the sewn seam (Photo 5). Follow the same process for the other three corners. Iron the seam open.

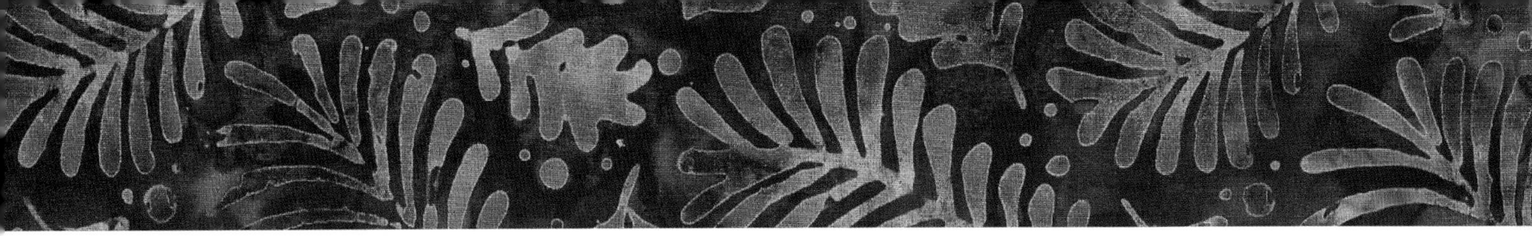

Backing

The same fabric can be used on the reverse of your quilt, or you can consider it another design opportunity, and piece a design on the back. Piecing the back is a good way to use up your left over fabrics. For quilting on a domestic machine, the backing should extend at least 2 inches around the outside dimensions of your finished top.

Longarm Info

More and more quilters are having their quilts quilted by a longarm professional. If you choose to go this route then you will need additional fabric for the backing. Longarmers recommend at least 5″ to 6″ larger than your quilt top on *all* sides.

It is best not to have a vertical seam running directly down the center of your backing; instead, off-set the seam. Longarmers prefer horizontal backing seams, due to the way the quilt is loaded into the machine.

If I have intricate piecing along the edges of the quilt, I use my walking foot and stay-stitch the edges down about 1/8″ from the raw edge. I have also added an extra border to the outside of my top, if I am planning to have the binding come right up to the edge of the piecing. This extra border is removed before binding.

It is very important to tell the longarmer exactly what you are looking for. Listen to their recommendations and ask to see their work. Remember you get what you pay for!

Batting

Choose a good quality batting. There are many different manufacturers and lofts. Batting comes in different colors; white, natural and black. Look for one that can be quilted at least 5 inches apart.

I like cotton batting the best, but the polyester battings are nice if your quilt is heavy. They retain their shape nicely.

Like the backing, you will need at least 2 inches around for domestic or hand quilting; or 5″ to 6″ if you are sending your quilt to the longarmer. Most longarm quilters have a favorite batting they like to use. Check with them first.

If domestic or hand quilting, layer the top, batting, and backing. Hand baste, or use safety pins to hold the layers together for quilting. No basting is necessary for longarm quilting.

Quilting

Throughout this book you will find close-ups of the quilting to give you ideas and hints on quilting designs to enhance your work.

Notice that the quilting motifs are varied throughout the quilts, making the most of the designs in the blank areas.

For the Picture Piecing designs, a monofilament thread was used to outline flowers and leaves. Expert longarm quilters, Richard Larson and Denise Green have some helpful tips.

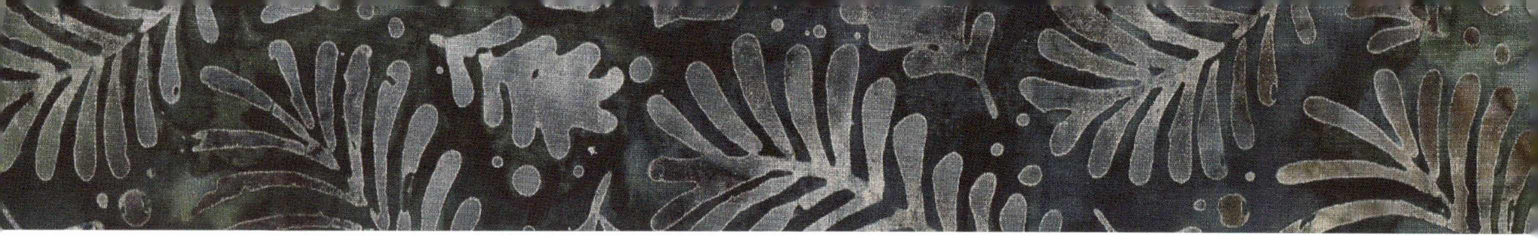

Richard recommends Superior Mono Poly thread, which is made out of polyester, not nylon. This thread is high-heat resistant, iron and dryer safe, will not become brittle over time, and will not discolor. He uses this thread when stitching around applique or places that need to be hidden. When stitching in the ditch he also uses a MR3.5 needle with Superior Sew Fine thread. It eliminates build up and does not show as much. He likes Superior's Omin Tex 30 weight thread and suggests using a MR4.0 needle for the majority of the quilting.

Denise's "go to" batting for most quilts is usually an 80/20 blend either from Hobbs Bonded Fibers or Pellon Legacy; however for a quilt that will hang as wall art or in a show, she prefers Quilters Dream Poly Select, or a dual batting of wool and a thin cotton for quilts that benefit from that extra bit of oomph. She prefers Superior Sew Fine thread for the majority of her work, as this thin thread allows for dense quilting without being too "thready".

Binding

There are two types of binding; straight of grain, and bias binding. The quilts in this book all use straight of grain binding. Bias binding is needed when the quilt has curves in the borders such as a scalloped border.

I like narrow binding and usually cut 2 1/4" wide binding strips. The strips are then folded in half when applied to the quilt. The finished size becomes about 3/8". Many quilters prefer wider binding; anywhere between 2 1/2" to 2 3/4".

Straight of Grain Binding

This type of binding works well for square or rectangular quilts.

Determining how much binding is needed:

- Measure the outside circumference of the quilt and add 10". This additional 10" will allow you to join the binding later.

  As an example: if I were binding the Autumn Leaves wall hanging, the finished size of the quilt is 55" X 55". You would need 220" for the circumference of the quilt, plus 10", making the total number of inches needed 230". Divide that number by 40" (WOF - width of fabric from bolt). So, you would need 5 3/4 strips of 2 1/4" binding. Round up to 6 strips.

- Sew these strips together using a 45 degree angle, so the seam will lay flat. Iron this seam open. Fold the entire strip of binding with wrong sides together, lengthwise; and press.

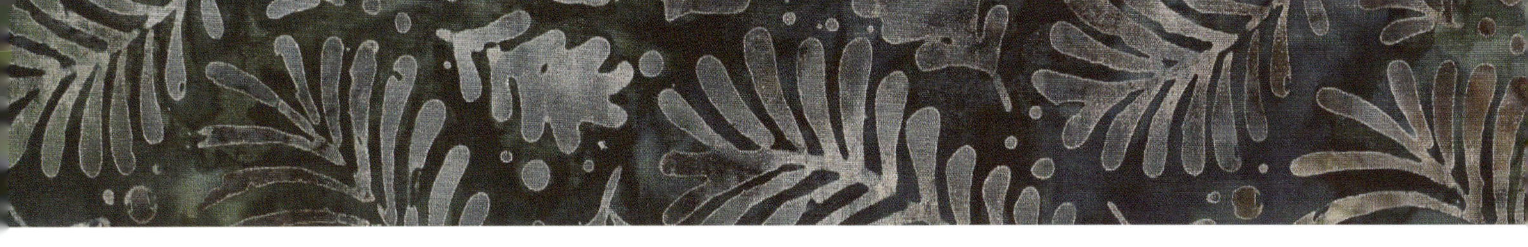

Hand or Machine Sewn?

Before applying the binding, square your quilt with the rotary cutter.

Traditionally, binding is sewn to the front of the quilt, turned to the back, and slip stitched to secure it. It is helpful to use a walking foot for this application. Make sure and tug the binding nice and tight when you turn the binding to the back. Judges check to see if the binding is full. If I am not planning to enter the quilt in a show, or if it is a community service quilt, I do not like to spend the time doing the hand work, especially if the entire quilt is machine made.

Here are two different techniques for applying binding with no handwork.

Top Stitched Binding

Stitching will be visible from the quilt top. Use a thread in the bobbin that matches the back of the quilt, and a thread in the top of the machine that matches the binding.

- Match raw edges of binding to raw edges of quilt on the ***back side*** of quilt. Use a walking foot and sew 1/4″ from the edge.
- Flip binding over to the ***right side*** of the quilt.
- Top stitch along the edge, securing the binding.

Stitch-in-the-Ditch Binding

This is my favorite way of finishing the binding. It looks the most like the traditional way of applying binding. The stitching is not visible from the front. Use a thread in the bobbin that matches the binding of the quilt, and a top thread that matches the quilt top. In the picture I used white thread so it is easier to see.

- Match raw edges of binding to raw edges of quilt on the ***right side*** of quilt. Use a walking foot and sew 1/4″ from the edge.
- Flip binding over to the ***back side*** of the quilt, and stitch-in-the-ditch from the right side. Sew next to the binding seam, securing the binding along the back. See Page 15, Photo 8.

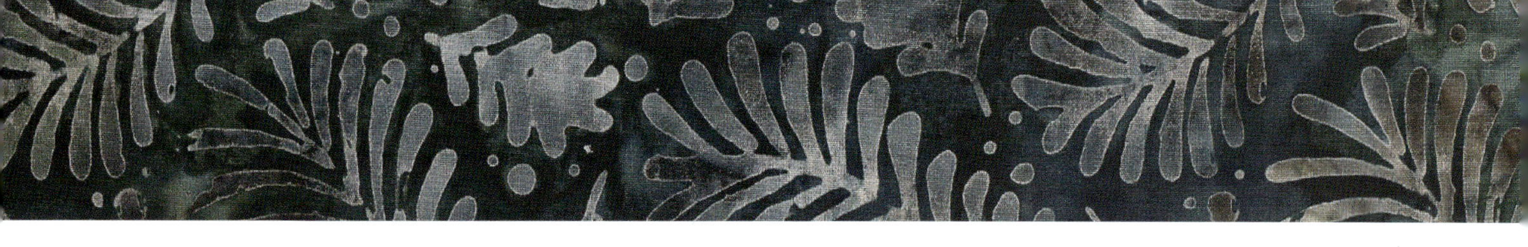

Applying Straight Binding

Whether you decide to sew the binding to the front or back, the technique is the same. Odd angle binding is described on Page 16.

Match raw edges of binding to raw edges of quilt. Use a walking foot and start binding about midpoint on one side of the quilt. Do not start too close to a corner, because the seam lines (that join the strips of binding) can cause a problem if they fall in a corner.

Begin sewing about eight inches from the end of the binding. Backstitch to secure the thread, and sew 1/4" from the raw edge. Continue sewing until 1/4" from the corner of the quilt. Sew out to the corner at a 45-degree angle. This angle is very helpful for the next step (Photo 1).

Fold binding up at a 45-degree angle (Photo 2). Then, fold it down on the angle that you just made, lining up the edge of the binding with the next side of the quilt (Photo 3). Hold the fold down so it lays flat. This extra fabric is needed for a neat corner when the binding is stitched down.

Begin sewing at the folded edge and backstitch to secure threads (Photo 4). Sew to the next corner, and repeat the process. Stitch all four corners in the same manner. When you get about ten to twelve inches from where the binding was originally sewn, stop and backstitch. Final seam directions on next page.

After seaming, flip over, and either machine or hand-stitch to secure (Photo 5).

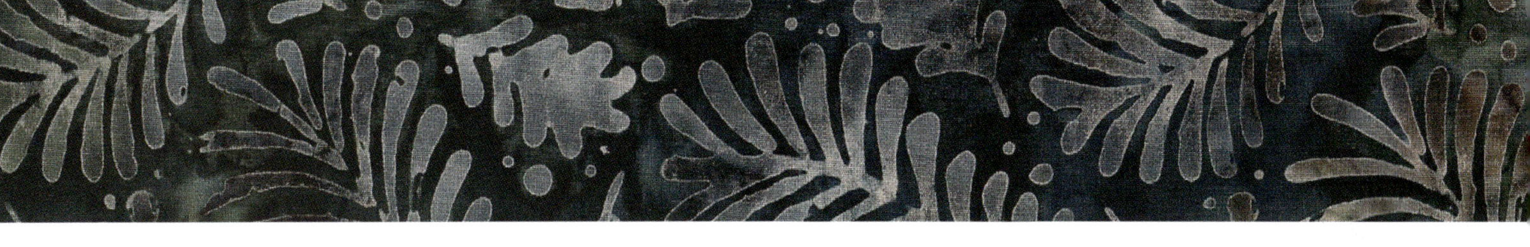

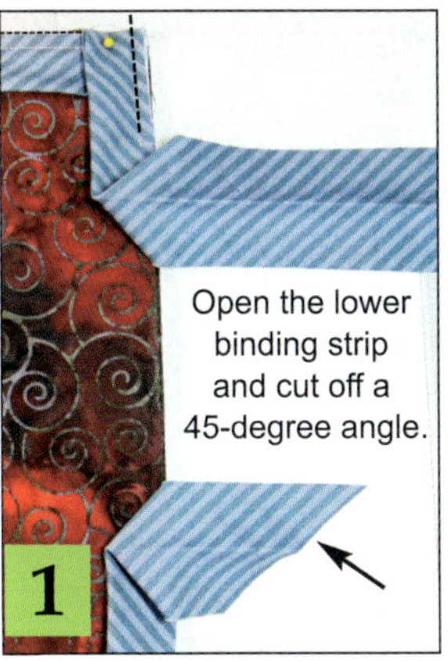

Final Seam for Binding

This technique is foolproof! The final seam must be cut and joined at a 45-degree angle. If it is joined with a straight seam it will contain excess fabric and will not lay flat. For professional results, lay the quilt on a flat surface.

1. Open the lower binding strip and cut off a 45-degree angle.

2. Place the lower binding strip along the edge of the quilt and insert a straight pin, horizontally, 1/2" from top of the cut angle.

3. Lay the top binding strip over the lower one. Place another straight pin through the *bottom layer* of the binding that is on top. Use the original pin as a guide for placement.

4. The second pin inserted becomes the marking place for cutting the 45-degree angle in the top binding strip.

5. Open the top binding and cut at a 45-degree angle using the pin as a starting point. ***Both 45-degree cuts must be made in the same direction.*** Remove the pin before cutting this angle.

6. Join the two binding ends as shown. Place the joined binding along the edge of quilt, and sew it to the quilt (Photo 7). Complete the binding by slip-stitching it on the back, or applying it by machine as described on Page 13. If using the stitch-in-the-ditch binding method, the back of the quilt will look like Photo 8.

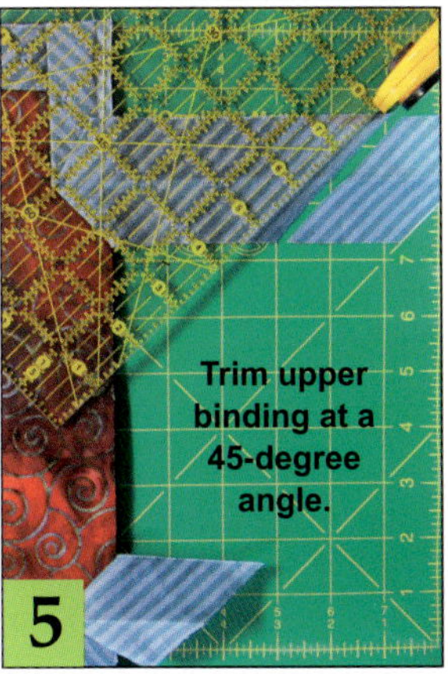

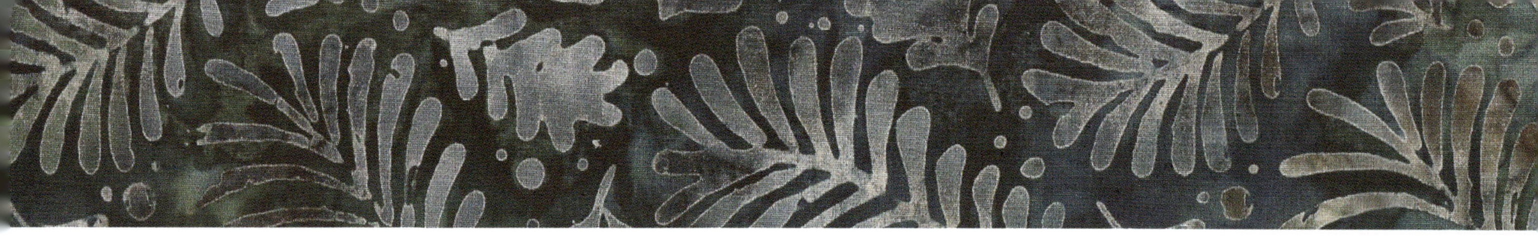

Odd Angle Binding

Several of the projects in this book have odd angles in them; Maple Leaf table runner, Hot Pink Roses runner, and Scarlett Pinwheels. When working with odd angles, the corners are folded a little differently.

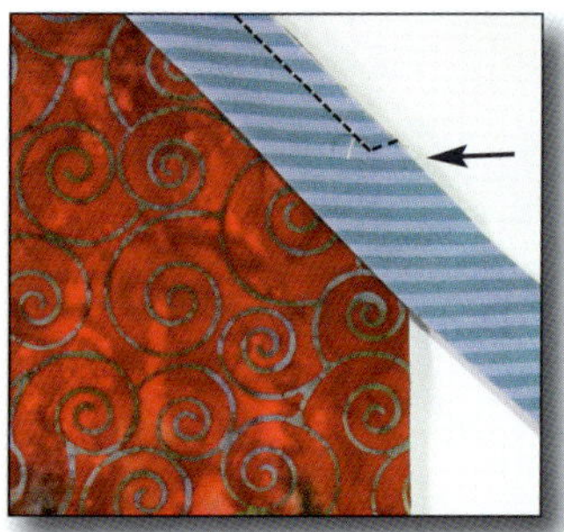

At the corner, angle out as pictured.

Fold back so the binding raw edge is even with the quilt top; not the 45-degree angle you would for traditional binding.

Start sewing from the end of the edge of the quilt (dotted line).

The finished corner will look like this from the front side of the quilt.

Blocking

Sometimes when the quilt is finished it doesn't hang as flat as you would like. Blocking a quilt is much like blocking needlework, the piece is pinned to the design wall, dampened, and then steamed. Test to make sure your fabrics are colorfast before blocking.

Display Sleeve

This sleeve evenly distributes the weight of the quilt and is a way to hang it with out placing holes in the quilt. The size of the quilt determines the type of sleeve that is used. Small wall hangings are light, and just require one sleeve, whereas a large quilt would benefit from two display sleeves.

Prepare The Sleeve

Measure the width of the quilt and subtract about $1^{1/2}$". Use a rotary cutter and ruler to cut a piece of fabric about $8\ ^{1/2}$" wide by the sleeve length. On the short end, with the right side facing the table, fold 1/4" in from the edge, then fold again. Sew along this edge, matching the thread to the sleeve fabric. Bring the

Front side of sleeve

two wrong sides together and stitch. Fold the sleeve in half, right sides out, and iron the seam open (see below). This seam will face the quilt backing and will not show. Now, you have a choice of how the sleeve is attached.

Back side of sleeve

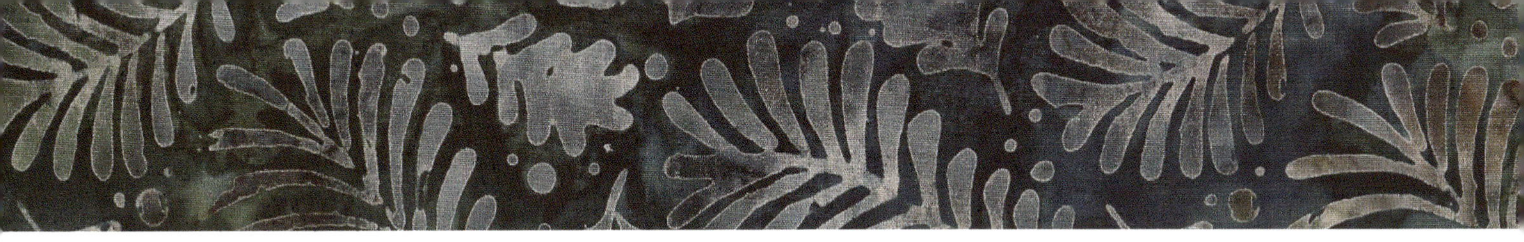

Large Display Sleeve

This method is commonly used for quilts that are exhibited in shows that need excess fabric within the sleeve to accommodate the rods used for hanging. It is the best kind of sleeve for large quilts. Place the sleeve seam side down on the back of the quilt, center it and place along the top edge of the quilt about 1/2″ from the top of the binding.

Use a slip-stitch and attach the top of the sleeve to the quilt. Try to make every third stitch go through the front of the quilt, but be careful that these stitches do not show. This will make the sleeve stronger, and help to distribute the weight. After the top line of stitching is completed on the sleeve, push the quilt tube up to extend over to the bottom edge of the binding. Pin it in place, and slip-stitch the bottom line of the quilt sleeve. Take a few extra stitches at the corners for reinforcement. Pushing the edge of the sleeve up will give the rod the extra space it requires without pulling on the quilt top.

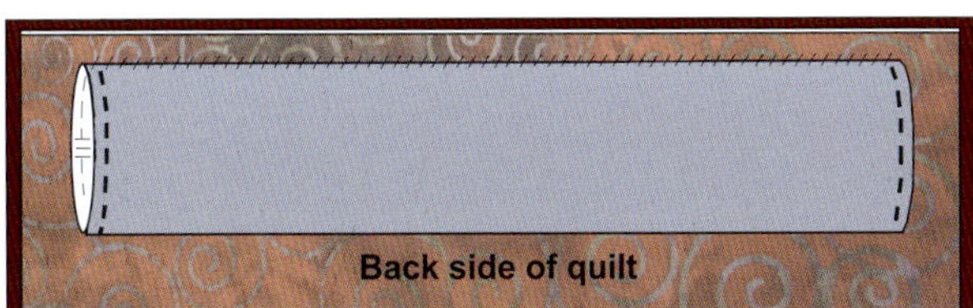

For large quilts, it is helpful to make two sleeves and leave a gap between them. Large quilts need additional hangers to sustain the weight. A nail can be placed in the wall at the gap for support. Make sure the nail hits a stud (this makes my Engineer husband happy).

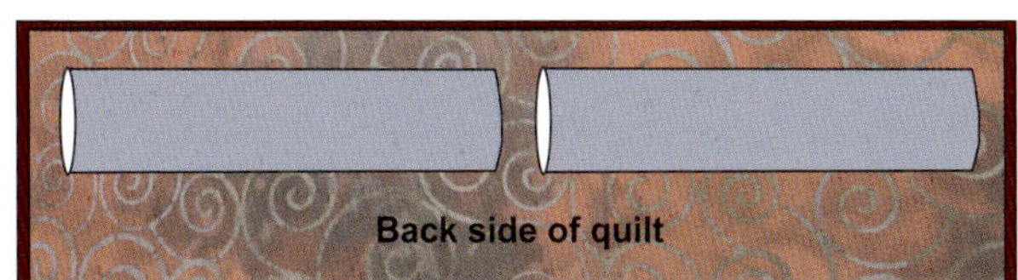

Cutting Down the Hand Sewing

If the wall hanging is small (less than 30″), the top edge of the sleeve can be sewn into the binding. To do this, position the sleeve along the back of the quilt before the binding is sewn. Pin it in place, and machine stitch through the sleeve at the same time the binding is stitched on. Slip-stitch the bottom of the sleeve. Keep the sleeve flat, and *do not* push up the sleeve when slip stitching as in the Display Sleeve method. If you choose to do this, use a small, thin dowel for hanging.

"If the entire quilt is machine made, why spend precious handwork on the sleeve?"

Eliminating Hand Sewing!

Recently, I discovered a "no hand-stitch sleeve" method. I make *many* wall hangings and am always trying to find a faster way of finishing. That last bit of hand stitching along the bottom of the sleeve is annoying. For this technique to work, the wall hanging must have at least one border. Here is how to get around that hand stitching.

Make the sleeve about 1″ to 2″ wider than needed. Turn in the short side edges at each side about 1/4″ and press. Fold over again and sew to finish the sleeve edges. Turn the

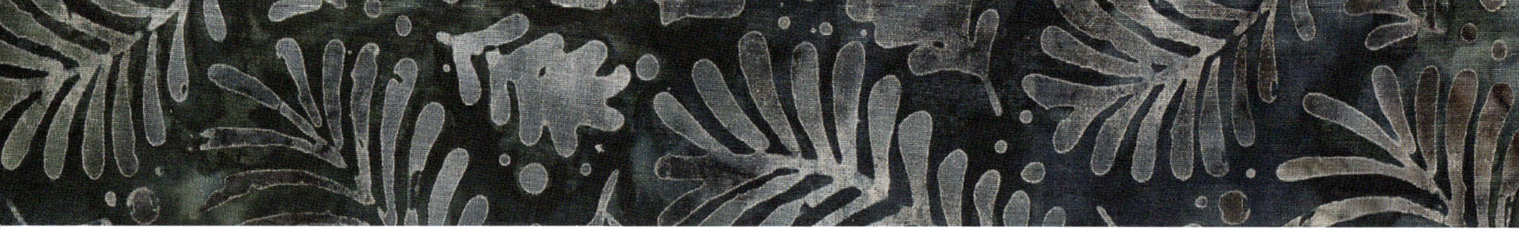

wall hanging with the back side facing up and position the sleeve open near the top of the wall hanging. Pin in place. Flip the wall hanging over to the *right side* and use a monofilament thread, and stitch in the ditch along one of the borders. Turn the wall hanging to the back side again, and press the sleeve up along this stitched line. Trim off the excess at the top, and secure the sleeve at the top when you sew the binding. This technique is not recommended for a large quilt, because there is no extra room in the sleeve except for a small dowel.

Labeling the Quilt

It is very important to label your quilt after it is completed. Include your name, the quilt's name, size, date completed, and the city and state. Consider including design inspirations and any anecdotes that you would like others to know about the quilt.

It can be written in permanent ink on muslin, embroidered, or the computer can print one for you. Test to make sure that the ink is permanent. Heat set any ink work with the iron.

------ About the Designs in this Book -------

There are many different kinds of fabrics used in the projects in this book. Some have a traditional feel, others a contemporary flare. This was intentional, so that you can see the same block in different color combinations and quilt styles.

We would love to see what you come up with! Feel free to email pictures of your finished quilts! Project pictures can be posted on the site to give others inspiration and ideas for their own quilts. We quilters like to share!

Everyone learns differently. I am a visual learner, so there are lots of illustrations and pictures throughout this book. There are free tutorials on the website at www.englanddesign.com. Enjoy!

Cynthia England

Picture Piecing Basics

Picture Piecing is frequently mistaken for another popular quilting technique called Paper Piecing or Foundation Piecing.

What's different?

1 In Picture Piecing, seams are sewn next to paper, rather than through it; therefore, there is **no paper to remove** from the seams. Foundation piecing requires you to remove all paper from seams regardless of how accurate the seam is.

2 In Picture Piecing there is **less fabric waste** because seam allowance is estimated from the *right* side. In foundation piecing, scraps of fabrics are used and the surplus is then cut away.

3 Pattern pieces are ironed **to the right side of the fabric** in Picture Piecing, rather than the wrong side. This enables you to use the fabric to its best advantage. In Foundation Piecing directional fabric, (such as a stripe fabric, water fabric, tree bark fabric) poses a problem. You have to guess which way the pattern piece will flip back to accommodate the directional fabric. In Picture Piecing, there is no flipping back. What you see is what you get.

4 In Picture Piecing, *any* two pattern pieces that make a pair can be sewn together. This allows **chain stitching** within a section, making construction faster. Sewing can be more assembly-line processed. Different parts of one section can be worked simultaneously. Foundation piecing requires sewing *only* one pattern piece at a time making sewing more time consuming.

"If the seam doesn't line up after sewing, don't rip the seam out! Either move the pattern pieces over or sew closer!"

5 The best reason for using the Picture Piecing technique: ***cheating is allowed and is encouraged!*** Most of the time seams do not have to line up exactly. If the seam is not sewn close enough to the edge of the paper, this technique allows repositioning of the pattern piece. Simply remove the pattern piece and iron again.

Working with the Patterns—

The Picture Piecing technique uses two patterns; a master pattern on bond paper and an identical pattern, this one on freezer paper. The master pattern will be used for sewing reference. The freezer paper pattern will be cut apart and used as iron-on templates. **Fabric notations** will be identical on the two patterns.

The pattern is traced onto plastic coated freezer paper, shiny side down. Look for freezer paper in your local quilt shop or the grocery store. Often it is located near the canning supplies.

3 ways to transfer pattern onto freezer paper.

- **Trace** by hand
- **Scan and print** from computer
- **Purchase** pre-printed from your favorite quilt shop or from our website: www.englanddesign.com

The back side is shiny and has a wax coating. This wax coating sticks to the fabric when heated with an iron.

The freezer paper (shiny side down) is placed on top of the pattern. Lines of the pattern will be visible through the freezer paper.

Adding the Fudge Factor

Got your attention with the idea of fudge, didn't I? Unfortunately not the sweet kind, but sweet in a "make it easier" way.

With a typical Picture Pieced design the finished wall hanging can be squared to any size when it is completed. In this book the finished size is *very* important because blocks in the traditional quilt must fit together. To make sure that the finished size of the block is correct the design floats in the background. The blocks have been designed larger and will be trimmed to exact size.

- When *hand tracing* the patterns use a pencil and straight edge and **add 1/4" all around the outer edges of the master pattern**. Trace all lines and notations. The traced pattern will be cut apart. The original that you traced from will be used as your Master Pattern.
- When *scanning from the computer,* center pattern and add an extra 1/2" all around with the computer or a straight edge.
- If purchasing pre-printed freezer paper patterns, no need to add this extra 1/2", it will already be included. Just start cutting.

Freezer paper patterns can be used multiple times. After sewing the block, save the pattern pieces and place each section in a labeled zipper-type sandwich bag to use again.

Basic Notations

Circled Numbers ——— ①

Circled numbers refer to where each pattern piece goes after it is cut apart. Unlike foundation piecing, this is not necessarily the order in which the pieces are sewn together. In foundation piecing, sewing is by number *only* in sequential order. With Picture Piecing, *any* two pattern pieces that share a common side can be sewn together. Circled numbers denote placement and give you an idea of what to sew next. Picture Pieced patterns in this book include *Sewing Sequence* information for each section. Once you understand the process, it will come naturally.

Bold Lines and Letters —A

Bold lines and letters indicate major sections. When breaking up a design, the first divisions usually become major sections. After the pattern is divided and notations are placed, these bold lines and bold letters are the first things that are marked. Major sections are the last seams to be joined. First, sew smaller pattern pieces within the major section together. Then, join the major sections to complete the piece.

Dashed Lines --------------------

Dashed lines indicate sub-sections within the bold-lined sections. These must be sewn together first before they can be joined to another group. Dashed lines help break up the pattern visually so smaller sub-sections can

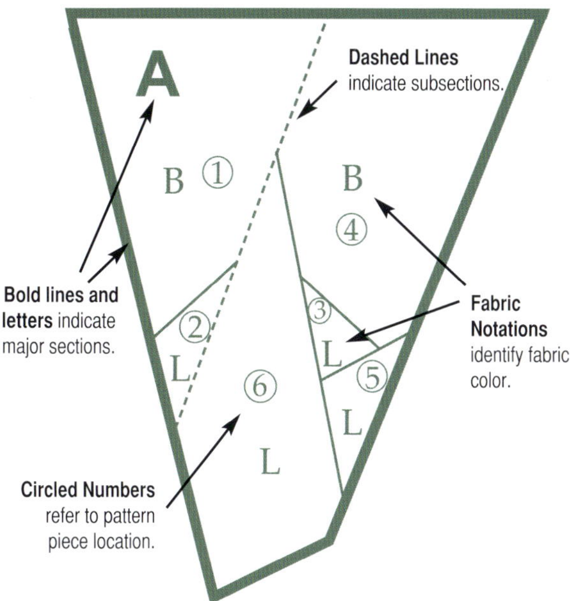

be spotted quickly. Dashed lines also indicate which pattern piece is to be sewn on next. Usually, solid lines are sewn together before dashed lines. Visualize a nine-patch block. The three squares must be sewn together before the rows are joined; Picture Piecing uses the same concept. In this technique, you look for two pieces that share a common seam.

In the illustration above, ① and ② share a common seam and circled numbers ③ and ④ share a common seam. Either of these pairs can be sewn. In the pattern above, pattern piece ③ and pattern piece ④ have to be sewn together first before adding ⑤.

Fabric Notations ——— B, G1

Fabric notations are indicated by small upper-case letters and letters with numbers. These correspond to the fabric selection chart. To make the fabric selection chart, clip a small triangle swatch from each fabric. Using a glue stick, attach the fabric swatches to a piece of white paper. Under each swatch write a letter. The more fabrics in a design the more valuable the color chart becomes.

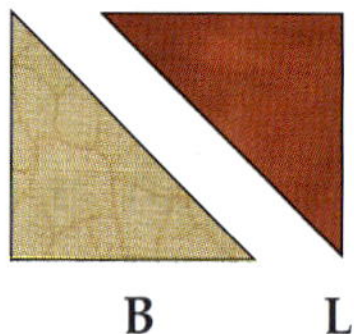

If there is more than one shade of a color, place the fabrics according to value (light to dark). If there are three greens; G1 for the lightest fabric, G2 for the medium, and G3 for the dark. The higher the number, the darker the fabric. If you are planning to use the front and back of the fabric, cut two swatches and place them according to value. There are beautiful fabrics which have varying shades in them. If using two or more parts of a single fabric, cut a swatch from each part.

Circle Over an Intersection 

A circle over an intersection is an important seam that must match. This is the **only** time a seam must match. For example, on Page 92 in the Violet Pattern, between section A and section C there is a circle over an intersection. There is a leaf on either side of the seam. It will look better if the seam matches when joined. Pin before sewing this seam.

Blender Arc ———————)

A blender arc is used to designate a seam where you may want the fabric color to match on either side. For instance the fabrics in the maple leaf block are batiks. These fabrics have color variations in them. When the leaves are constructed it looks best to have the same shade of fabric on each side of the leaf division. The blender arc was placed over the subdivided line to help with color placement.

Pre-Sewing Strips ———————

Each Picture Piecing design in this book provides "Pre-Sewing Recommendations" in the directions. To make the small pieces easier it is recommended to pre-sew fabric strips together before beginning. Sew 1/4" seam allowance along the length of the strip. Press open. Pre-sewing is optional. The technique works fine if you cut each pattern piece individually as well.

**Please note that directional fabrics can be difficult to pre-sew and they are sometimes easier to work with if the pattern pieces are all cut apart.*

When cutting out the freezer paper pattern, leave small pattern pieces that share a common seam together. Iron the pattern pieces along the sewn seam on the right side of the fabric as shown in the illustration above.

Maple Leaf Sewing Sequence

Note: If you have presewn strips you will already have prepped some of the sewn pieces. For instance, 1 and 2 will already be sewn.

Section A: Sew 1 to 2, 3 to 4. Add 5 to 3/4, then add 6. Join 1/2 to 3-6.
Section B: Sew 1 to 2, 6 to 7. Sew 1/2 to 3, add 4, then 5. Join 1-5 to 6/7.
Section C: Sew 1 to 2 add 3, add 4, add 5, then 6.
Section D: Sew 1 to 2 add 3, add 4, then 5.
Section E: Sew 1 to 2, add 3.
Sew Sections A to B. Sew Section C to D. Join AB to CD. Add E.

Maple Leaf Pattern

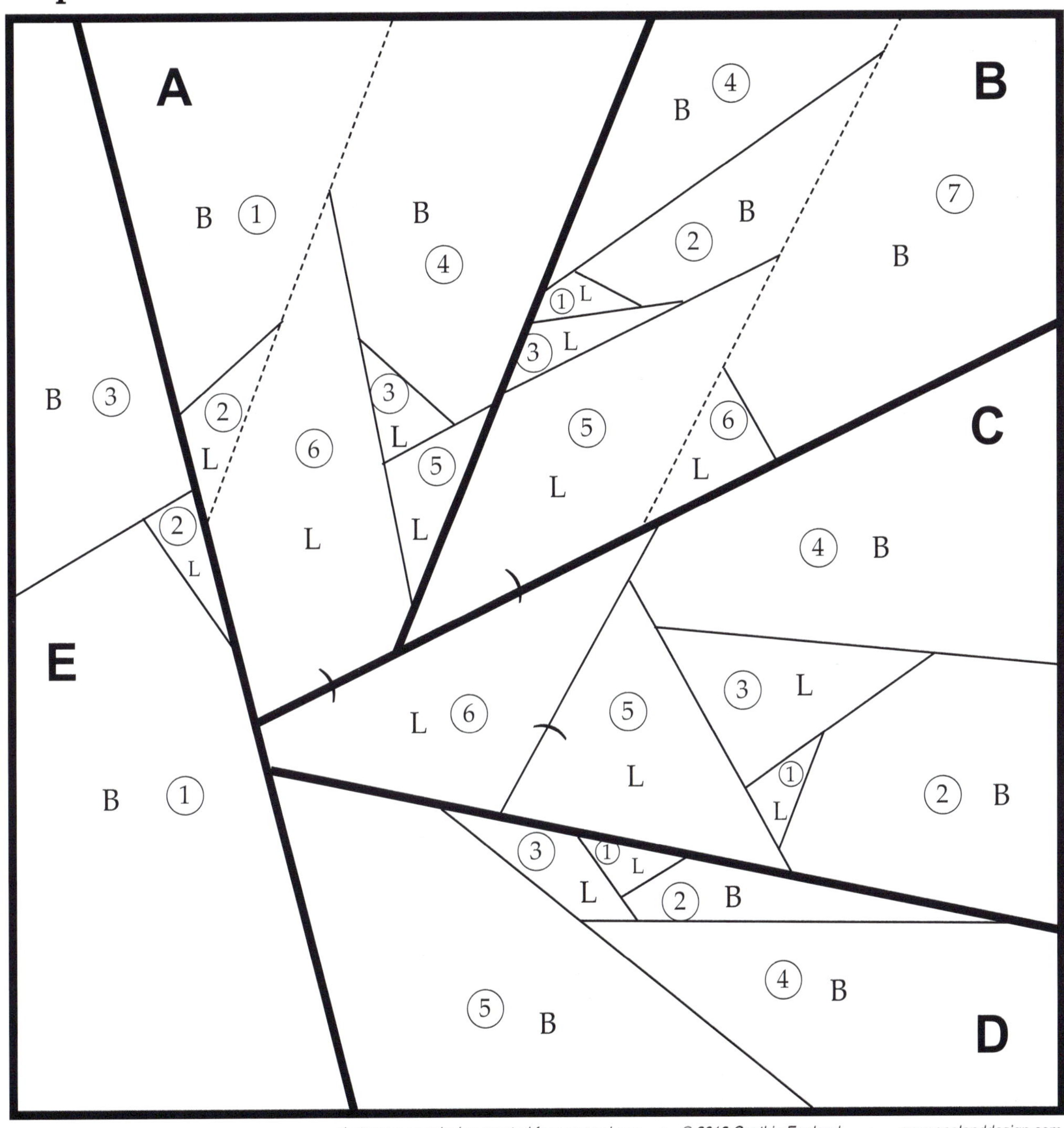

IMPORTANT:
When tracing onto freezer paper ADD 1/4″ extra all around for squaring outer edges.
Note: If you are using pre-printed freezer paper cut on lines. NO EXTRA needed.
After trimming, the block will measure 6 1/2″ X 6 1/2″.

Sewing

It is important to have the pattern pieces and the Master Pattern next to each other. Do not tape your pattern to the wall in front of you or place it on the opposite side of the sewing machine. You will constantly be verifying placement of pattern pieces by putting them on top of the Master pattern.

The construction method is different in Picture Piecing. With traditional piecing you strive for very accurate piecing. The more precise you are with your 1/4″ seams the easier it will go together. Accuracy is not as important in Picture Piecing. Basically, you sew a seam. If you didn't sew close enough you pull the pattern piece off and reposition it. More details to follow, read on.

Prep Work

There are a few items that I use on a constant basis that I find helpful for Picture Piecing.

- Use the top side of a plastic tray or plastic shoebox lid to lay out the pattern pieces while working with them. Pattern pieces will slide and will be easy to sort. Pick a tray that is not deep and one that is smooth on one side.
- This technique is ironing intensive. Make sure your iron is located near by. If possible, use a travel iron for the piecing. When the project gets larger use the full-size iron. Choose a travel iron that has small holes or no holes on the sole plate. If small pattern pieces fall under one of the holes they will not heat up.

- There is more scissor cutting than rotary cutting in this technique. I prefer to use serrated scissors. Serrated scissors have one blade that is smooth and one blade that is serrated like a knife. They allow very fine trimming.

Serrated Scissors have a blade that is like a knife. Makes cutting easier.

Some sewers use two different pairs of scissors to cut paper and fabric. With serrated scissors, I have not had any trouble with the blades dulling any differently when cutting either paper or fabric. I just use the one pair. There are several good brands out there, but I *love* Karen K. Buckley's Perfect Scissors pictured above. There are several sizes. I prefer the longer blade. When serrated blade scissors are sharpened they sharpen the smooth side.

- Use zipper-type baggies to organize the pattern pieces by section. The freezer paper pattern pieces can be used multiple times and are easily stored in labeled baggies.

- Index cards or sticky notes are helpful to block off the sections that you are *not* working on, allowing you to concentrate on the area you *are* working on.

Getting Started

Note: If you are using pre-printed freezer paper you can skip this tracing step.

- Place freezer paper over the Master Pattern and trace all lines. Add an outside border of 1/2″ all around to include extra seam allowance in case you need some fudge room later.
- Place a plastic tray or shoebox lid under your work area and use paper scissors to cut out the **freezer** paper pattern (not the Master Pattern) on the bold lines.

Referring to the Maple Leaf pattern, Section A, you should have five separate bold-lined sections A through E. Starting with A, identify which pattern pieces can be left together that share a common seam. Use the pre-sewn strips you have already prepared. Pattern pieces ① and ② are a pair and can be cut out as one piece and pattern pieces ③ and ④ can be cut out as one piece.

Cut out all of the pieces in Section A, place them in a sandwich bag, and label it **Section A**. Repeat this process with each section identifying which pattern pieces share the common seam, and cut the remaining pattern pieces out separately. Place each section in its own bag, and label them with a permanent marker. Feel free to use a rotary cutter when cutting apart large sections.

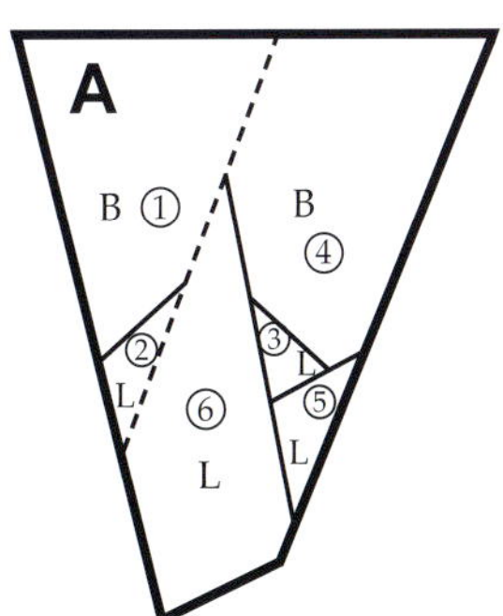

Ironing and Cutting

Use a cotton setting when ironing the pattern pieces to the fabric. No steam. Work with one section at a time, sorting the pattern pieces by color notation. Press the pattern pieces to the *right* side of the fabric, leaving 1/4″ around each piece. If there are two pattern pieces of the same color, place them at least 1/2″ apart, allowing for a 1/4″ seam allowance around each pattern piece. Try placing a finger in between the pattern pieces to determine the amount of space needed.

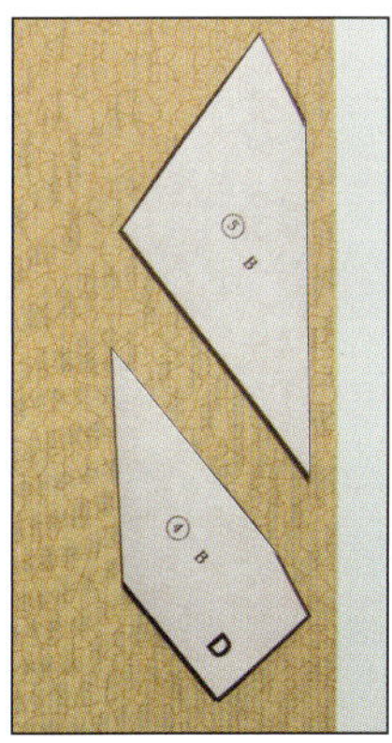

To save time, use the edge of the fabric for one side of the 1/4″ seam allowance. Cut a generous 1/4″. This allows room for repositioning the pattern piece, after sewing, if necessary. Avoid the tendency to cut a proportionally smaller seam allowance on small pattern pieces. Trim as neatly as possible, keep the fabric edges parallel with the pattern piece edges.

Square off and clip any long points to 1/4". The more accurately the pattern pieces are cut, the easier it will be to sew them together. However, there is no need to measure and cut them out with a rotary cutter. The plan is to move them *over* if the seam isn't perfect. The important thing to remember is to keep seam lines straight and parallel while you work with them. Trim seams

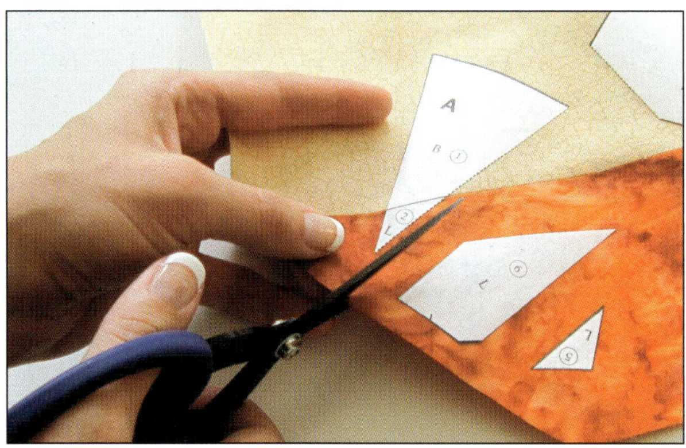

straight while sewing to maintain a straight line. If the seam lines are cut neat and straight the pattern pieces can be butted up at the top. So, if you can't see the fold you can sew a scant 1/4" from the top.

Sewing

If you are a visual learner, there are free videos on the sewing process on the website: www.englanddesign.com

Refer to the Sewing Sequence on Page 22 as needed. As you get familiar with the technique you will not need to reference the numbers. For large sections try chain stitching as many pattern pieces together as possible. Lay out the pattern pieces from one section in the tray. Keep them in a single

layer (do not overlap them). It is not necessary to lay them out in exact numeric order, but place them so you can spot the **circled numbers** quickly.

Use a normal stitch length (12 to 14 stitches per inch) throughout. Unlike foundation piecing, (where stitch length is shortened to allow for paper removal), stitching is made next to the freezer paper pattern pieces rather than through them. Place the Master Pattern close to the sewing machine, as it will be referred to constantly. During construction, lay the pattern pieces directly on top of the Master Pattern to check placement. Sticky notes are helpful to block off sections. Work only one section at a time. Each section has its own set of sequential numbers. If more than one section is sewn at a time, there will be duplicate **circled numbers** which will be confusing.

Use a scant 1/4" when sewing. It is better to sew too far away than over the paper. Sew from end to end without backstitching. When the pattern pieces are sewn together,

Match the corners of the freezer paper, not the whole line.

right sides will face one another (freezer paper to freezer paper). Pull back the corner of the top pattern piece, and make sure the end points of the freezer paper match. Check only the corners of the pattern pieces. If you pull back on the whole line, the freezer paper will pop off.

When pinning, sometimes it is easier to see one end point of a pattern piece than another due to the odd angles. If so, align the side that is the *easiest* to see. Remember, the seam does not need to be perfect. The pattern piece can be moved. Pin in the center of the pattern piece, keeping the pin vertical. Pin *down* through the fabric seam allowance, and come *up* through the freezer paper. When placing the pin through the seam allowance, try to insert the pin near the paper edge but not through it (see left photo). After the pair is pinned, it will dent slightly away from where the pin goes through and comes up. Take your fingers and place them on either side of the pin. Fold the fabric back along the edge of the freezer paper and pinch to make a visible fold. This fold will be your sewing guideline. You may find it helpful to use more than one pin for longer pattern pieces. Try to avoid sewing over pins.

Pin matched pieces. With the pin, go through the fabric and come up through the paper.

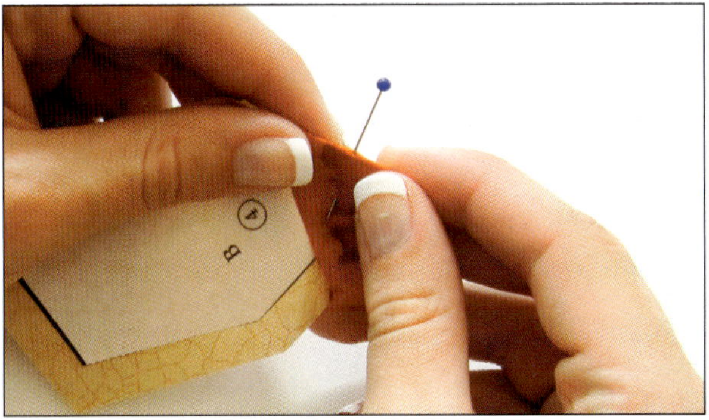

Use your fingers and fold back pinching down along the freezer paper edges.

Use the folded line as a sewing guide.

The Fudge Factor

Do not stress about sewing along the fold perfectly. If the fold isn't readily visible, sew a scant 1/4" seam and hope for the best. If the seam allowances were cut a little larger than 1/4", your seam should not be too far off.

After sewing the seam, check to see how close the freezer paper pattern pieces are to each other. They must meet along the edges with no fabric showing between the pattern pieces. If they are not aligned, this technique allows you to move the pattern pieces rather than resew the fabric.

If there is too much space between the pieces after you have sewn them, remove the freezer paper, reposition the pattern pieces closer to the seam, and iron again. Do not feel guilty! This fudging is encouraged! This will not change the outcome of your design. Seams do not have to align perfectly for the design to look correct. The block will be squared after all sewing is completed and it WILL be the correct size.
Here is an example. Let's say you are working on leaves in a violet block. There are two greens, G1 and G2, and you just finished sewing two pattern pieces together; they are too far apart. There are ways to correct this (See Repositioning Pattern Pieces below). Pattern pieces can be repositioned exactly on either side of the sewn seam, or, you have the choice of moving just one pattern piece over the seam to touch the other. This change would not affect the overall look of the design. It doesn't matter if you have a little more G1 fabric than G2 fabric.

Pattern pieces could also be repositioned in the opposite manner, for example, you could have more G2 than G1. It is fine to move the pattern piece *over* the seam. Remember that the pattern pieces need to touch after every sewn seam. The pattern will maintain its size if the pattern pieces are aligned. If too much space is allowed between pattern pieces, the next pattern piece to be sewn on will not align.The only time repositioning a pattern piece over another color is *not* a good idea is in the case of a **circle over an intersection** notation. This notation means

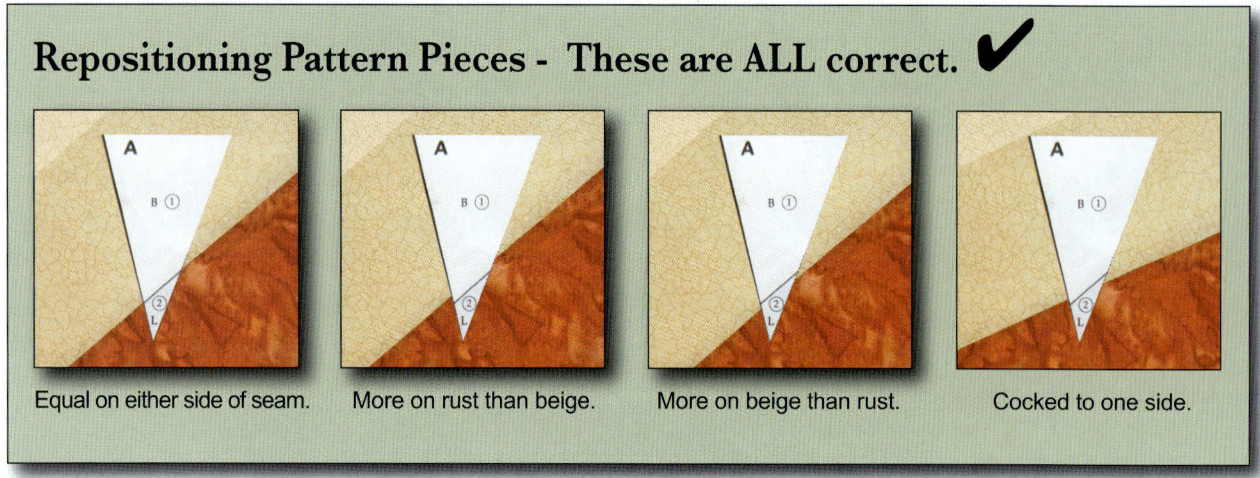

Equal on either side of seam. More on rust than beige. More on beige than rust. Cocked to one side.

that there is a color change here that matters. If there is space between the two pattern pieces, you must sew a new seam closer to the pattern to align the seam closer (see Tightening Up on Page 32). There is no need to remove the stitching already there.

During construction, pin **circle match notations** first, then align the end points of the pattern pieces. It is helpful to remove the paper when matching **circles over intersections**. This notation is a seam matching point. If needed, the pattern pieces can be ironed on again. Continue sewing, adding the pattern pieces to complete the sections. After a section is complete, remove as much paper as possible. Remove those pieces that are surrounded by sewn seams. You can also remove any pattern pieces that are on the outside edges that are not needed for reference. Leave on pattern pieces that must be referred to later; for example, leave the corners and edge pattern pieces. Some quilters like to leave all of the pattern pieces on until the very end. I find they get in my way. Plus, if you have the wrong color in the wrong place you can correct the mistake at the section level rather than when the entire block is finished.

" It is ALL about the paper touching. As long as the paper touches, the pattern stays the same size."

After major sections are complete, look for two sections that share a common side. Join the rest of the major sections in the same manner. After sewing, check to see that the outside edges of the freezer paper visually line up. If the freezer paper is not straight, remove the offending piece and reposition it. Trim threads and dog ears as you go. When joining large sections, it helps to trim these long seams using a rotary cutter and quilters' ruler. Trim to 1/4" seam allowance.

When all sections are joined, use steam and/or spray starch and press the front and the back of the block. Before trimming to size, embroider the stem details found on the corresponding pattern Trim Guide.

What NOT to do. Try to avoid these situations. ∅

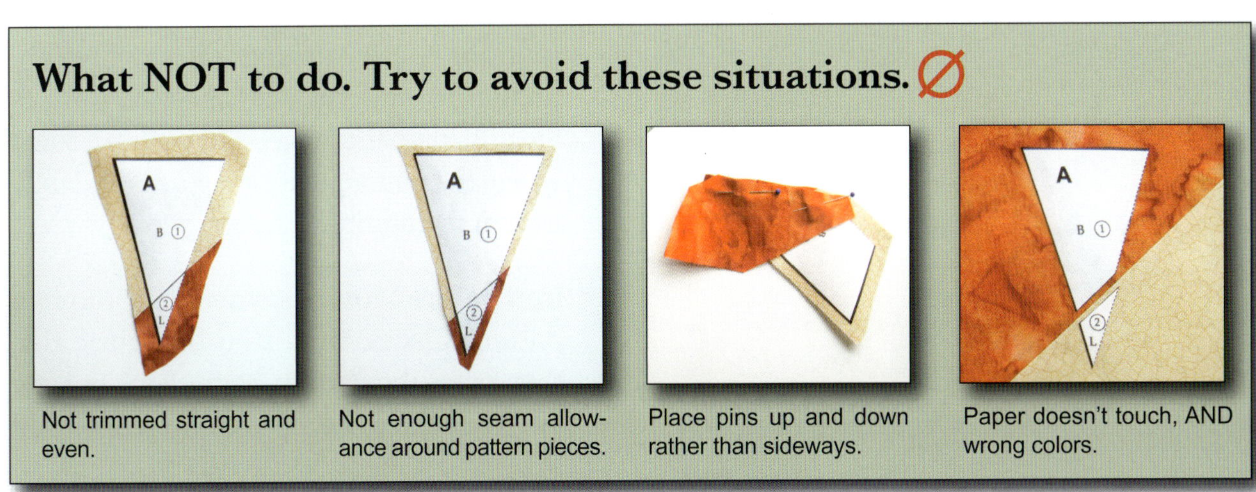

Not trimmed straight and even.

Not enough seam allowance around pattern pieces.

Place pins up and down rather than sideways.

Paper doesn't touch, AND wrong colors.

Troubleshooting Tips

- **Use Scraps:** Avoid small pattern pieces by sewing a scrap of fabric to the larger pattern piece. Then press the small pattern piece into position and trim.

- **Ate Too Much Paper:** If the sewn seam goes *over* the freezer paper slightly and paper is caught in the seam, gently tug on both sides of the seam. Usually the freezer paper will release itself. Remove excess paper from the seam allowance from the back, before sewing another seam, otherwise, it will be buried and will be difficult to remove. If there is a good amount of paper stuck in the seam and tugging doesn't work, refold the paper back along the edge to obtain a new fold. Resew along this new fold, and then take out the original seam.

Can't see where to sew?

- Try ironing the seam back along the freezer paper edge. Sew along the pressed line.

- Try folding back the seam of the top pattern piece with your finger, and align it. Lift the seam allowance of the pattern piece on top, align, and then sew along the folded line.

- Don't look for the fold. Just sew a skinny seam and then plan on removing the pattern pieces and repositioning them!

- **Push Away:** To get a seam back and out of the way, try using the tip of the iron to push the seam allowance away. When the next pattern piece is sewn on, this seam allowance will be moved aside. If the iron trick doesn't work, try taking out the last few sewn stitches, and the seam allowance can then be pressed out of the way.

- **Pivot Seam Out and Away:** Here is another way to deal with long, thin pattern pieces. When the seam is about 1/4" from the end, start pivoting the seam outward at an angle (yellow dot). When the seam allowance is ironed, it will fall back and out of the way for the next seam.

- **Lost a Pattern Piece:** If you misplace a pattern piece simply place freezer paper (shiny side down) over the pattern and trace that single piece. You can also pretend that the pattern piece is still there. All seam lines are straight. If the surrounding pattern pieces are sewn, eventually the empty space takes the form of the missing pattern piece. Just place a scrap where the missing pattern piece is and then trim out straight as you go.

- **Iron Before Moving:** When repositioning pattern pieces, first, iron the fabric flat, then press the pattern pieces back on, one at a time. Use the tip of a finger to hold the pattern piece in place.

Maple Leaf Trim Guide

Outside solid line is rotary cut squaring size 6 1/2" X 6 1/2".

Finished Block size is 6" X 6".

- Dashed line is sewing line.
- Diagonal lines for placement reference.
- Small dashed lines are quilting suggestions for leaf veins.
- Larger zig-zag line indicate stem to be embroidered.

With a permanent marker, trace the Trim Guide onto template plastic and place over finished Picture Pieced block. Design was intentionally made larger. Trim away excess.

- **Remove Paper Beforehand:** If a seam needs to be tightened up, remove the paper near it, sew closer to the fold, then press the pattern pieces on again.

- **Fold Back:** This works well for small pattern pieces and I frequently use it when I want to leave three pattern pieces together. Cut out three pattern pieces as one piece. Iron two of them on the presewn strips (Fig 1). Cut out with the seam allowance and don't worry about the third piece at this point. Fold the third piece on the line towards the other two pattern pieces (Fig 2). Cut away about 1/4" past that fold. Use a strip of fabric that is the same color as the third pattern pieces and align the strip at the top (Fig 3). Pin and pinch fold as usual. Sew along the fold.

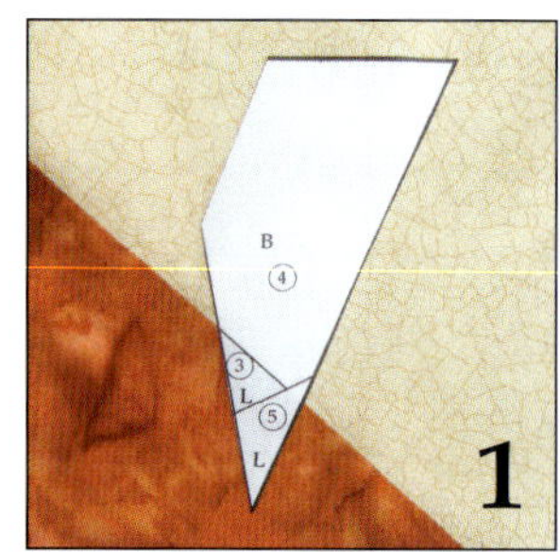

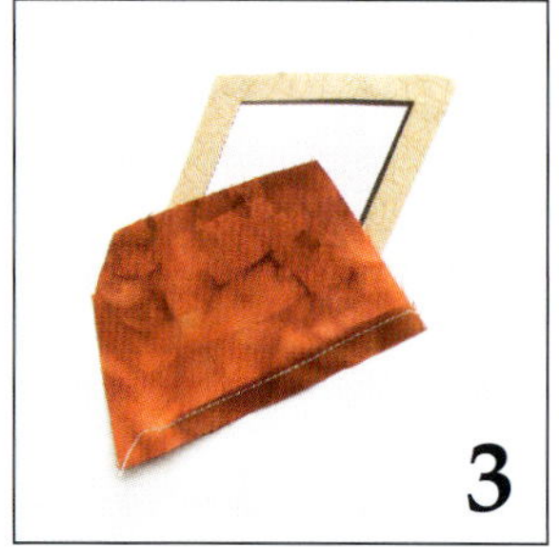

The Fold Back technique works great for adding very small pattern pieces.

Press back and then trim around the third small pattern piece (Fig 4).

Tightening Up - Pulling it All Together

This is a great tip for sewing large sections together. When joining sections, *intentionally* sew a skinny seam, well away from where it should be (Fig 1).
If you open it up, the two section papers will be too far away (Fig 2). From the right side of the fabric, push the two paper sections together, so that the papers touch and press with a hot iron (Fig 3). This will form a fold on the back, and will leave a crease to sew next to (Fig 4). After sewing, the sections will be next to each other (Fig 5). It's much easier to sew closer than to unsew! Leave that first sewn line in. This makes it stronger.

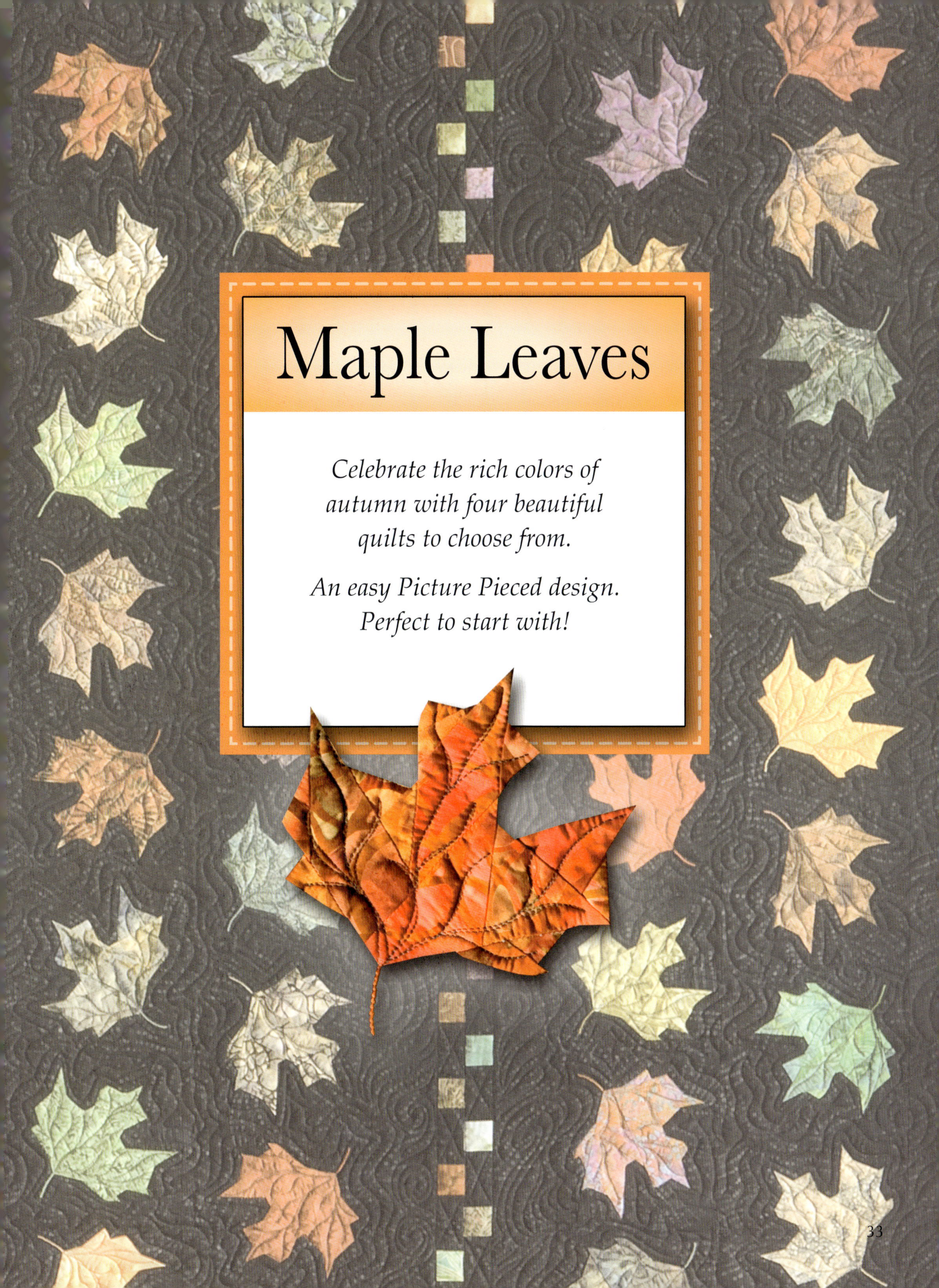

Maple Leaves

Celebrate the rich colors of autumn with four beautiful quilts to choose from.

An easy Picture Pieced design. Perfect to start with!

Canadian Maple Leaf

Finished Quilt Size: 23″ X 23″
Finished Picture Piecing Block Size: 6″ X 6″

Designed and Pieced by Cynthia England — Quilted by Denise Green

Picture Piecing Material Requirements

For Four Leaf blocks you will need:

- **B -** Four different creams for background for *each* block........................ 4 1/2″ X 42″
- **L -** Four different reds for *each* leaf.......................... 4 1/2″ X 22″

Make a color chart for the leaf fabrics as pictured.

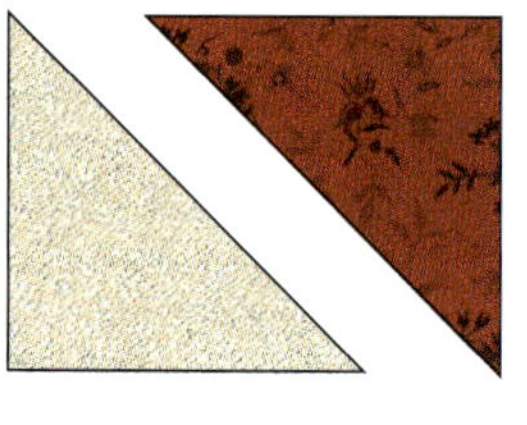

Traditional Quilt Material Requirements

- **A** - Black .... 1/3 yard
- **B** - Red print...............................2/3 yard
  Includes binding
- **C** - Cream................................ 1/4 yard
- **Backing** - Something pretty!.........1 yard

Make a color chart for these fabrics as pictured below.

Fabric Color	Size	Shape	Number Needed	Number To Cut
A	$2^{7/8}$" X $2^{7/8}$"		24	12
	$1^{1/2}$" X $6^{1/2}$"		4	4
	1" X $13^{1/2}$"		2	2
	1" X $14^{1/2}$"		2	2
B	$1^{1/2}$" X $1^{1/2}$"		1	1
	$2^{7/8}$" X $2^{7/8}$"		28	14
	2" X $20^{1/2}$"	*borders	2	2
	2" X $23^{1/2}$"	*borders	2	2
	$2^{1/4}$" X WOF	*binding	98"	3 strips
C	$2^{1/2}$" X $2^{1/2}$"		24	24

Rotary Cutting Traditional Quilt

*Before beginning, cut Fabric B border strips and binding strips. Set aside.

Picture Piecing Block Info —

Finished Block Size: 6″ X 6″

Picture Piecing sewing directions begin on Page 19. See Pages 22-23 for Maple Leaf sewing sequence and block pattern.
Don't forget! There are free videos on the website, ***www.englanddesign.com***

Pre-Sewing Recommendations

This makes the little pieces *so* much easier!

- Place Fabric B and Fabric L right sides together and sew a 1/4″ seam allowance along the length of the strip for each leaf. If the strips are different lengths along the bottom it doesn't matter.
- Press open.

B to L

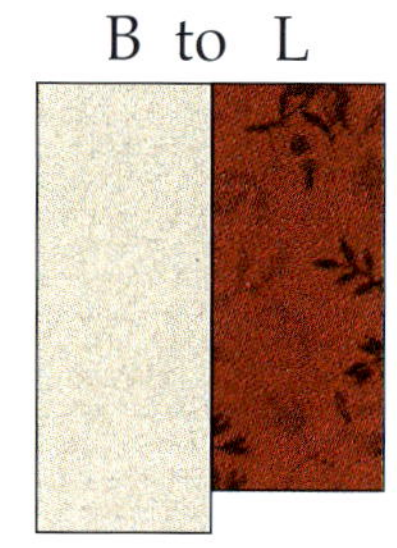

Note: *Pre-sewing strips is not recommended for directional fabrics.*

Piece 4 leaf blocks.
Refer to Trim Guide on Page 31 before cutting to size.

Embroidery Details

Use 3 strands of embroidery floss which match Leaf fabric and stem stitch the stems as indicated on the Trim Diagram on Page 31.

Traditional Set Info

Sew right sides together using a scant 1/4″ seam allowance.

1 Sew one $1^{1/2}$″ X $6^{1/2}$″ Fabric A strip between two red leaf blocks.
Note rotation of leaf blocks.

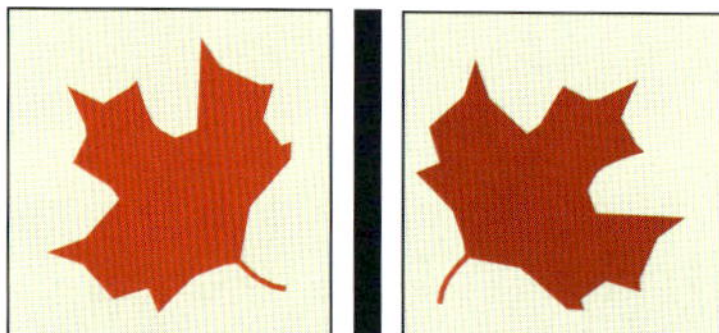

Make 2 of these leaf sash units.

2 Sew one $1^{1/2}$″ X $6^{1/2}$″ Fabric A strip to either side of the red $1^{1/2}$″ X $1^{1/2}$″ Fabric B square.

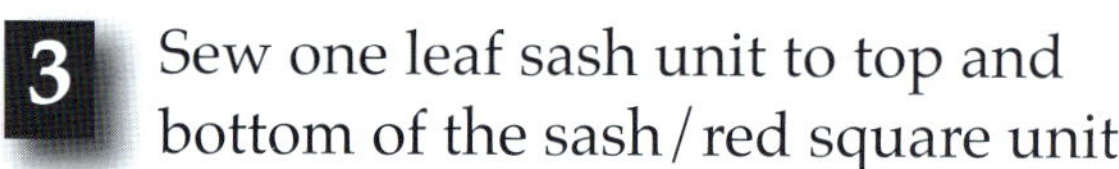

3 Sew one leaf sash unit to top and bottom of the sash/red square unit.

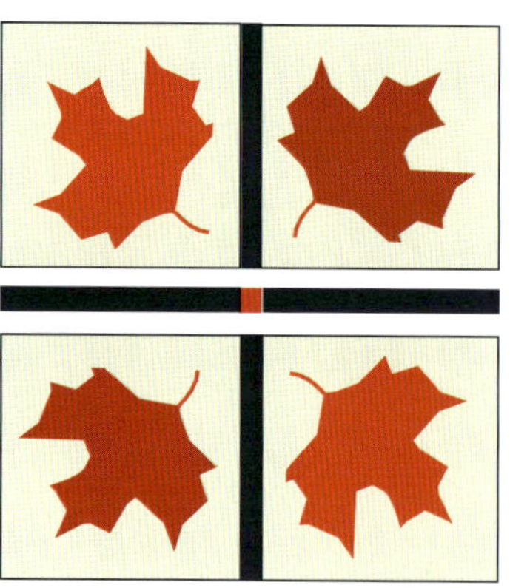

4 Add the inner border:
Sew one 1" X $13^{1/2}$" Fabric A strip to each side of the 4 Leaf block unit.

Sew one 1" X $14^{1/2}$" Fabric A strip to the top and bottom of the 4 Leaf block unit.

5 Construct the pieced border, **Unit A**:
Select one $2^{1/2}$" X $2^{1/2}$" square of Fabric C, one $2^{7/8}$" triangle of Fabric B and one $2^{7/8}$" triangle of Fabric A and sew together as indicated.

Make 14 Unit A border units of this color combination.

6 Construct the border corners, **Unit B**:
Select one $2^{1/2}$" X $2^{1/2}$" square of Fabric C, three $2^{7/8}$" triangles of Fabric B and sew together. Rotary cut excess fabric away as indicated by yellow dotted line. Be sure to leave 1/4" seam allowance beyond the square points.

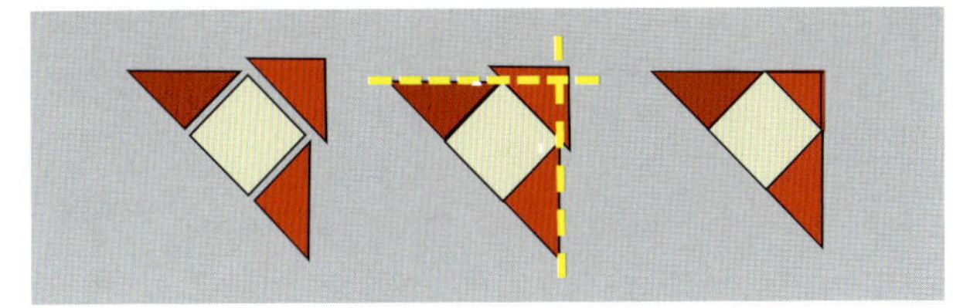

Rotary cut excess fabric away.

Make 4 Unit B border corner unit.

7 Make the triangles, **Unit C:**
Select one $2^{1/2}$" X $2^{1/2}$" square of Fabric C and two 2 $^{7/8}$" triangles of Fabric A.

Make 2 Unit C triangle border units.

8 Make the sides **Unit D**:
Select one $2^{1/2}$" X $2^{1/2}$" square of Fabric C, one $2^{7/8}$" triangle of Fabric A and one $2^{7/8}$" triangle of Fabric B sew together as indicated. Rotary cut excess fabric straight as indicated on the diagram with yellow dashed lines.

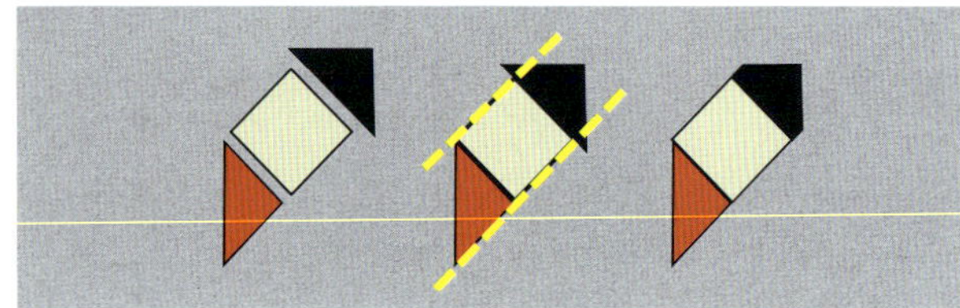

Make 2 Unit D pieced border units of this color combination.

9 Make the side triangles, **Unit E**: Select one 2$^{1/2}$" X 2$^{1/2}$" square of Fabric C, two 2$^{7/8}$"triangles of Fabric A. Sew together as indicated. Rotary cut excess fabric straight as indicated with yellow dashed line.

Make 2 Unit E side triangle border units.

- Refer to the illustration at right for the border setting. Work in diagonal rows, matching seams.

Note placement of color.

- Sew one Unit C to four Unit As. Sew to the top.

- Sew four Unit As to one Unit C. Sew to the bottom. Add the corners, Unit Bs.

Outer border:

- Sew one 2" X 20$^{1/2}$" Fabric B strip to each side of the quilt top.

- Sew one 2" X 23$^{1/2}$" Fabric B strip to the top and bottom of the quilt top.

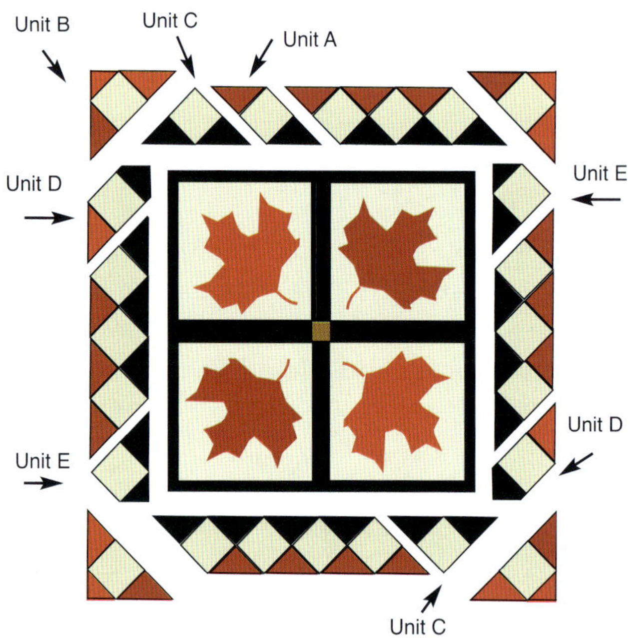

Canadian Maple Leaf Layout

- Begin with the sides. Sew one Unit E to three Unit As. Add Unit D. Sew to right side of Maple Leaf unit.

- Sew one Unit D to three Unit As. Add Unit E. Sew to left side of Maple Leaf unit.

Finishing

- To quilt, use a monofilament thread on top and in the bobbin to outline the pieced maple leaf designs.
- For the binding: Cut three strips Fabric B 2 $^{1/4}$" X WOF.

Maple Leaf Runner

Finished Quilt Size: 17 1/2″ X 43″
Finished Picture Piecing Block Size: 6″ X 6″
Finished Traditional Block Size: 6″ X 6″

Picture Piecing Material Requirements

For ten leaf blocks you will need:

- **B -** Black for background.............1 1/4 yard
  each leaf uses about 4 1/2″ X 42″
- **L -** Ten different fall fabrics
  for *each* leaf.......................... 4 1/2″ X 22″

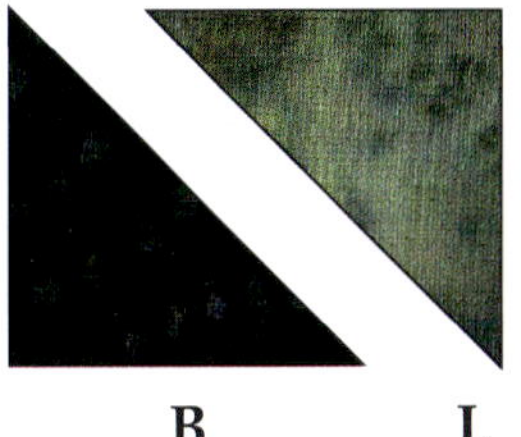

Make a color chart for the leaf fabrics as pictured to the right.

Designed by Cynthia England

Pieced by Ronda Stockton

Traditional Quilt Material Requirements

- **A** - Black .... 1/8 yard
  Same as Fabric B - Picture Piecing yardage
- **B** - Rust focus fabric................7/8 yard
  Includes binding
- **C** - Cinnamon............................ 1/4 yard
- **Backing** - Something pretty!......3/4 yard
  for pieced back

Make a color chart for these fabrics as pictured below.

Fabric Color	Size	Shape	Number Needed	Number To Cut
A	2 3/4" X 2 3/4"	⊠⊠	32	8
B	3 1/2" X 3 1/2"	□	4	4
	2 3/4" X 2 3/4"	⊠⊠	32	8
	9 3/4" X 9 3/4"	⊠⊠ *setting triangles	10	3
	2 1/4" X WOF	▭ *binding	130"	4 strips
C	4 1/4" X 4 1/4"	⊠⊠	16	4
	2" X 2"	□	16	16

Rotary Cutting

*Before beginning, cut outside setting triangles and binding. Set aside.

Picture Piecing Block Info

Finished Block Size: 6″ X 6″

Picture Piecing sewing directions begin on Page 19. See Pages 22-23 for Maple Leaf sewing sequence and block pattern.

Don't forget! There are free videos on the website, ***www.englanddesign.com***

Pre-Sewing Recommendations

This makes the little pieces *so* much easier!

- Place right sides together and sew a 1/4″ seam allowance along the length of the strip. If the strips are different lengths don't worry. They do not need to be even along the bottom.
- Sew black to each leaf fabric and press open.

B to L

Note: *Pre-sewing strips is not recommended for directional fabrics.*

Embroidery Details

Use 3 strands of embroidery floss which match your Leaf fabric and stem stitch the stems as indicated on the Trim Diagram on Page 31.

Traditional Block Info

Finished Block Size: 6″ X 6″
Ohio Star

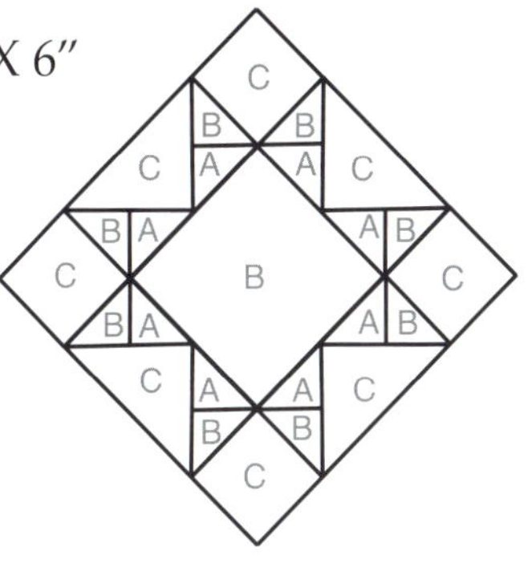

Sew right sides together using a scant 1/4″ seam allowance.

1 Make the quarter square triangle units: Sew one Fabric A triangle (cut from 2 3/4″ square twice on the diagonal) to one Fabric B triangle (cut from 2 3/4″ square twice on the diagonal) to create a larger triangle.

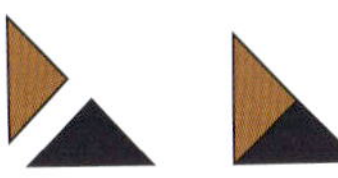

Make 16 pieced AB triangle units with the light fabric at the top.

Repeat, reversing the two triangles colors.

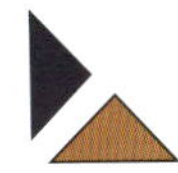

Make 16 pieced AB triangle units with the dark fabric at the top.

2 Make the flying geese units: Sew one AB triangle unit to each side of the Fabric C triangle (cut from 4 1/4″ square twice on the diagonal) as pictured. *Note color placement.*

Make 16.

3 Make the star point rows:
Sew one 2″ X 2″ Fabric C square to each side of 8 ABC flying geese units.

Make 8 pieced star point rows.

4 Make the center square units:
Sew one flying geese ABC unit to each side of a $3^{1/2}$″ Fabric B square.

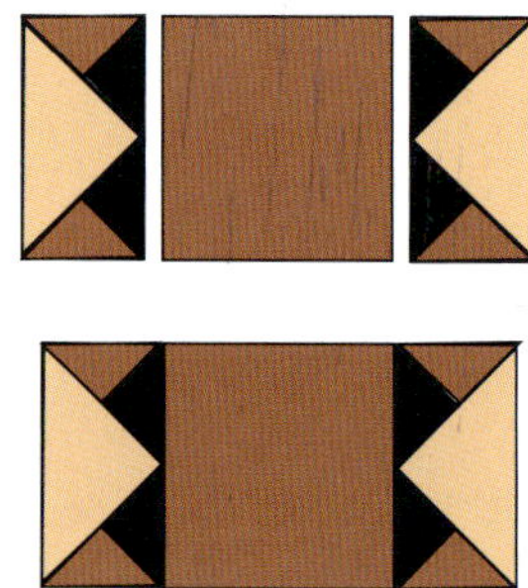

Make 4 pieced center square units.

5 Sew one star point unit to the top and bottom of each pieced center unit. Square to $6^{1/2}$″.

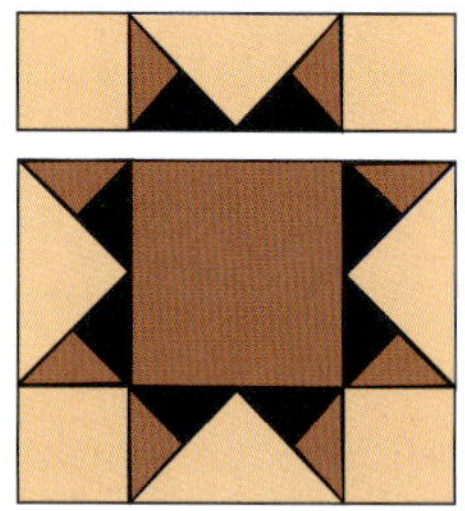

Complete 4 Ohio Star blocks.

Finishing

- Refer to the illustration below for the block setting. Work in diagonal rows, pointing the blocks as indicated.
- Bind runner with Fabric B strips cut 2 $^{1/4}$″ X WOF.

Detailed finishing instructions on binding angles are on Page 16.

Falling Leaves

Designed and Pieced by
Rhonda Gabriel and Cynthia England

Quilted by Denise Green

Falling Leaves

Finished Quilt Size: 71″ X 97″
Finished Picture Piecing Block Size: 6″ X 6″

Picture Piecing Material Requirements

Break out those rich colors of fall and have fun making this contemporary colorful quilt!

Make use of the scrap bag; the brighter the better! Aim for a variety of fabrics. When making your fabric choices look for good contrast between the leaves and your background.

You don't need much fabric for the leaves. This would be a great exchange with your quilting friends!

For 78 leaf blocks you will need:

- **B -** Black for background............9 3/4 yards
  each leaf uses about 4 1/2″ X 42″
- **L -** Variety of fall fabrics
  for *each* leaf.......................... 4 1/2″ X 22″

Make a color chart for the leaf fabrics as pictured.

B **L**

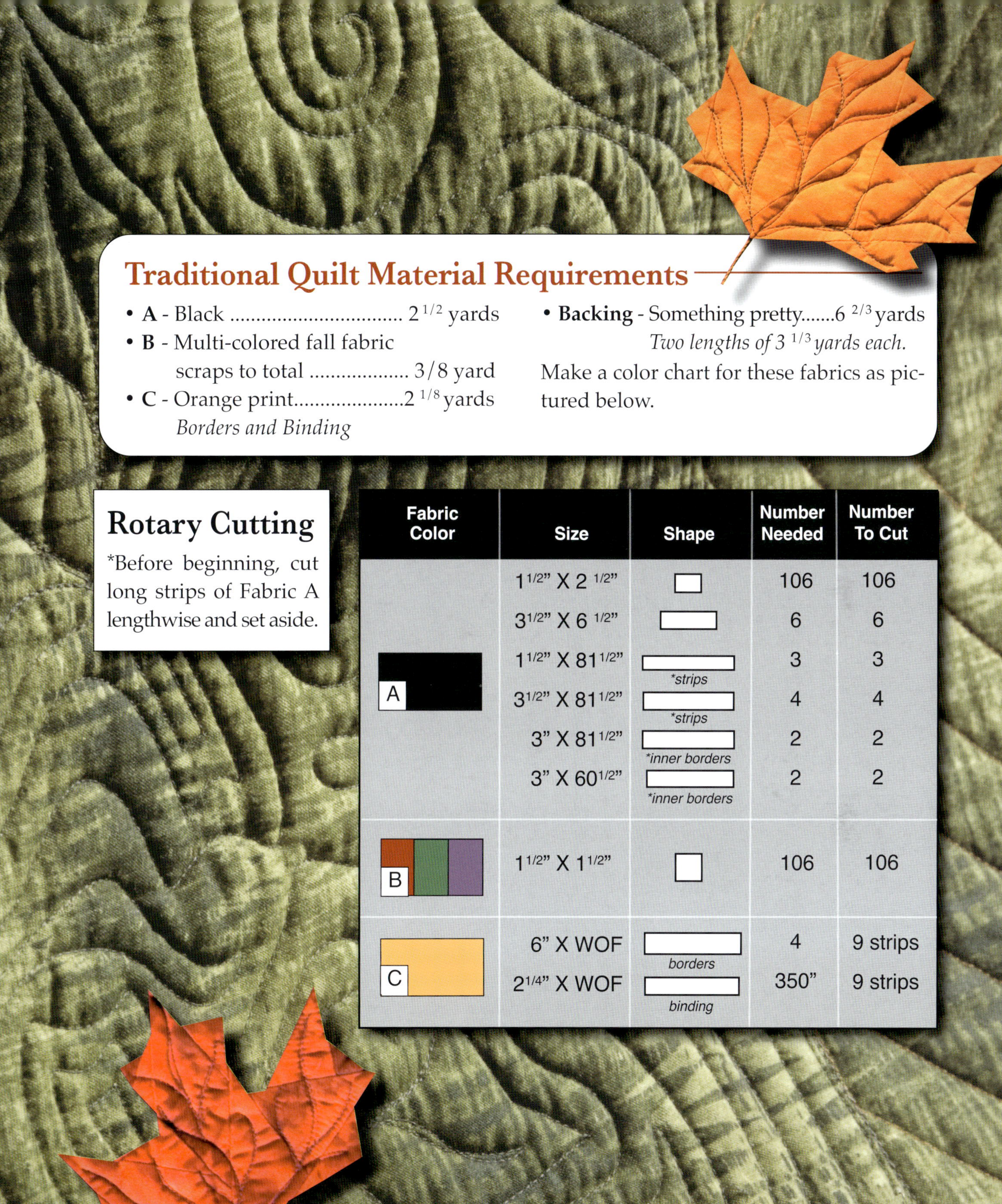

Traditional Quilt Material Requirements

- **A** - Black .... $2^{1/2}$ yards
- **B** - Multi-colored fall fabric scraps to total .... 3/8 yard
- **C** - Orange print.....................$2^{1/8}$ yards
  Borders and Binding
- **Backing** - Something pretty.......$6^{2/3}$ yards
  Two lengths of $3^{1/3}$ yards each.

Make a color chart for these fabrics as pictured below.

Rotary Cutting

*Before beginning, cut long strips of Fabric A lengthwise and set aside.

Fabric Color	Size	Shape	Number Needed	Number To Cut
A	$1^{1/2}$" X $2^{1/2}$"		106	106
	$3^{1/2}$" X $6^{1/2}$"		6	6
	$1^{1/2}$" X $81^{1/2}$"	*strips	3	3
	$3^{1/2}$" X $81^{1/2}$"	*strips	4	4
	3" X $81^{1/2}$"	*inner borders	2	2
	3" X $60^{1/2}$"	*inner borders	2	2
B	$1^{1/2}$" X $1^{1/2}$"		106	106
C	6" X WOF	borders	4	9 strips
	$2^{1/4}$" X WOF	binding	350"	9 strips

Picture Piecing Block Info —

Finished Block Size: 6″ X 6″

Picture Piecing sewing directions begin on Page 19. See Pages 22-23 for Maple Leaf sewing sequence and block pattern.

Don't forget! There are free videos on the website, ***www.englanddesign.com***

Pre-Sewing Recommendations

This makes the little pieces *so* much easier!

- Place Fabric B and L strips right sides together and sew a 1/4″ seam allowance along the length of the strip for each leaf. If the strips are different lengths don't worry. They do not need to be even along the bottom. Press open.

B to L

Note: *Pre-sewing strips is not recommended for directional fabrics.*

Make 78 leaf blocks.

- Use 3 strands of embroidery floss which match your Leaf fabric and stem stitch the stems as indicated on the Trim Diagram on Page 31.

Traditional Set Info

Sew right sides together using a scant 1/4″ seam allowance.

1 Sew 6 long strips of leaves in groups of **13**, turning the blocks a quarter turn each time. Vary colors as you go. See Page 48 for complete layout of each row.

2 Add the six spacer bars. These alternately start and end the rows. Sew one $3^{1/2}$″ X $6^{1/2}$″ Fabric A rectangle to *one end* of the corresponding leaf block strip pairs.

3 Make the confetti strips:
Sew one $1^{1/2}$" X $2^{1/2}$" Fabric A rectangle in between one colorful Fabric B $1^{1/2}$" X $1^{1/2}$" square. Continue adding rectangles and squares until there are a total of 26 colorful squares. Finish the strip with a rectangle.
See diagram.

Make 2 strips.

4 Make the long confetti strips:
Repeat step 3. This time, finish the strip with a colorful square. Making a total of 27 colorful squares with rectangles.
See diagram.

Make 2 strips.

5 Sew the confetti strips together:
Select one 26 and one 27 confetti strip. Sew together, offsetting the patches. The colorful square should fall between the rectangle. Excess at top and bottom will be trimmed away after the top is completed.

Make 2 pairs.

Photo by Julie Moser

Assembling the Quilt Top —

Refer to the illustration on Page 48.

- Sew one 1 $^{1/2}$" X $81^{1/2}$" Fabric A strip in between Row 1 and Row 2 of the leaf strips.
- Repeat with Row 4 and Row 5 leaf strips.
- Repeat with Row 7 and Row 8 leaf strips.
- Sew one 3 $^{1/2}$" X $81^{1/2}$" Fabric A strip to each side of the 2 confetti strip pairs.
- Sew one 3" X $81^{1/2}$" Fabric A strip to the left side of Row 1 and Row 2 group.
- Sew one 3" X $81^{1/2}$" Fabric A strip to the right side of Row 7 and Row 8 group.
- Sew all rows together. Trim away excess from the ends of confetti strips. Add one 3" X $60^{1/2}$" Fabric A strip to the top and the bottom.

Finishing

Detailed finishing instructions on Page 7.

- Sew one 6″ X 86 1/2″ Fabric C to each side. Sew one 6 ″ X 71 1/2″ Fabric C to the top and bottom.
- Bind quilt using 9 strips of Fabric C strips cut 2 1/4″ X WOF.
- Sleeve and label your quilt.

Autumn Leaves

Designed and Pieced by Cynthia England

Quilted by Denise Green

Autumn Leaves

Finished Quilt Size: 55″ X 55″
Finished Picture Piecing Block Size: 6″ X 6″

Picture Piecing Material Requirements

Here is an excuse to use some of those beautiful fall prints you have been saving! We chose a scrappy look and a mix of rich variety of shades.

In this quilt we used the following:
7 Reds to burgundies
7 Greens
4 Oranges
5 Golds
8 Tan to browns
5 Blacks

When laying out colors, sprinkle the lights and darks throughout. Scatter the blocks so two of the same color are not next to each other.

For 36 leaf blocks you will need:

- **B -** Beige for background........................$4^{1/2}$ yards
  each leaf uses about $4^{1/2}$″ X 42″
- **L -** Variety of fall prints for *each* leaf........................ $4^{1/2}$″ X 22″

Make a color chart as pictured.

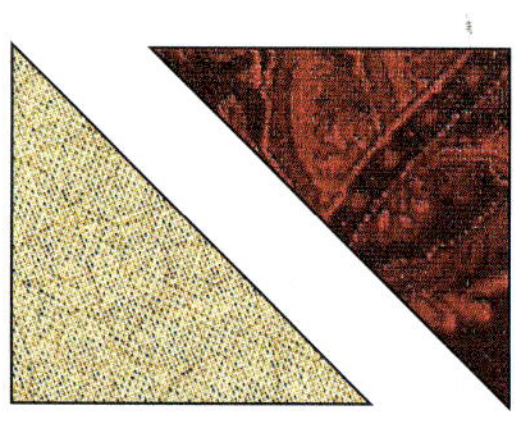

B **L**

Traditional Quilt Materials Requirements

- **A** - Orange border print............$1^{1/2}$ yards
- **B** - Black print..........................$1^{1/4}$ yards
  Includes binding
- **C** - Red print...............................3/8 yard
- **D** - Scraps......................to total 1/3 yard
- **E** - Orange print.........................1/8 yard
- **Backing** - Something pretty!.....$3^{1/2}$ yards

Make a color chart for these fabrics as pictured below.

Rotary Cutting

*Before beginning, rotary cut strips of Fabric A lengthwise and set aside for borders.

Fabric Color	Size	Shape	Number Needed	Number To Cut
A	$4^{1/2}$" X 47 $^{1/2}$"	*borders	4	4
B	$2^{1/2}$" X $13^{1/2}$" $2^{1/4}$" X WOF	sashing binding	24 230"	8 strips 6 strips
C	$2^{1/2}$" X $2^{1/2}$" $1^{1/2}$" X $6^{1/2}$"	 sashing	8 36	8 6 strips
D	$1^{1/2}$" X $1^{1/2}$"	multi-colored 4-patches	96	96
E	$1^{1/2}$" X $1^{1/2}$"	cornerstones	9	9

Picture Piecing Block Info

Finished Block Size: 6″ X 6″

Picture Piecing sewing directions begin on Page 19. See Pages 22-23 for Maple Leaf sewing sequence and block pattern.
Don't forget! There are free videos on the website, ***www.englanddesign.com***

Pre-Sewing Recommendations

This makes the little pieces *so* much easier!

- Place right sides together and sew a 1/4″ seam allowance along the length of the strip. The strips do not need to be even along the bottom.
- Sew beige to each leaf fabric and press open.
- Make 36 Leaf blocks and use 3 strands of embroidery floss which match your Leaf fabric and stem stitch the stems as indicated on the Trim Diagram on Page 31.

Traditional Set Info

Sew right sides together using a scant 1/4″ seam allowance.

1 Select one $1^{1/2}$″ X $6^{1/2}$″ Fabric C sashing strip between two Leaf blocks. Note rotation of leaf blocks.

 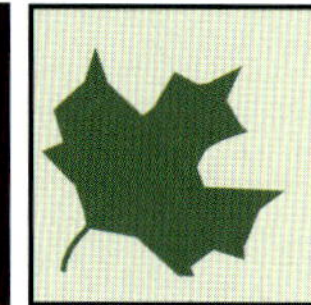

Make 2 leaf sash units.

2 Sew one $1^{1/2}$″ X $6^{1/2}$″ Fabric C sashing strip to either side of a $1^{1/2}$″ X $1^{1/2}$″ Fabric E square.

3 Sew one leaf sash unit to the top and bottom of the sash/square unit. Square to $13^{1/2}$″ X $13^{1/2}$″.

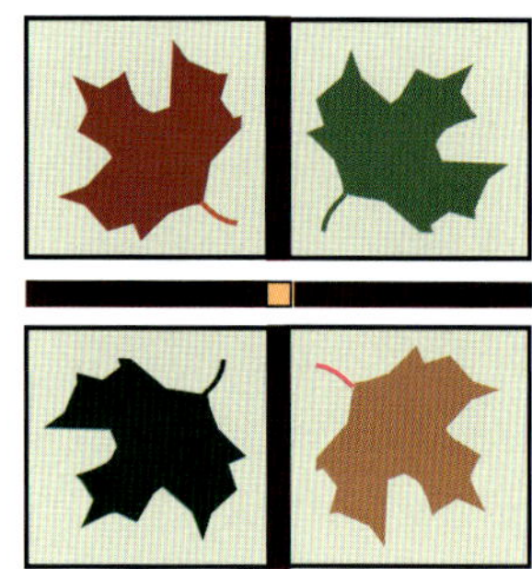

Complete 9 four-leaf blocks.

4 Select four different $1^{1/2}$″ Fabric D squares and sew together to make a four-patch unit as shown. Press seams in opposite directions.

Make 24 four-patch units. Square to $2^{1/2}$″ X $2^{1/2}$″. Set aside 8 for corner units.

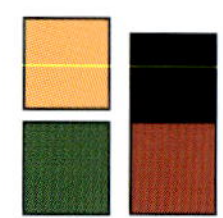

5 Make the corner four-patch blocks: Sew 2 four-patch units and two Fabric C $2^{1/2}$″ X $2^{1/2}$″ squares together as shown. Square to $4^{1/2}$″.

Make 4 corner units. Set aside.

6 Sew 4 four-patch units and 3 Fabric B $2^{1/2}$″ X $13^{1/2}$″ sashing strips as shown in diagram.

Make 4 sashing strip units.

7 Join 3 four-leaf block units with four $2^{1/2}$″ X $13^{1/2}$″ Fabric B sashing strips.

Make 3 rows consisting of 3 leaf blocks and 4 sashing strips.

Assembling the Quilt Top

Use the illustration and join the sashing/ four-patch units and the leaf block rows.

- Sew 1 Fabric A $4^{1/2}$" X 47 $^{1/2}$" border strip to each side of the quilt top.
- Sew 1 four-patch corner block to each end of the remaining Fabric A $4^{1/2}$" X 47 $^{1/2}$" border strips. Sew to top and bottom.

Finishing

Detailed finishing instructions on Page 7.

- Bind quilt using 6 strips of Fabric B, cut $2^{1/4}$" X WOF.
- Sleeve and label your quilt.

Roses

Four romantic rose designs are waiting for you.

This classic rose design fits every decor.

Change the orientation of the blocks for a completely different look!

Hot Pink Roses

Finished Quilt Size: 17″ X 43″
Finished Picture Piecing Block Size: 6″ X 6″
Finished Traditional Block Size: 6″ X 6″

Picture Piecing Material Requirements

For four rosebud blocks you will need:

- **B** - Very dark blue for bkg......... 1/2 yard
  each rosebud uses about $4^{1/2}$″ *X 42″*
- **R1** - Pink for roses......................... 4″ X 42″
- **R2** - Medium pink for roses......... 4″ X 22″
- **R3** - Very dark pink for roses...... 4″ X 11″
- **G1** - Green for leaves................... 4″ X 42″
- **G2** - Dark green for leaves......... 4″ X 22″

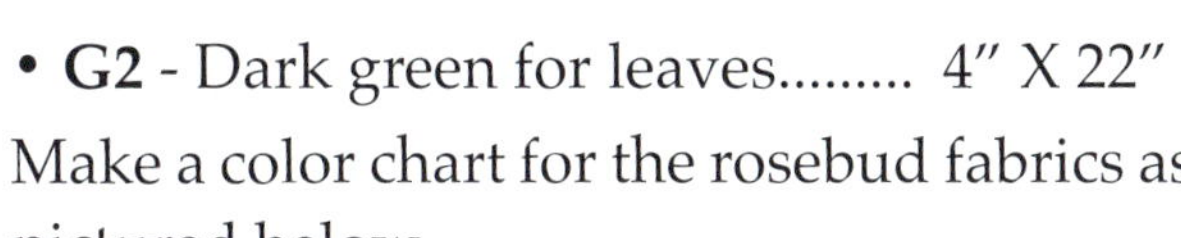

Make a color chart for the rosebud fabrics as pictured below.

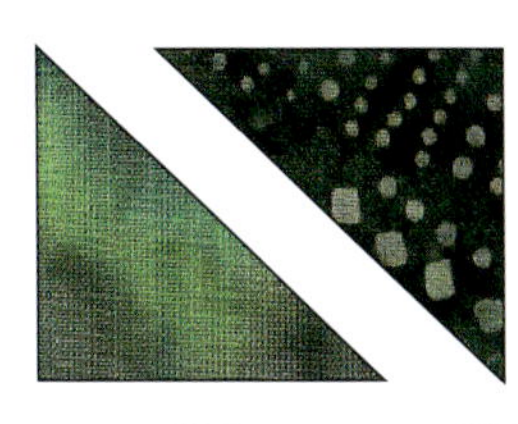

B **R1** **R2** **R3** **G1** **G2**

Cynthia England

Picture Piecing Block Info —

Finished Block Size: 6″ X 6″

Picture Piecing sewing directions begin on Page 19. See next page for Rosebud block pattern. *Don't forget! There are free videos on the website,* ***www.englanddesign.com***

Pre-Sewing Recommendations

This makes the little pieces *so* much easier!

- Place right sides together and sew a 1/4″ seam allowance along the length of the strip. Some of the strips may be different lengths. Just sew along the side to the end. Press open.

- Sew the following strips together:

B to R1 to R2 to R3

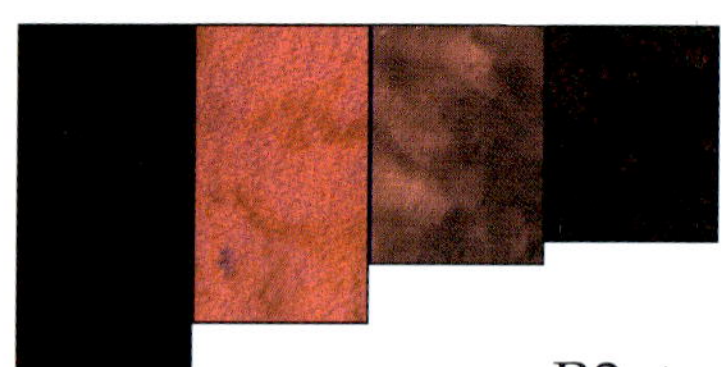

R2 to B to G1 to G2

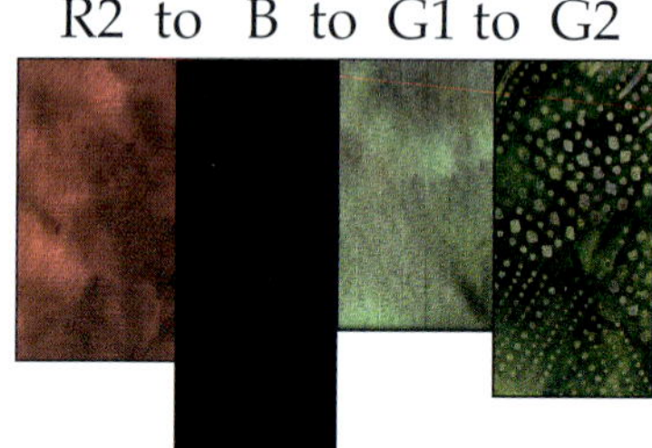

Note: *Pre-sewing strips is not recommended for directional fabrics.*

Sewing Sequence:

Note: If you have pre-sewn strips you will already have prepped some of the sewn pieces. For instance, 1 and 2 will already be sewn.

Section A: Sew 1 to 2, 3 to 4, 5 to 6, 11 to 12, 14 to 15. Join 1/2 to 3/4, 11/12 to 13. Join 1-4 to 5/6. Add 7 to 1-6. Add 8, 9 and 10. Join 1-10 to 11-13. Join 1-13 to 14/15.

Section B: Sew 1 to 2, 8 to 9. Add 3 to 1/2, Add 10 to 8/9. Add 4 to 1-3. Add 5, 6 then 7. Join 1-7 to 8-10.

Section C: Sew 1 to 2, 4 to 5, 6 to 7. Add 3 to 1/2. Join 4/5 to 6/7. Add 8, 9 and then 10. Join 1-3 to 4-10.

Section D: Sew 1 to 2, add 3. Add 4, 5, then 6.

Section F: Sew 1 to 2; add 3, then 4.

Section E: Sew 1 to 2, 5 to 6. Add 3 to 1/2, add 7 to 5/6. Add 4 to 1-3. Join 1-4 to 5-7. Add 8, then 9.

Sew Sections A to B, add C. Sew Section D to E, add F. Join ABC to DEF.

Piece 4 rosebud blocks. Refer to Trim Guide on Page 58 before cutting to size.

Rosebud Pattern

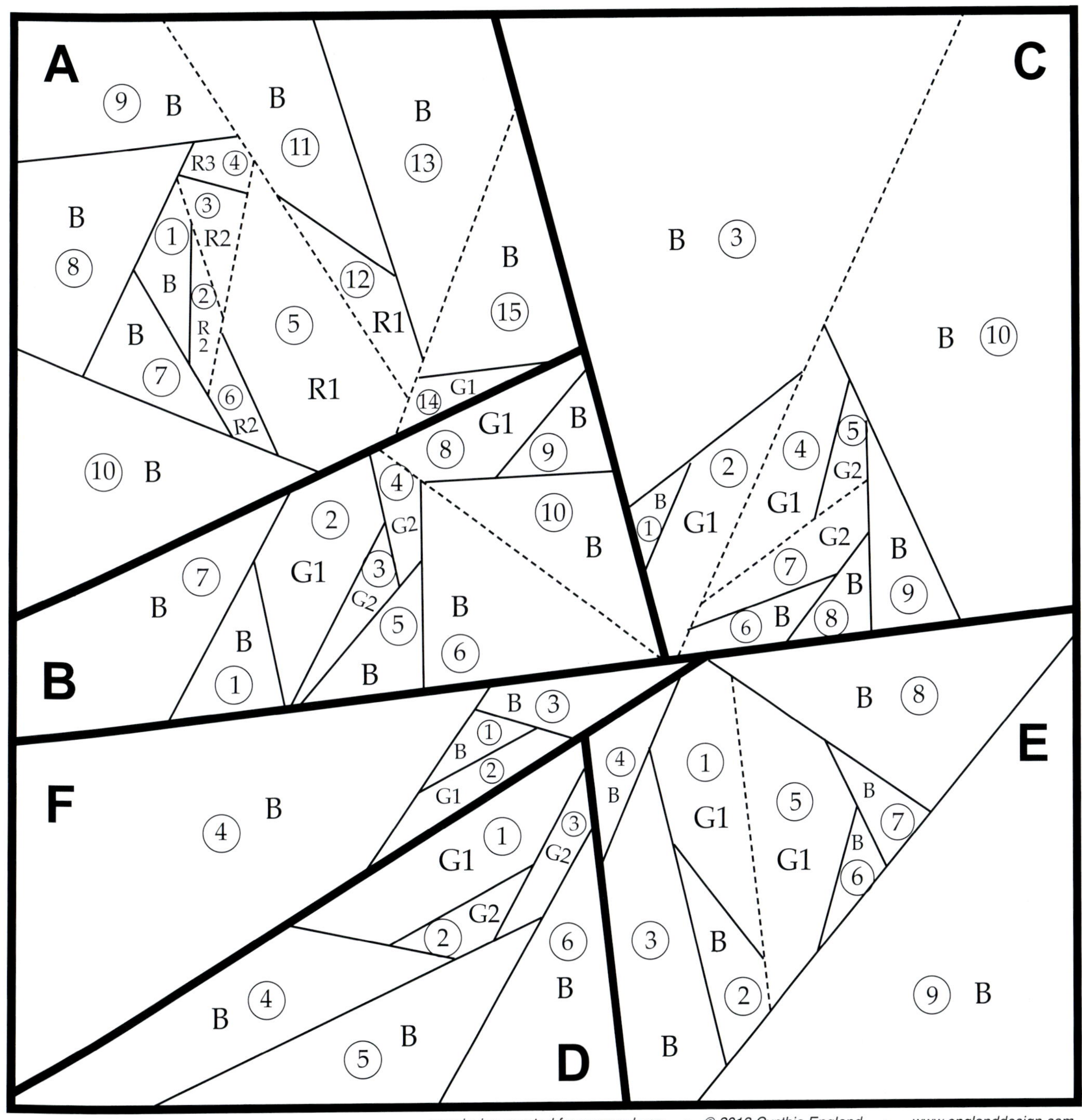

IMPORTANT:
When tracing onto freezer paper ADD 1/4″ extra all around for squaring outer edges.
Note: If you are using pre-printed freezer paper cut on lines. NO EXTRA needed.
After trimming, the block will measure 6 1/2″ X 6 1/2″.

Rosebud Trim Guide

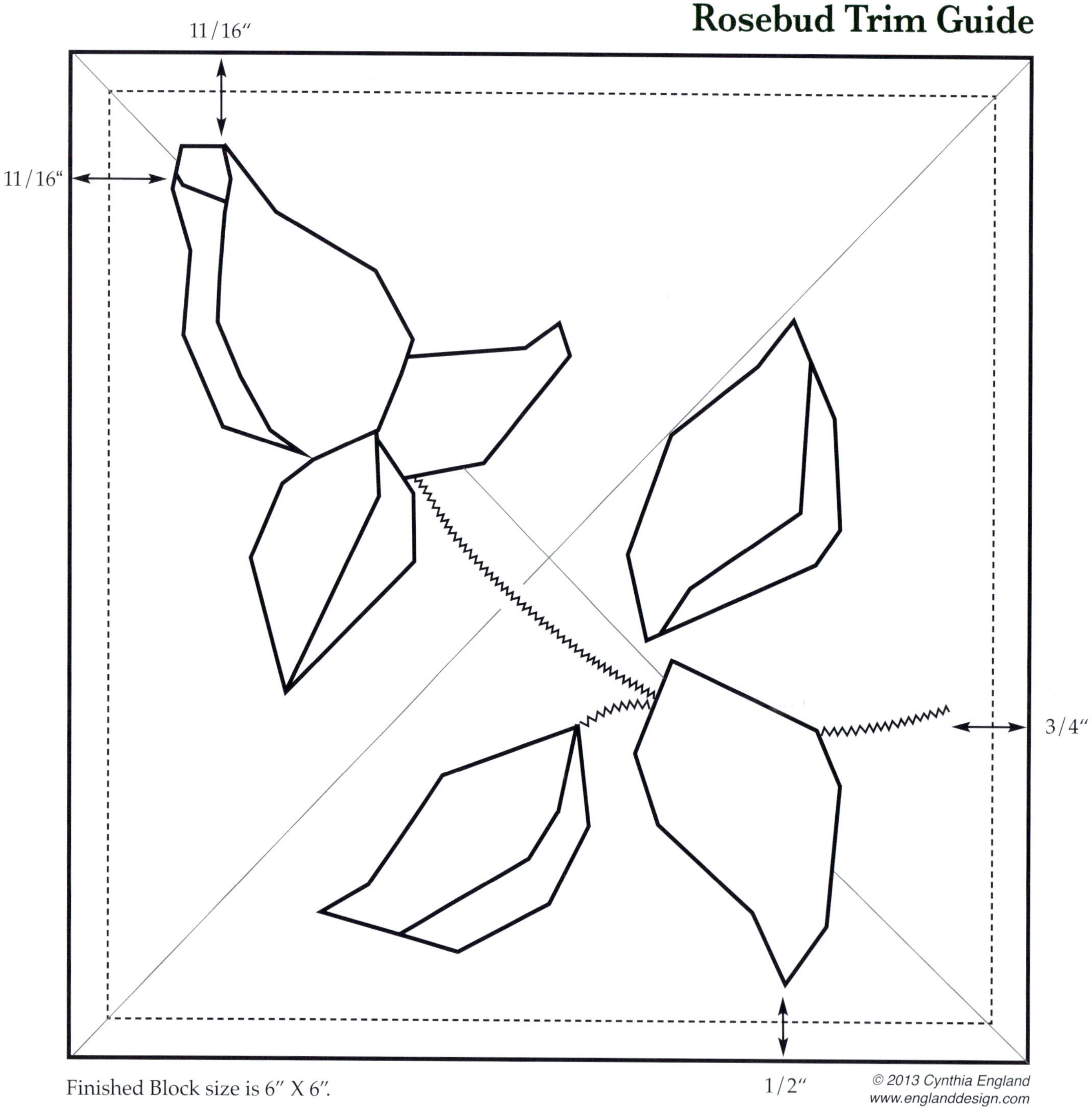

Finished Block size is 6" X 6".

Note the amount of space around the rosebud when trimming.

- Outside solid line is rotary cut trim size 6 1/2" X 6 1/2".
- Dashed line is sewing line.
- Diagonal lines for placement reference.
- Larger zig-zag lines indicate stems to be embroidered. Use 3 strands of green embroidery floss which match your light green fabric and stem stitch the lines for the rose stems.

With a permanent marker, trace the Trim Guide onto template plastic and place over finished Picture Pieced block. Design was intentionally made larger. Trim away excess.

Traditional Quilt Material Requirements

- **A** - Dark blue for background.......3/4 yard
  Includes binding
- **B** - Dark green .... 1/3 yard
- **C** - Pink....................................... 1/4 yard
- **D** - Dark pink................................1/4 yard
- **Backing** - Something pretty!.......1 1/4 yard *for pieced back*

Make a color chart for these fabrics as pictured below.

Rotary Cutting

*Before beginning, cut outside setting triangles and binding of Fabric A.

Fabric Color	Size	Shape	Number Needed	Number To Cut
A	9 3/4" X 9 3/4" 2 1/4" X WOF	*setting triangles *binding	10 130"	3 4 strips
B	7 1/4" X 7 1/4"		10	3
C	2 1/2" X 2 1/2"		20	20
D	2 1/2" X 2 1/2"		20	20

Traditional Block Info

Shaded Square Finished Block Size: 6″ X 6″

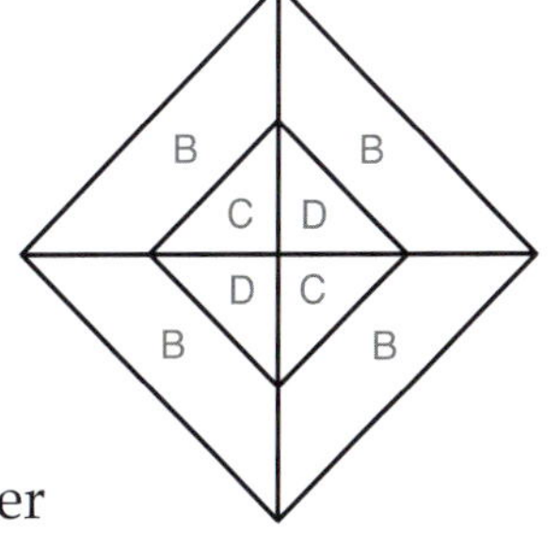

Sew right sides together using a scant 1/4″ seam allowance.

Making the Traditional Blocks

1 Make the BC triangle units: Select one triangle of Fabric B and one 2 1/2″ square of Fabric C. Draw a line diagonally across the square and stitch. Press and cut away excess.

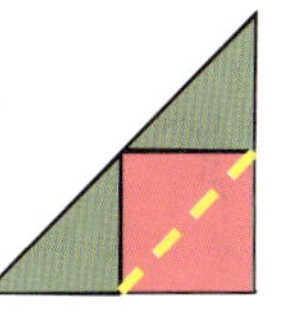

Make 20 pieced BC triangle units.

2 Make the BD triangle units: Select one triangle of Fabric B and one 2 1/2" square of Fabric D. Draw a line diagonally across the square and stitch. Press and cut away excess.

Make 20 pieced BD triangle units.

3 Select two BC triangle units and two dark BD triangle units and sew together as pictured.

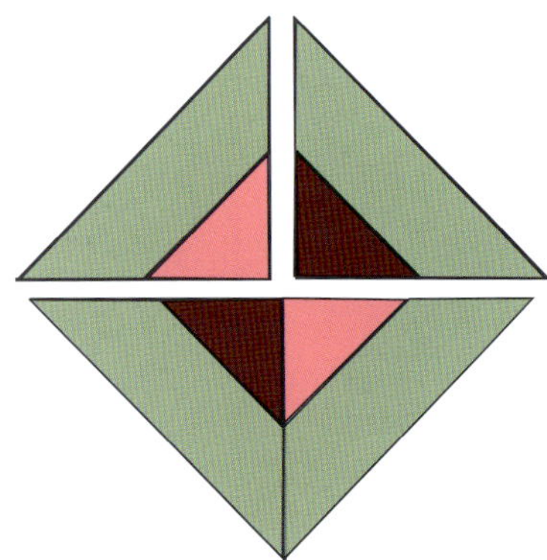

Make 10 Shaded Square blocks.
Square to 6 1/2" X 6 1/2".

Finishing

- Refer to the illustration at right for the block setting. Work in diagonal rows, pointing the rose blocks facing each other.

Be careful to place the light Fabric C triangles facing the correct direction.

- Cut three 2 1/4" X WOF Fabric A strips for the binding.

Detailed finishing instructions on odd angle binding are on Page 16.

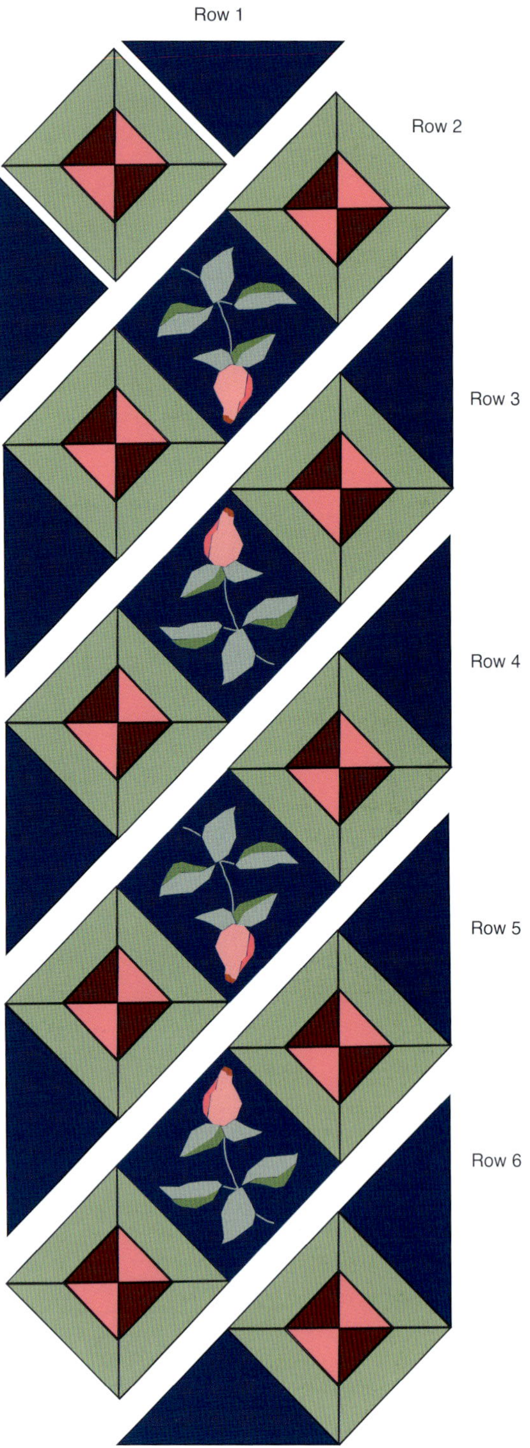

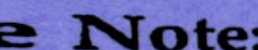

se Note:
re are measurement corrections on this design,
dswept Roses (page 61) and Field of Violets (page
. See our website for updates
w.englanddesign.com

Windswept Roses

Designed and Pieced by Cynthia England

Quilted by Denise Green

Windswept Roses

Finished Quilt Size: 46 1/2″ X 46 1/2″
Finished Picture Piecing Block Size: 6″ X 6″

Picture Piecing Material Requirements

For four rosebud blocks you will need:

- **B** - Beige for background............ 1/2 yard
- **R1** - Bright red for roses.............. 4″ X 22″
- **R2** - Dark red for roses.............. 4″ X 22″
- **R3** - Very dark red for roses...... 4″ X 11″
- **G1** - Green for leaves................... 4″ X 22″
- **G2** - Dark green for leaves........... 4″ X 22″

Make a color chart for the rosebud fabrics as pictured below.

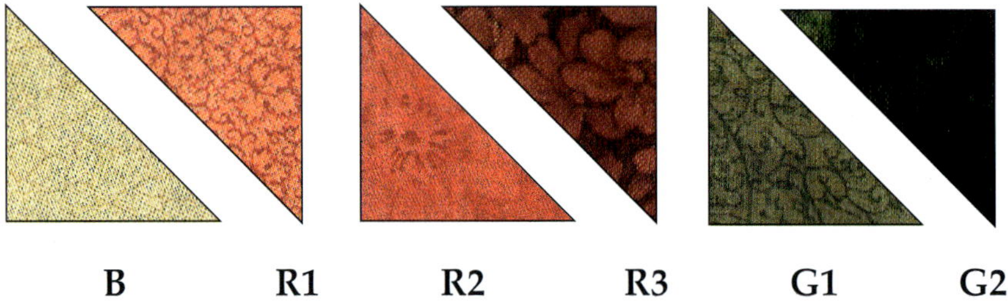

Traditional Quilt Materials Requirements

- **A** - Beige......................................5/8 yard
- **B** - Tan paisley........................... 1/3 yard
- **C** - Red floral.............................3/4 yard
- **D** - Green accent..........................1/2 yard
- **E** - Med/dk red........................1 1/2 yard
- **F** - Dark gold accent.................1/8 yard
- **G** - Burgundy............................1/2 yard
- **Backing** - Something pretty!.....3 1/2 yards

Two lengths of 1 3/4 yards.

Make a color chart for these fabrics as pictured below.

Rotary Cutting

*Before beginning, cut Fabric E outside borders lengthwise. Set aside.

Fabric Color	Size	Shape	Number Needed	Number To Cut
A	8 7/8" X 8 7/8"		4	2
	6 7/8" X 6 7/8"		4	4
	2 1/2" X 2 1/2"		20	10
B	2 1/8" X WOF		144"	4 strips
C	9 1/4" X 9 1/4"		8	2
	2 1/8" X 2 1/8"		16	1 strip
	2 1/8" X 5 1/2"		8	8
	2 1/8" X WOF	border	4	4 strips
D	2 1/8" X 2 1/8"		20	2 strips
	2 1/8" X WOF	border	4	4 strips
E	9 1/4" X 9 1/4"		8	2
	4" X LOF	*border lengthwise	4	4 strips
F	2 1/8" X 2 1/8"		4	4
G	*2 1/4" X WOF	binding	200"	5 strips

Picture Piecing Block Info —

Finished Block Size: 6″ X 6″

Picture Piecing sewing directions begin on Page 19. See Pages 56-57 for Rosebud sewing sequence and block pattern.

Don't forget! There are free videos on the website, ***www.englanddesign.com***

Pre-Sewing Recommendations

This makes the little pieces *so* much easier!

- Place right sides together and sew a 1/4″ seam allowance along the length of the strip. Some of the strips will be different lengths so they will not be even along the bottom. Press open.
- Sew the following strips together:

B to R1 to R2 to R3

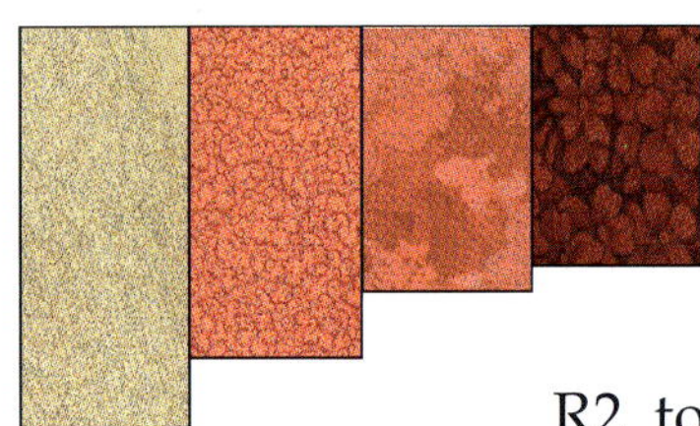

R2 to B to G1 to G2

Note: *Pre-sewing strips is not recommended for directional fabrics.*

Use three strands of embroidery floss and stem stitch rosebud stems.

After sewing four Rosebud blocks, use the Trim Guide on Page 58 and square up to $6^{1/2}$″X $6^{1/2}$″.

Traditional Piecing

1 Sew right sides together using a scant 1/4″ seam allowance. Sew two Rosebud blocks together facing the buds as shown. Repeat. Sew the four blocks together. Press. Set aside.

2 Piecing the inner setting triangles: Select two 2 $^{1/2}$″ Fabric A (diagonally cut) triangles and sew one to each side of one 2 $^{1/8}$″ Fabric C square. *Note placement of angles.*

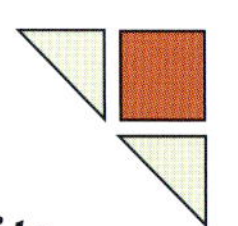

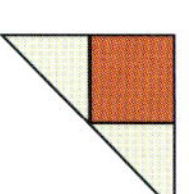

Make 4 ACA units.

3 Sew one 2 $^{1/2}$″ Fabric A triangle to one 2 $^{1/8}$″ Fabric C square. Add one 2 $^{1/8}$″ Fabric D square.

Make 4 ACD units.

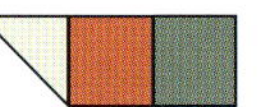

4 Sew one 2 $^{1/2}$″ triangle of Fabric A to the ***right*** side of one $2^{1/8}$″X $5^{1/2}$″ Fabric C rectangle.

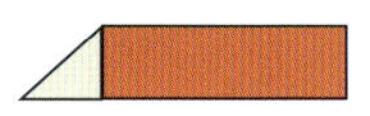

Make 4 AC rectangle units.

5 Repeat step four adding one 2 $^{1/8}$″ Fabric D square at the end.

Make 4 ACD rectangle units.

6 Put the units together to create pieced triangle units. Sew ACA unit to ACD unit. Press, add AC rectangle unit. Sew ACD rectangle unit to the top.

Make 4 pieced inner setting triangles.

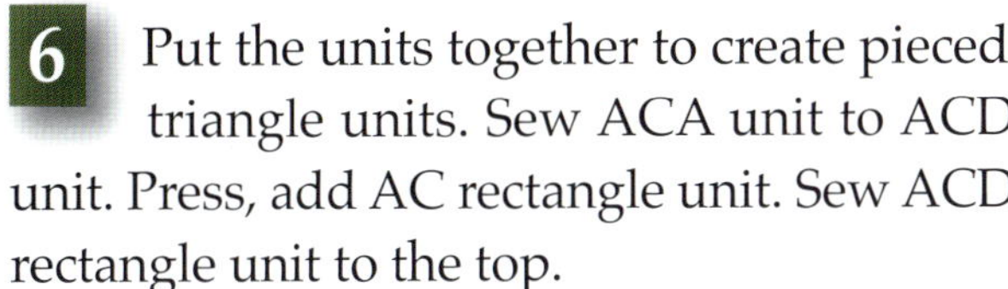

7 Sew pieced inner setting triangles to center rosebud medallion. Align center Fabric A triangle to the seam between roses.

Pieced Setting Units

1 Sew one Fabric C triangle (from quarter cut 9 1/4″ square) to one Fabric E (from quarter cut 9 1/4″ square) triangles. Align along short side as pictured.

Make 4 CE triangles with C on left.

2 Repeat step one reversing the Fabric C triangle.

Make 4 CE triangles with C on right.

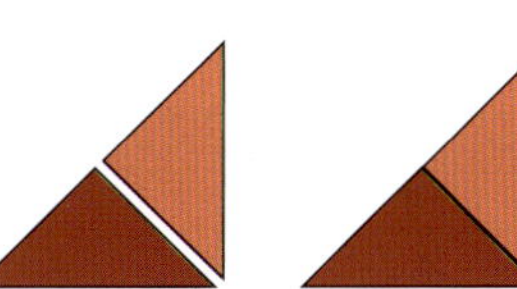

3 Subcut Fabric B into eight rectangles 2 1/8″ X 6 7/8″. Sew one 2 1/8″ Fabric D square to the right side of four of them.

Make 4.

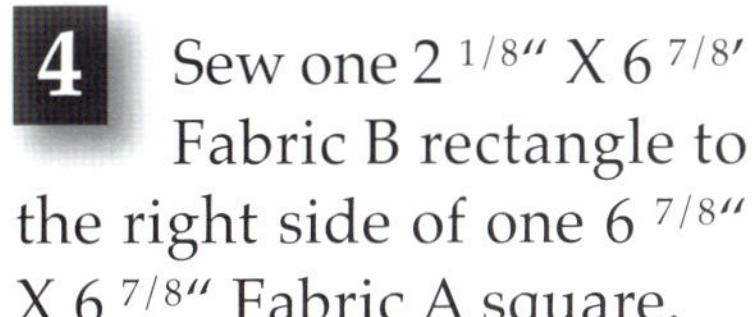

4 Sew one 2 1/8″ X 6 7/8′ Fabric B rectangle to the right side of one 6 7/8″ X 6 7/8″ Fabric A square.

Make 4.

5 Sew the BD rectangle unit to the top of the BA square unit.

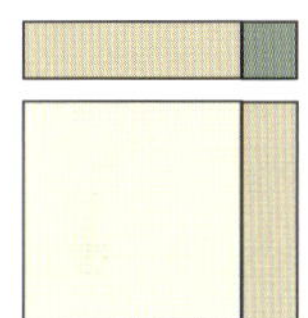

6 Subcut Fabric B into eight 2 1/8″ X 11″ rectangles. Sew one 2 1/8″ Fabric F square to the right side of four of them.

Make 4.

7 Sew one 2 1/8″ X 11″ Fabric B strip to the right side of one Fabric A triangle (diagonally cut from the 8 7/8″ square. Align at top. The strip will be longer than the triangle at the bottom.

Make 4.

8 Sew BF strip unit to the top of BA triangle unit. The additional Fabric B will be trimmed off before adding borders.

Make 4.

Assembling the Quilt Top

Refer to the illustration below for setting and color placement.

- Sew one large square unit to each side of two large triangle units to make the top and bottom rows. *Note placement of green squares.*

- Sew one large triangle unit to each side of the center rosebud medallion to create the center row. Sew rows together.

After top is complete, trim excess Fabric B even with the bottom of the triangle on all sides. See black dotted line; should measure $33^{1/2}$" square.

Finishing

Detailed finishing instructions on Page 7.

- Using two $2^{1/8}$" Fabric C squares and two $2^{1/8}$" Fabric D squares make four 4-patch units. Square each 4 - patch to $3^{3/4}$".
- Sew one $2^{1/8}$" X $33^{1/2}$" Fabric D strip to one $2^{1/8}$" X $33^{1/2}$" Fabric C strip. Make 4.
- Sew one DC strip to each side of the rose-bud medallion unit.
- Sew two CD 4-patches to each end of two DC strips. Sew one border unit to the top and one to the bottom.
- Use four strips of Fabric E 4" X LOF and add the borders, mitering corners. Directions on Page 9.
- Bind quilt using 5 strips of Fabric G, cut $2^{1/4}$" wide.

Christine's Rose Garden

Designed and Pieced by Cynthia England

Quilted by Denise Green

Christine's Rose Garden

Finished Quilt Size: 70″ X 79″
Finished Picture Piecing Block Size: 6″ X 6″
Finished Traditional Block Size: 6″ X 6″

Picture Piecing Material Requirements

For twenty rosebud blocks you will need:

- **B** - Beige for background........ $2^{1/2}$ yards
- **R1** - Red for roses....................... $1^{1/3}$ yards
- **R2** - Medium red for roses........ $1^{1/3}$ yards
- **R3** - Dark red for roses............. 2/3 yards
- **G1** - Green for leaves.................. $1^{1/3}$ yards
- **G2** - Dark green for leaves........ $1^{1/3}$ yards

Make a color chart for the rosebud fabrics as pictured below.

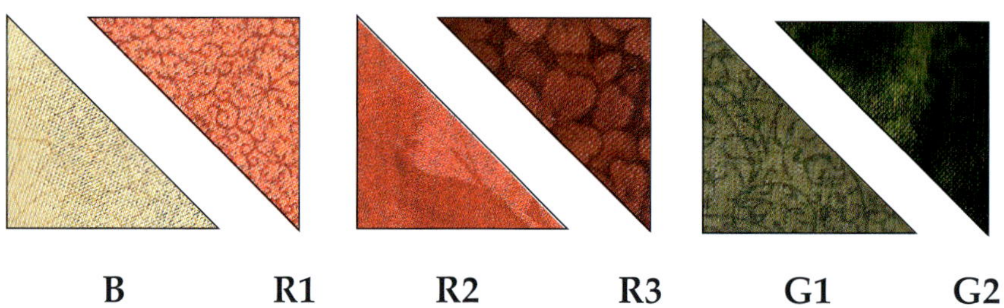

B **R1** **R2** **R3** **G1** **G2**

Traditional Quilt Material Requirements

- **A** - Red................1 yard
- **B** - Dk red......... 1 yard
- **C** - Beige............ 1 yard
- **D** - Gold..........2 5/8 yard
  Includes borders
- **E** - Green.............1 yard
- **F** - Black.......... 1 1/4 yard
  Includes binding
- **G** - Focus.......2 5/8 yards
  Includes borders

- **Backing** ....5 yards

Make a color chart for these fabrics as pictured.

Rotary Cutting

*Before beginning, cut inner border strips of Fabric D and outer border strips of Fabric G lengthwise. Set aside.

Fabric Color	Size	Shape	Number Needed	Number To Cut
A	1 7/8" X 1 7/8"		40	20
	1 1/2" X 2 1/2"		10	10
	1 1/2" X 4 1/2"		10	10
	2 1/2" X 2 1/2"		24	24
	2 7/8" X 2 7/8"		72	36
B	1 7/8" X 1 7/8"		40	20
	1 1/2" X 2 1/2"		10	10
	1 1/2" X 4 1/2"		10	10
	5 3/8" X 5 3/8"		24	12
	7 1/4" X 7 1/4"		32	8
C	6 7/8" X 6 7/8"		20	10
	7 1/4" X 7 1/4"		16	4
	6 1/2" X 6 1/2"		4	4
	2 1/2" X 2 1/2"		8	8
D	6 7/8" X 6 7/8"		4	2
	2 7/8" X 2 7/8"		24	12
	*2" X LOF	*borders	4	4
E	2 1/2" X 2 1/2"		16	16
	9 3/4" X 9 3/4"	side triangles	22	6
	9 3/8" X 9 3/8"	corners	4	2
F	2 1/2" X 2 1/2"		5	5
	1 7/8" X 10 1/4"		32	32
	*2 1/4" X WOF	binding	320"	8 strips
G	2 1/2" X 2 1/2"		48	48
	7 1/4" X 7 1/4"		16	4
	5 3/8" X 5 3/8"		8	4
	6 7/8" X 6 7/8"		16	8
	*4 1/2" X LOF	*borders	4	4

Picture Piecing Block Info —

Finished Block Size: 6″ X 6″

Picture Piecing sewing directions begin on Page 19. See Pages 56-57 for Rosebud sewing sequence and block pattern.

Don't forget! There are free videos on the website, ***www.englanddesign.com***

Pre-Sewing Recommendations

This makes the little pieces *so* much easier!

- Place right sides together and sew a 1/4″ seam allowance along the length of the strip. Some of the strips will be different lengths so they will not be even along the bottom. Press open.

- Sew the following strips together:

B to R1 to R2 to R3

R2 to B to G1 to G2

Note: *Pre-sewing strips is not recommended for directional fabrics.*

Use three strands of embroidery floss and stem stitch rosebud stems.

After sewing twenty Rosebud blocks, use the Trim Guide on Page 58 and square up to $6^{1/2}$″X $6^{1/2}$″.

Traditional Block Info

Box-in-a-Box Block

Finished Block Size:

6″ X 6″

Making the Traditional Blocks

Sew right sides together using a scant 1/4″ seam allowance.

1 Select one $1\ ^{7/8}$″ triangle of Fabric A one $1\ ^{7/8}$″ triangle of Fabric B. Sew together to make a square. Square to $1\ ^{1/2}$″.

Make 40 AB squares.

2 Sew one AB square to either side of one $1^{1/2}$″X $2^{1/2}$″ Fabric A rectangle to make the short AB rows.

Note diagram for color placement.

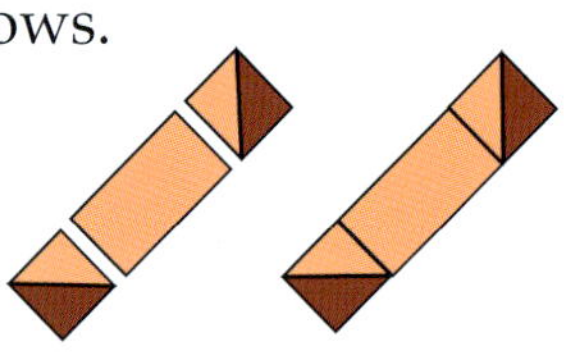

Make 10 short AB rows.

3 Repeat Steps 1 and 2 using Fabric A and B in *reverse*. This time, use a long $1^{1/2}$″X $4^{1/2}$″ Fabric B rectangle in the middle.

Note diagram for color placement.

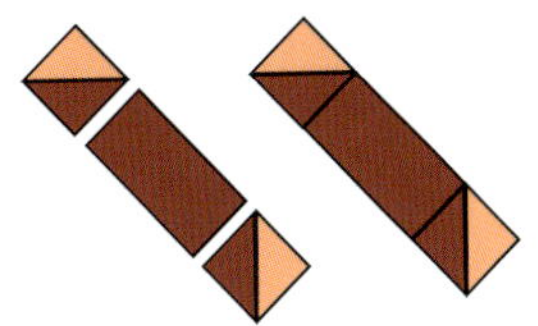

Make 10 long BA rows.

4 Sew one 1 1/2" X 2 1/2" strip of Fabric B to each side of one 2 1/2"X 2 1/2" Fabric F square.

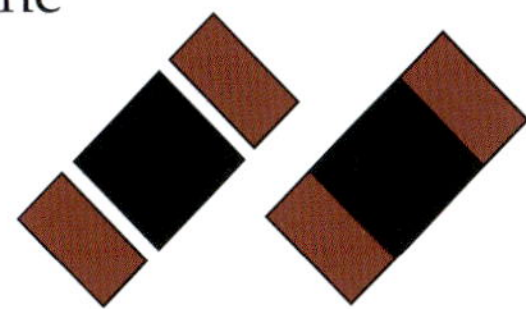

Make 5 BFB square units.

5 Sew one short AB row to each side of one BFB square unit.

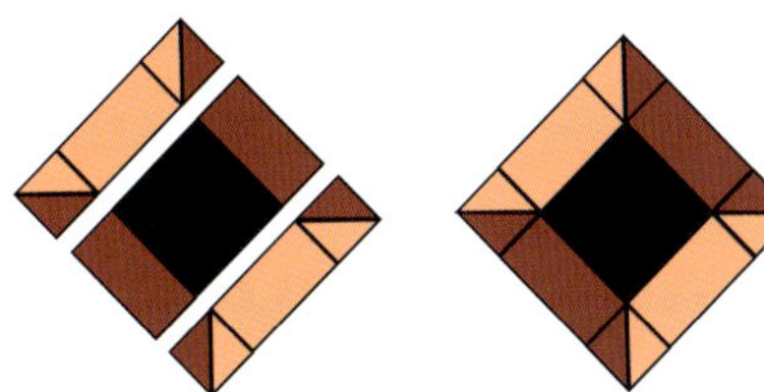

Make 5 ABF square unit centers.

6 Sew one 1 1/2" X 4 1/2" strip of Fabric A to each side of one ABF square unit center.

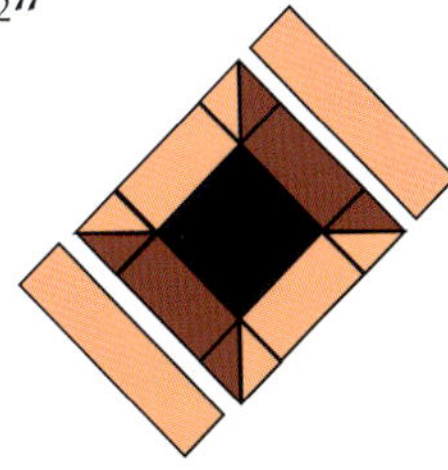

Make 5.

7 Sew one long BA row to each side of one center square unit. Square to 6 1/2".

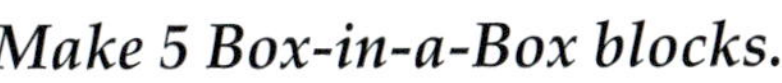

Make 5 Box-in-a-Box blocks.

8 Make the large half square triangles. Sew one 6 7/8" triangle of Fabric C to one 6 7/8" triangle of Fabric D. Square to 6 1/2".

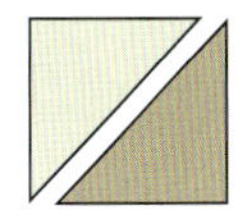

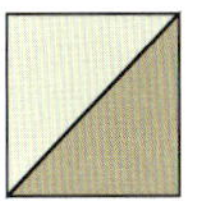

Make 4 CD half square triangles.

9 Repeat Step eight using one 6 7/8" triangle of Fabric C to one 6 7/8" triangle of Fabric G. Square to 6 1/2".

Make 16 CG half square triangles.

10 Make the inner border units: Select two 2 7/8" Fabric D (diagonally cut) triangles and sew one to each side of one 2 1/2" Fabric E square. *Note placement of colors.*

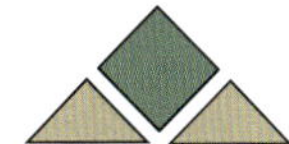

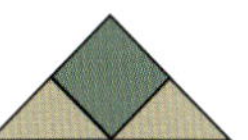

Make 8 DED units.

11 Sew one 2 7/8" Fabric D triangle to one 2 1/2" Fabric E square. Add one 2 1/2" Fabric C square.

Make 8 CDE units.

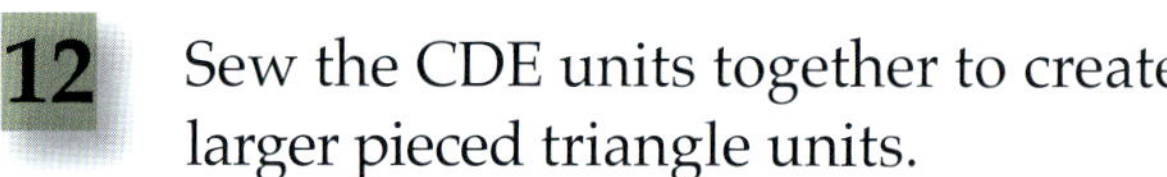

12 Sew the CDE units together to create larger pieced triangle units.

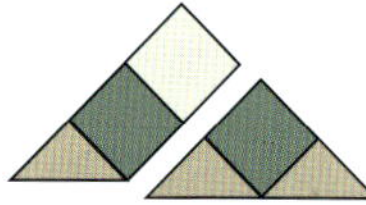

Make 8 CDE inner border pieced triangles.

13 Repeat steps ten through twelve using Fabrics A and G.

Note diagram for color placement.

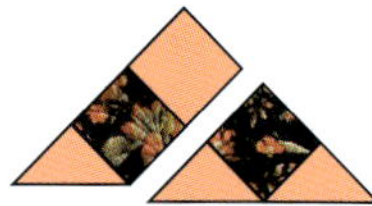

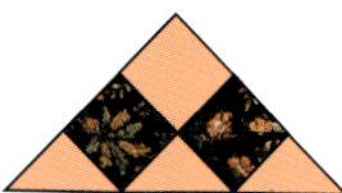

Make 24 AG border triangle units.

14 Sew one triangle of Fabric G (from diagonally cut 5 3/8" square) to one 1 7/8" X 10 1/4" Fabric F strip. Center triangle over strip. After sewing, trim away excess as indicated in the diagram.

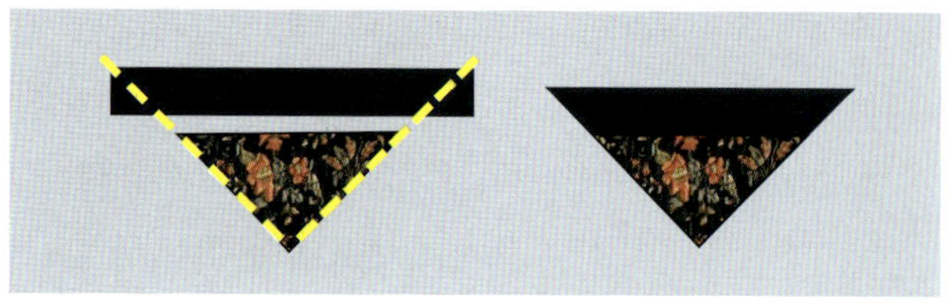

Make 8 GF inner border units.

15 Repeat Step 14 using Fabric B triangle and Fabric F strip. Trim away excess.

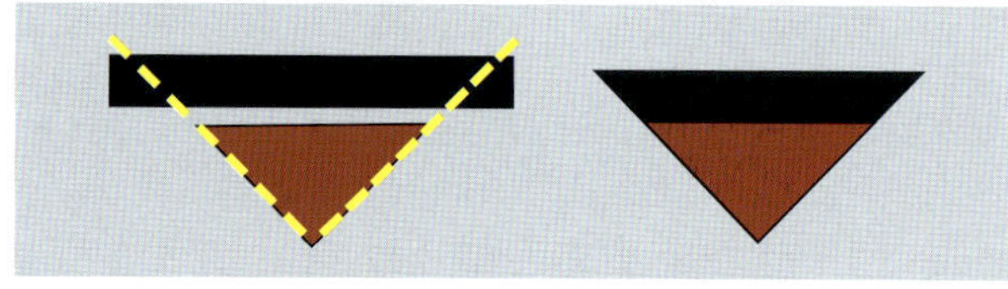

Make 24 BF border triangle units.

16 Sew one CDE inner border pieced triangle unit to one GF inner border unit. Square to 6 1/2".

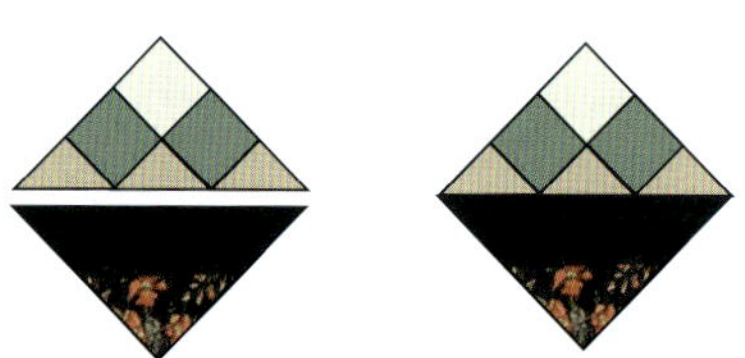

Make 8 pieced CDE/GF square units.

17 Sew one AG border triangle unit to one BF border unit. Square to 6 1/2".

Make 24 AF/BF square units.

18 Sew one triangle of Fabric C (from 7 1/4″ square cut twice on the diagonal) to one triangle Fabric B (from 7 1/4″ square cut twice on the diagonal). *Note diagram for angle placement.*

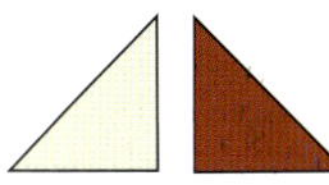
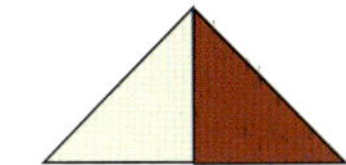

Make 16 CB triangle units.

19 Repeat step eighteen using Fabric B and Fabric G. *Note diagram for angle placement.*

Make 16 BG triangle units.

20 Sew one CB triangle unit to one BC triangle unit. Square to 6 1/2″.

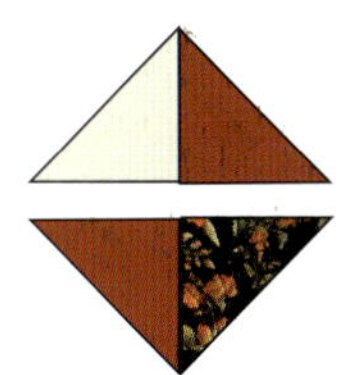

Make 16 CB/BG square units.

Putting the Units Together —

- Sew two Rosebud blocks together facing buds as indicated. Repeat. Sew the four blocks together. Press. Square to 12 1/2″.

  Complete 4 blocks.

Prepare two rosebud rows:

- Sew one CDE/GF square unit to one CB/BG square unit.
  Make 2.

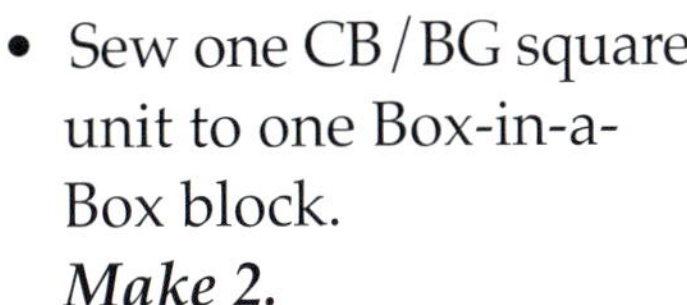

- Sew one CB/BG square unit to one Box-in-a-Box block.
  Make 2.

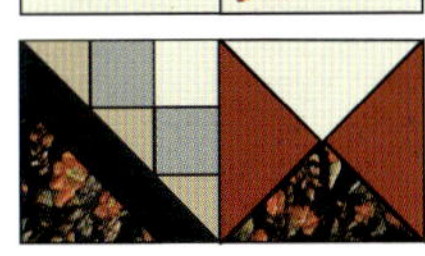
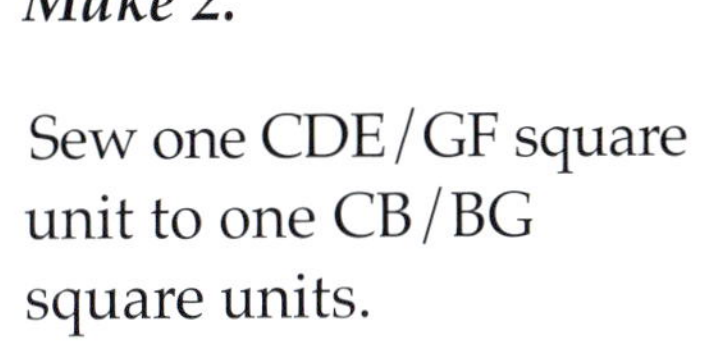

- Sew one CDE/GF square unit to one CB/BG square units.
  Note block positions.
  Make 2.

- Sew one 12 1/2″ Rosebud block to each end of rows as pictured in the diagram.
  Make 2 Rosebud Rows.

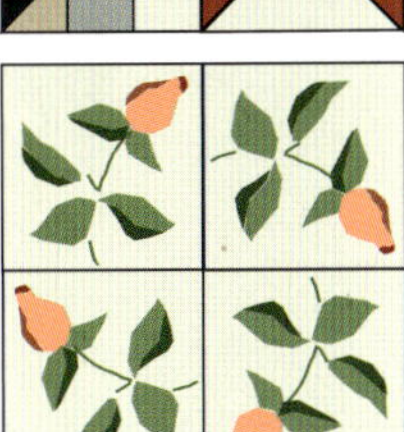

Join Rows

Follow illustration pictured on Page 74. *Important! Note block orientation.*

Square quilt to 42 1/2″ X 42 1/2″.

Start with the center square of the quilt.

- Sew Rosebud row at bottom left corner and join rows to the right ending with second Rosebud row.

- After center square of the quilt is complete, add top left corner rows and bottom right corner rows.

- Add lower left corner rows and upper right corner rows. Use four Fabric C triangles cut once diagonally from the 9 3/8″ squares.

Finishing

For the borders, place Fabric D and Fabric G strips together and sew. Press. Following mitering directions on Page 9, center sides first, and sew. Center top and bottom border strips and sew. Miter corners.

Detailed finishing instructions on Page 7.

- Bind quilt using 8 strips of Fabric F, cut 2 1/4" X WOF.
- Sleeve and label your quilt.

Sweetheart Roses

Designed and Pieced by Cynthia England

Quilted by Richard Larson

Sweetheart Roses

Finished Quilt Size: 53″ X 53″
Finished Picture Piecing Block Size: 6″ X 6″
Finished Traditional Block Size: 10″ X 10″

Picture Piecing Material Requirements

For four rosebud blocks you will need:

- **B** - Beige for background........... 1/2 yard
- **R1** - Bright red for roses...............1/4 yard
- **R2** - Dark red for roses................ 1/4 yard
- **R3** - Very dark red for roses....... 1/8 yard
- **G1** - Green for leaves....................1/4 yard
- **G2** - Dark green for leaves..........1/4 yard

Make a color chart for the rosebud fabrics as pictured below.

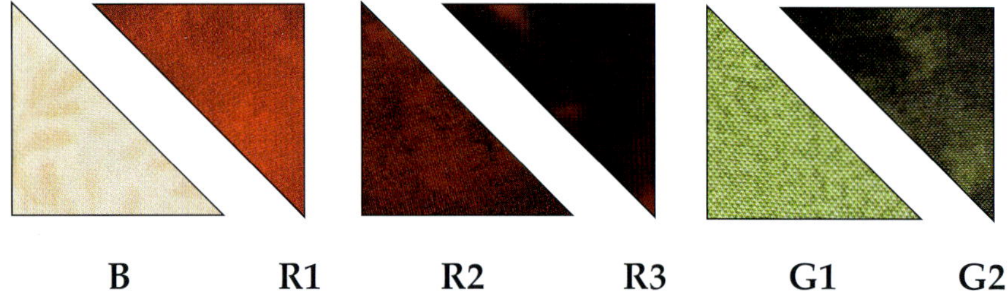

Traditional Quilt Materials Requirements

- **A** - Cream/red shirting................1 yard
- **B** - Beige for background.........1/8 yard
- **C** - Red with cream....................1 yard
- **D** - Red plaid............................1/2 yard
- **E** - Med/dk red.......................3/8 yard
- **F** - Dark red............................ 1/3 yard
- **G** - Very dark red.................1 3/4 yards
  Includes borders and binding
- **R1** - Bright red ....1/8 yard
  Same color as R1, Picture Piecing
- **Backing** - Something pretty!....3 1/2 yards
  Two lengths of 1 3/4 yards.

Make a color chart for these fabrics as pictured below.

Rotary Cutting

*Before beginning, cut outside borders and binding of Fabric G, lengthwise. Set aside.

Note:
In order for clarification in the illustrations we have used different colors, however, the actual quilt is different shades of red. Very important to make the color chart with actual fabric swatches!

Fabric Color	Size	Shape	Number Needed	Number To Cut
A	4 7/8" X 4 7/8"		28	14
	2 7/8" X 2 7/8"		28	14
	4 1/2" X 4 1/2"		8	8
B	2 1/2" X 2 1/2"		8	8
C	2 1/2" X 40"		4 strips	4 strips
	1 1/2" X 10 1/2"	sashing	40	40
D	4 7/8" X 4 7/8"		24	12
	2 7/8" X 2 7/8"		32	16
E	2 7/8" X 2 7/8"		84	42
F	2 1/2" X 40"		3 strips	3 strips
G	2 7/8" X 2 7/8"		80	40
	*4 1/2" X LOF	*borders	4	4
	*2 1/4" X LOF	*binding	4 strips	4 strips
R1	1 1/2" X 1 1/2"		25	25

The background fabric and the shirting background color are close to the same shade.

Picture Piecing Block Info

Finished Block Size: 6″ X 6″

Picture Piecing sewing directions begin on Page 19. See Pages 56-57 for Rosebud sewing sequence and block pattern.
Don't forget! There are free videos on the website, ***www.englanddesign.com***

Pre-Sewing Recommendations

This makes the little pieces *so* much easier!

- Place right sides together and sew a 1/4″ seam allowance along the length of the strip. Some of the strips will be different lengths so they will not be even along the bottom. Press open.

- Sew the following strips together:

B to R1 to R2 to R3

R2 to B to G1 to G2

Note: *Pre-sewing strips is not recommended for directional fabrics.*

Use three strands of embroidery floss and stem stitch rosebud stems.

After sewing four Rosebud blocks, use the Trim Guide on Page 58 and square up to $6^{1/2}$″X $6^{1/2}$″.

Traditional Block Info

Finished Block Size: 10″ X 10″

Nine Patch Variation

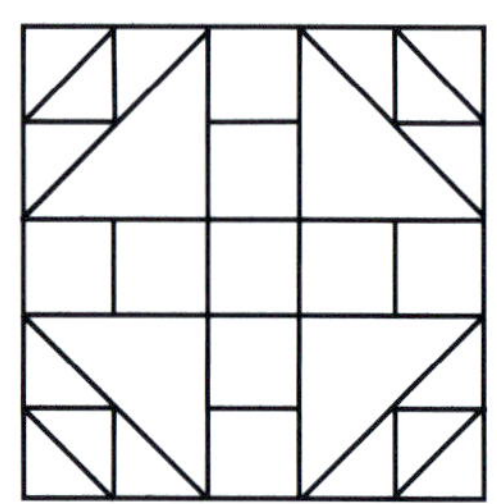

Careful color placement makes this quilt special. To create the effect, **three** different color variations of the same block were used.

They are:

Corner Blocks.................................. 4 needed
Side Blocks..................................... 8 needed
Picture Pieced Set Blocks............... 4 needed

Check out Indigo Lights on Page 115.
The same Nine-Patch block was used as in Sweetheart Roses. Blocks are set on-point in shades of blue.

Making the Traditional Blocks

Sew right sides together using a scant 1/4" seam allowance.

1 Sew one 2 7/8" triangle of Fabric D to one 2 7/8" triangle of Fabric G to create a DG half square triangle. Square to 2 1/2".

Make 8 DG squares.

2 From one of the 2 1/2"X 40" strips of Fabric C, subcut twelve 2 1/2" X 2 1/2" squares. Set aside.

3 Make the square units:
Sew one 2 1/2" X 40" strip of Fabric C to one 2 1/2"X 40" strip of Fabric F. Make 3 strip sets. Crosscut the strip sets into 48 units. Each unit should measure 2 1/2"X 4 1/2"

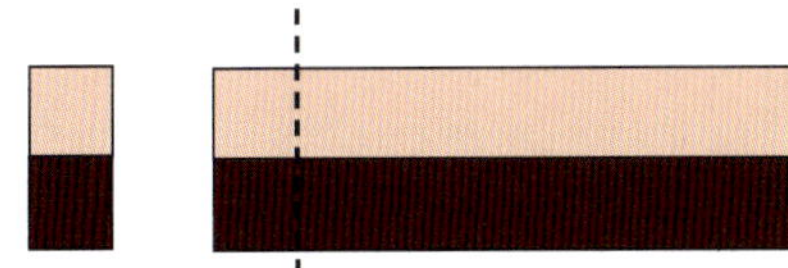

Make 48 CF square units.

4 Sew two of the CF square units to each side of one 2 1/2"X 2 1/2" Fabric C square.

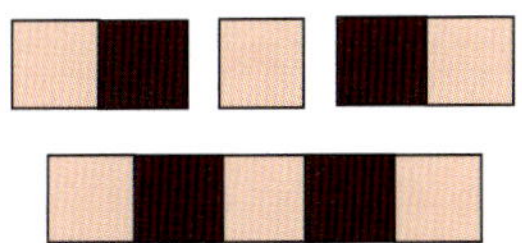

Make 12 CF square set rows.

5 Make the light triangle units:
Select one 2 7/8" triangle of Fabric A
three 2 7/8" triangles of Fabric E
one 4 7/8" triangle of Fabric A
Layout fabrics as pictured. Sew.

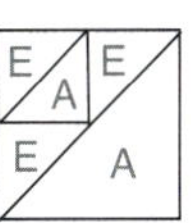

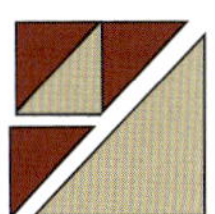
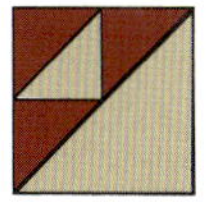

Make 28 light triangle units.

6 Make the dark triangle units:
Select one 2 7/8" triangle of Fabric D
three 2 7/8" triangles of Fabric G
one 4 7/8" triangle of Fabric D
Layout fabrics as pictured. Sew.

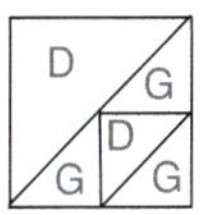

Make 24 dark triangle units.

7 Make the Corner Blocks:
Sew one light triangle unit to each side of one CF square unit. Sew one light triangle unit and one dark triangle unit to each side of a CF square unit. Join as pictured. *Note orientation of units in bottom row.* Square to 10 1/2".

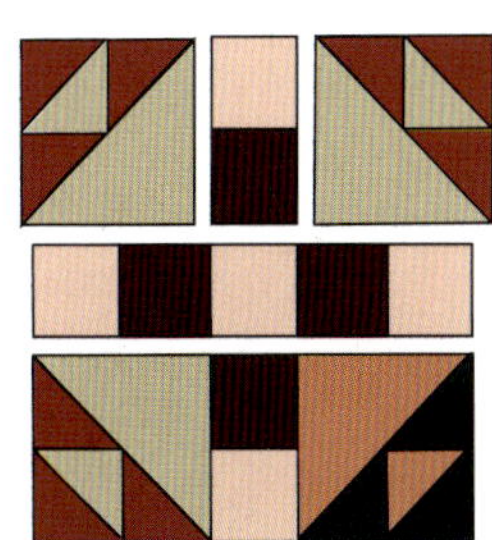

Complete 4 Corner Blocks.

8 Make the Side Blocks:
Sew one light triangle unit to each side of a square unit. Sew one dark triangle unit to each side of a square unit. Sew these units on either side of a square row as pictured. Square to 10 1/2".

Complete 8 Side Blocks.

9 Make the Picture Pieced Set Blocks:
Sew one dark triangle unit to one 4 1/2" Fabric A square. Sew two DG half square triangles to two 2 1/2" Fabric B squares. Sew one DG square unit to right side of a Fabric A square. Sew one 4 1/2" Fabric A square to one DG square unit. Sew one Rosebud block to the right side as indicated in illustration. Square to 10 1/2".

Complete 4 Picture Pieced Set Blocks.

Assembling the Quilt Top

1 Join two Corner blocks and two Side blocks with five 1 1/2" X 10 1/2" Fabric C sashing rectangles. Take care that the corners are arranged correctly with the dark triangle unit facing in (white boxes in diagram). When joining blocks together, make sure that visually the block seams align (yellow dotted line). The skinny sashing will be in between so there will not be seams that line up exactly. But, they need to look close.

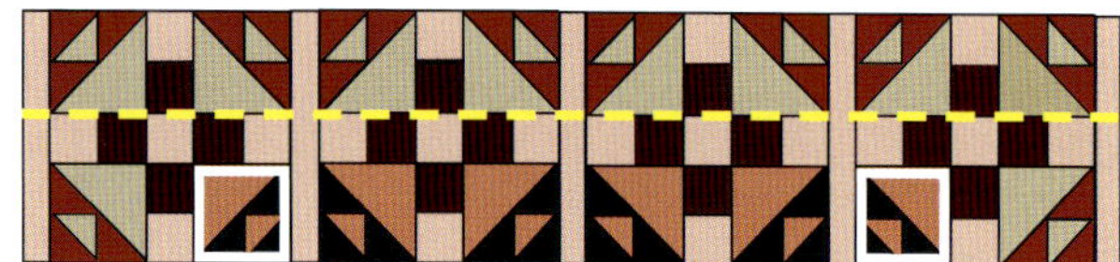

Make 2 rows with this combination.

2 Join two Side blocks and two Picture Pieced Set Blocks with five 1 1/2" X 10 1/2" Fabric C sashing rectangles.

Make 2 rows with this combination.

3 Use the remaining 1 1/2" X 10 1/2" Fabric C sashing strips combined with the 1 1/2" Fabric R1 squares to make sashing rows.

Make 5 rows.

4 Join rows as pictured, placing the dark dark triangle units to form a dark inner border surrounding the Picture Pieced Roses.

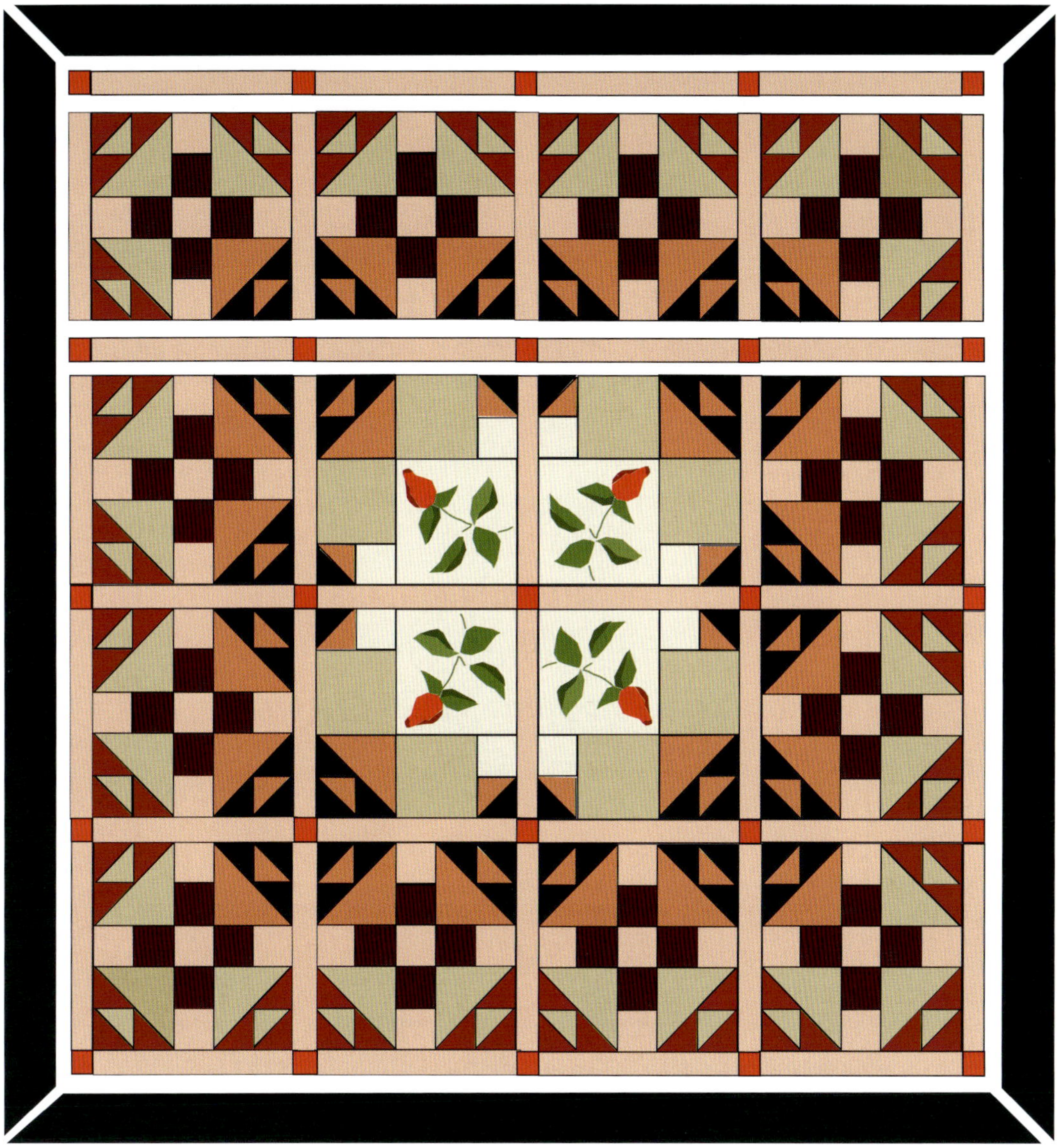

Outer Borders

Detailed finishing instructions on Page 7.

- Add the borders, using four strips of Fabric G $4^{1/2}$" X LOF. Miter corners.
- Bind quilt using 4 strips of Fabric G, cut $2^{1/4}$" X LOF.
- Sleeve and label the quilt.

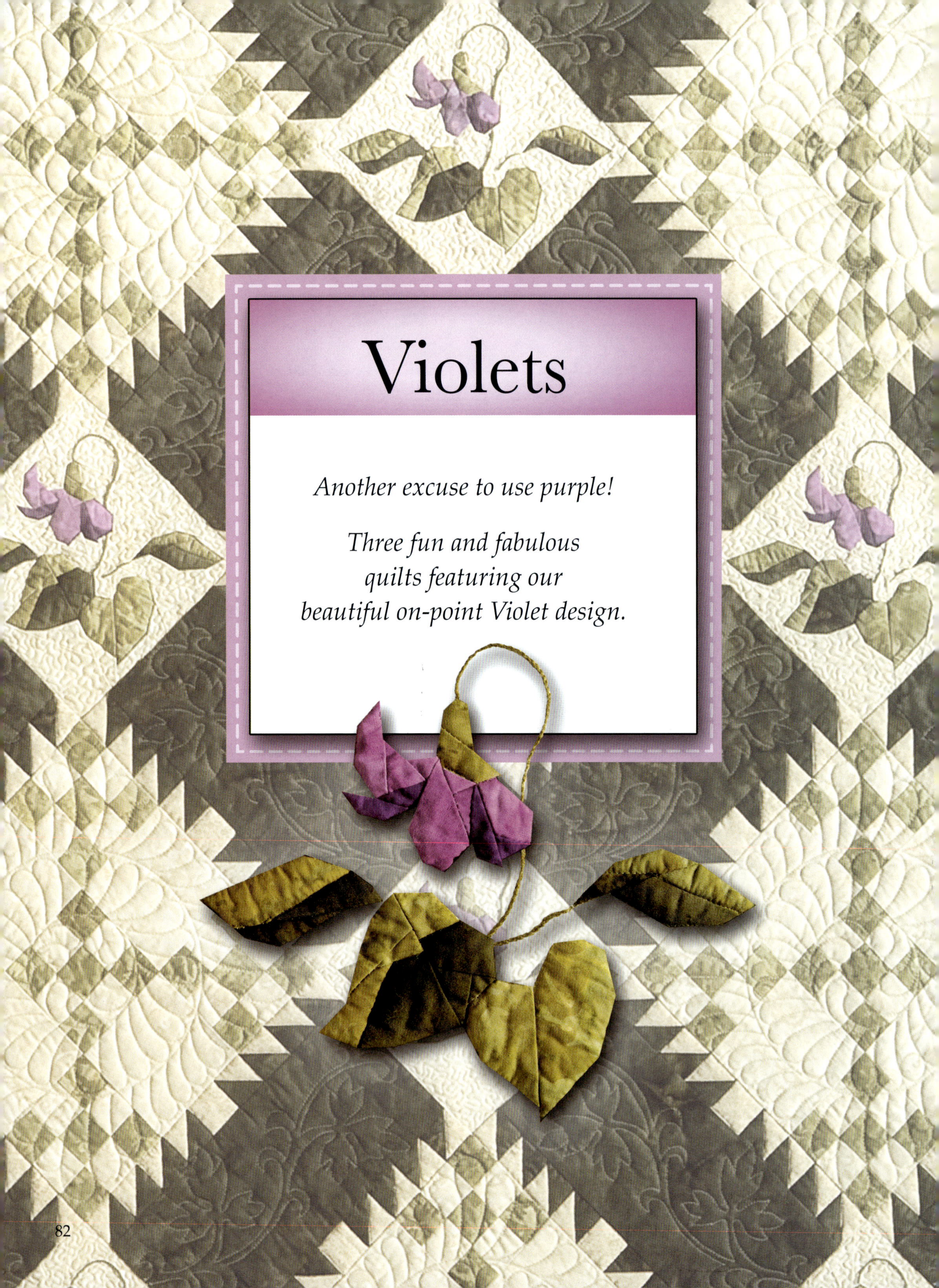

Violets

Another excuse to use purple!

Three fun and fabulous quilts featuring our beautiful on-point Violet design.

Aunt Wanda's Violets

Finished Quilt Size:
36″ X 36″

Finished Picture Piecing Block Size: 6″ X 6″

Designed and Pieced
by Cynthia England
Quilted by Richard Larson

Picture Piecing Material Requirements

For four violet blocks you will need:

- **B** - Black for background.............. 1/2 yard
  Same as Fabric A - Traditional Yardage
- **P1** - Purple for flowers.................. 4″ X 22″
- **P2** - Dark purple for flowers....... 4″ X 22″
- **G1** - Green for leaves.................. 4″ X 42″
  Same as Fabric C - Traditional Yardage
- **G2** - Dark green for leaves......... 4″ X 22″

Make a color chart for the violet fabrics as pictured below.

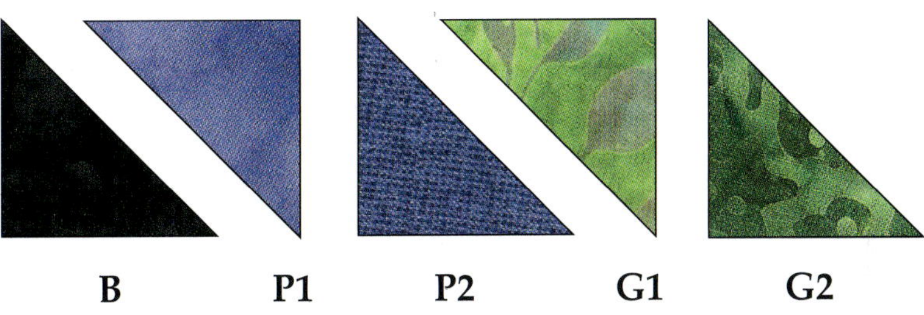

Traditional Quilt Material Requirements

- **A** - Black ....1 yard
  used for setting triangles / inner border
- **B** - Lavender.............................. 3/8 yard
- **C** - Lime green.......................... 2/3 yard
- **D** - Purple ....1 3/4 yards
  used for setting triangles and binding

- **Backing** - Something pretty!....1 1/4 yards

Make a color chart for these fabrics as pictured below.

Rotary Cutting

*Before beginning, cut 1 yard of Fabric D and set aside for setting triangles and binding.

** Note:*
Suggest using half square triangle unit grid papers for the 2″ finished half squares. For this, use sheets of 8 1/2″ X 11″ paper. See Page 6.
Or.....
Use the 2 7/8″ X 2 7/8″ measurements and cut squares, then cut diagonally.

Fabric Color	Size	Shape	Number Needed	Number To Cut
A	*8 1/2" X 11"	rectangle	36	3 sheets
	or			or
	2 7/8" X 2 7/8"	half-square triangles	36	3 strips
	2 1/2" X 20 1/2"	strip	4	4
	9 3/4" X 9 3/4"	quarter-square triangles	8	2
B	*8 1/2" X 11"	rectangle	36	3 sheets
	or	or		or
	2 7/8" X 2 7/8"	half-square triangles	36	3 strips
C	*8 1/2" X 11"	rectangle	60	5 sheets
	or	or		or
	2 7/8" X 2 7/8"	half-square triangles	60	5 strips
D	*8 1/2" X 11"	rectangle	60	5 sheets
	or	or		or
	*2 7/8" X 2 7/8"	half-square triangles	60	5 strips
	10" X 10"	half-square triangles *setting	4	2
	13" X 13"	quarter-square triangles corners	4	1
	2 1/4" X WOF	strip *binding	154"	4 strips

Picture Piecing Block Info —

Finished Block Size: 6″ X 6″

Picture Piecing sewing directions begin on Page 19. See Pages 92-93 for Violet sewing sequence and block pattern.
*Don't forget! There are free videos on the website, **www.englanddesign.com***

Pre-Sewing Recommendations

This makes the little pieces *so* much easier! Cut all strips in half (they will be around 4″ X 22″ long).

- Place right sides together and sew a 1/4″ seam. Some of the strips may be different lengths. Just sew along the side to the end. Press open.
- Sew the following strips together:

B to P2 to P1 to B

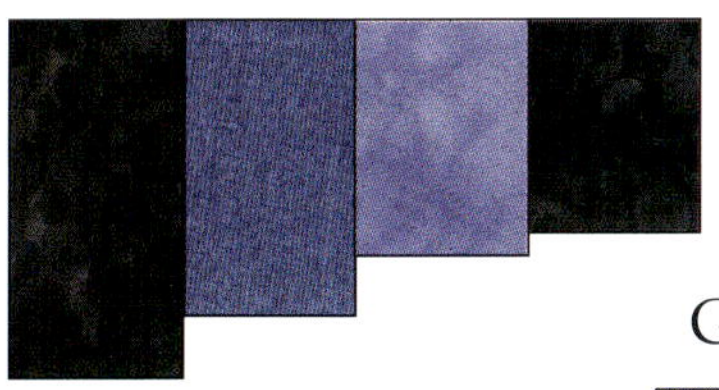

G1 to G2 to B

***Note:** Pre-sewing strips is not recommended for directional fabrics.*

Eventually you will need to sew more combinations of colors together for pre-sewing.

Use 3 strands of green embroidery floss which match your Light Green fabric to stem stitch the lines indicated on the Violet Trim Guide on Page 94.

Traditional Set Info

1 Sew two Violet blocks together facing the buds inward. Repeat. Sew the four blocks together. Press.

2 Add the Violet setting triangles: Select four large triangles of Fabric D (cut once on diagonal from 10″ X 10″), and sew one to each side of the group of four Violet Blocks. These blocks were intentionally cut larger than needed. Square to $16^{1/2}$″ X $16^{1/2}$″.

3 Make the AB half-square triangles: Using Fabric A and Fabric B make the 2″ finished half square triangle units. Either use the triangle unit grid papers as described on Page 6.... OR...
from 2 strips cut 18 squares ($2^{7/8}$″ X $2^{7/8}$″) once diagonally to yield 36 triangles. Sew right sides together. Press. Square to $2^{1/2}$″.

Make a total of 36 AB half squares.

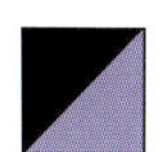

4 Make the half square triangle border: Select 16 Fabric AB half square triangles. Use eight half square triangles *reversing directions* in the center and sew into rows.

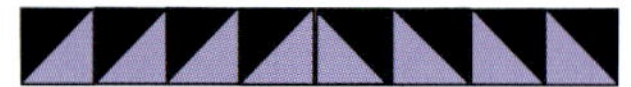

Make two rows of 8 AB half squares.

5 Select 20 Fabric AB half square triangles. Use ten half square triangles *reversing directions* in the center and sew into rows.

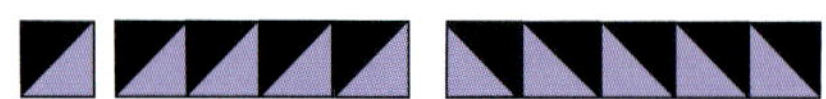

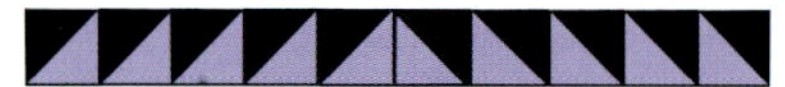

Make two rows of 10 AB half squares.

6 Sew the half square triangle border to the Violet block unit:

Sew one of the eight AB half square units to opposite sides, aligning center seam.

7 Sew one of the ten AB units to each of the remaining sides. Align center and corner seams.

Square to $20^{1/2}$″ X $20^{1/2}$″.

8 Make the CD half square triangles:

Using Fabric C and Fabric D, make the 2″ finished half square triangle units. Either use the triangle unit grid papers as described on Page 6... OR...

from 3 strips of each fabric cut 30 squares ($2^{7/8}$″ X $2^{7/8}$″) once diagonally to yield 60 triangles. Sew right sides together.

Press. Square to $2^{1/2}$″.

Make a total of 60 CD half squares.

9 Add the inner borders:

Select 4 Fabric A, $2^{1/2}$″ X $20^{1/2}$″ rectangles. Sew one on opposite sides of the center Violet unit.

Select 4 CD half square triangles and the remaining two Fabric A rectangles. Sew one half square triangle to either end of the Fabric A rectangle, placing the Fabric C triangle pointing *towards the center* of the quilt.

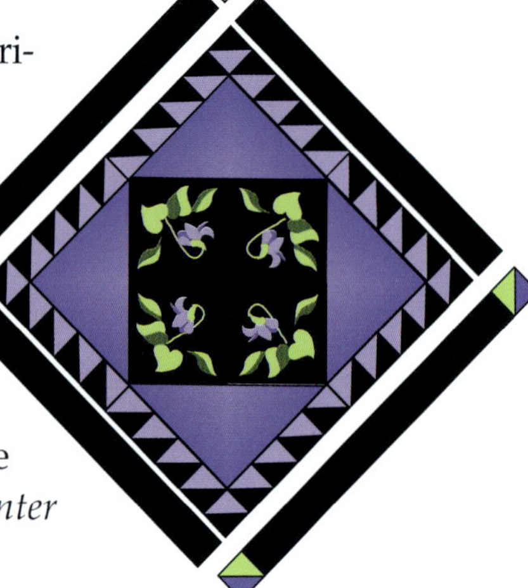

10 Make CD half square triangle outside border units of three:
Make the short sides. Select 12 Fabric CD half square triangles and sew into units of three. Make sure that the Fabric C triangles are at the top.

Make 8 CD units of three.

11 Select one Fabric A triangle (diagonal cut from the 9 3/4″ X 9 3/4″squares) and sew one CD unit of three to the right side.

Make 4 ACD units of 3.

12 Make half square outside border units of three with a triangle. Select 4 CD units of three and add one Fabric D triangle to the *right* end of each set.

Make 4 CD units of three with Fabric D triangle.

13 Select one Fabric A triangle (diagonal cut from the 9 3/4″ X 9 3/4″squares) and sew one CD unit of three with Fabric D triangle to the right side.

Make 4 ACD units of 3 with triangle at the end.

14 Make the long side half square triangle outside units of four:
Select 32 Fabric CD half square triangles and sew into rows of four. Add one Fabric D triangle at the *left* end. Make sure that the Fabric C triangles are at the top. *See diagram.*

Make 8 CD units of four with Fabric D triangle.

15 Add the long side half square triangle CD units of four to the ACD units of 3:
Select one ACD unit of 3 and one CD unit of four and sew to the *left* side as pictured.

Make 4.

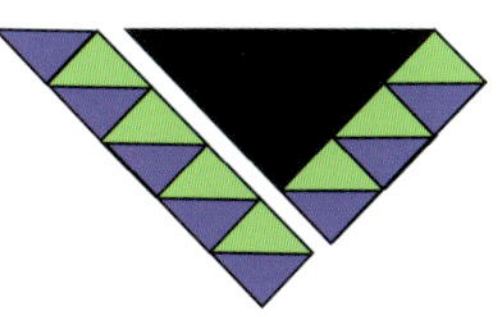

Repeat, using one ACD unit of 3 with Fabric D triangle and sew to the *left* side of the ACD unit of 3 with Fabric D Triangle.

Make 4 with triangle as pictured to the right.

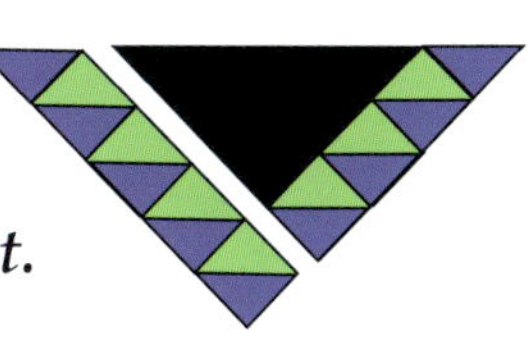

16 Sew one Fabric D setting triangle (cut twice on the diagonal from 13″ X 13″ square) between two of the Fabric A triangle units.

Make 4 triangle unit rows.

Assembling the Quilt Top

Refer to the illustration at right for the border setting. Match up center Fabric D triangle to center of Fabric A inner border strip using the red dots as reference.

Match seams where the lime green triangles meet.

After sewing two sides on there will be two points to trim off (see arrow and red dashed line).

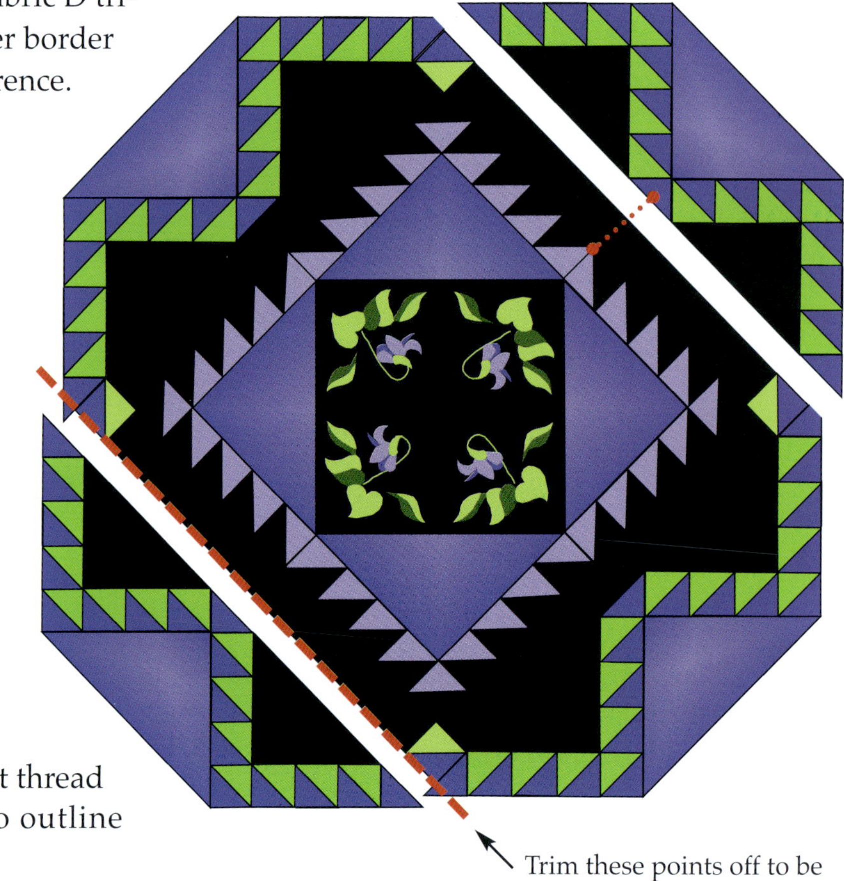

Trim these points off to be even with border edge before adding final sides.

Finishing

- Bind quilt using four strips Fabric D 2 1/4″ X WOF.
- To quilt, use a monofilament thread on top and in the bobbin to outline the pieced violet designs.

African Violets

Designed and Pieced by Cynthia England

Quilted by Denise Green

African Violets

Finished Quilt Size: 38″ X 38″
Finished Picture Piecing Block Size: 6″ X 6″
Finished Traditional Block Size: 12″ X 12″

Picture Piecing Material Requirements

For four violet blocks you will need:

- **B** - Light gray for background.... 1/2 yard
- **P1** - Purple for flowers................. 4″ X 22″
- **P2** - Dark purple for flowers....... 4″ X 22″
- **G1** - Green for leaves................... 4″ X 42″
- **G2** - Dark green for leaves......... 4″ X 22″
  Same as Fabric F in Traditional yardage.

Make a color chart for the violet fabrics as pictured below.

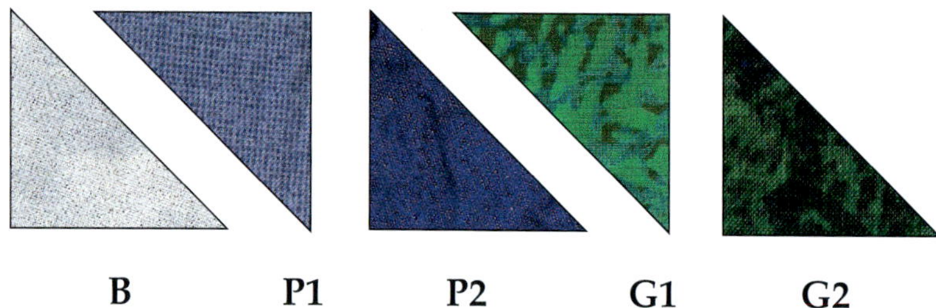

Picture Piecing Block Info —

Finished Block Size: 6″ X 6″

Picture Piecing sewing directions begin on Page 19. See Pages 92-93 for Violet sewing sequence and block pattern.

Don't forget! There are free videos on the website, ***www.englanddesign.com***

Pre-Sewing Recommendations

This makes the little pieces *so* much easier! Cut all strips in half (they will be around 4″ X 22″ long).

- Place right sides together and sew a 1/4″ seam. Some of the strips may be different lengths. Just sew along the side to the end. Press open.

- Sew the following strips together:

B to P2 to P1 to B

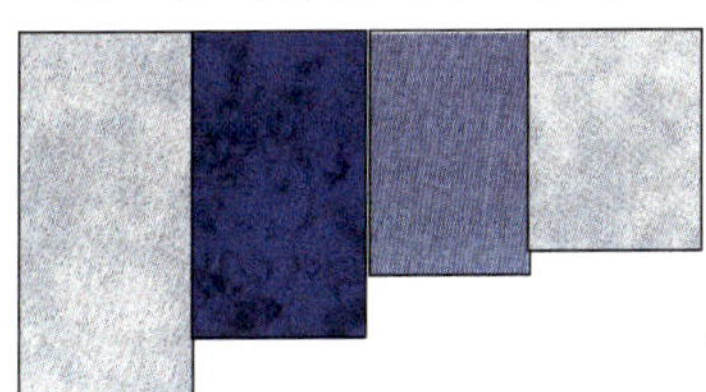

G1 to G2 to B

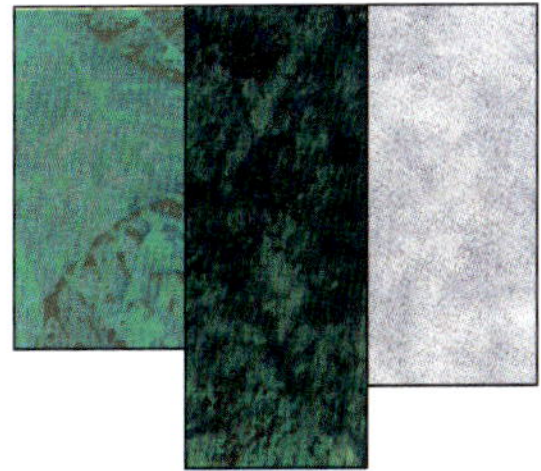

Note: *Pre-sewing strips is not recommended for directional fabric.*

Eventually you will need to sew more combinations of colors together for pre-sewing.

Use 3 strands of green embroidery floss which match your light green fabric to stem stitch the lines indicated on the Violet Trim Guide on Page 94.

Another option! Point violets in for a new design.

Another Look! Make a single violet a focus point. Combine with the Double X Block on Page 112.

Violet Pattern

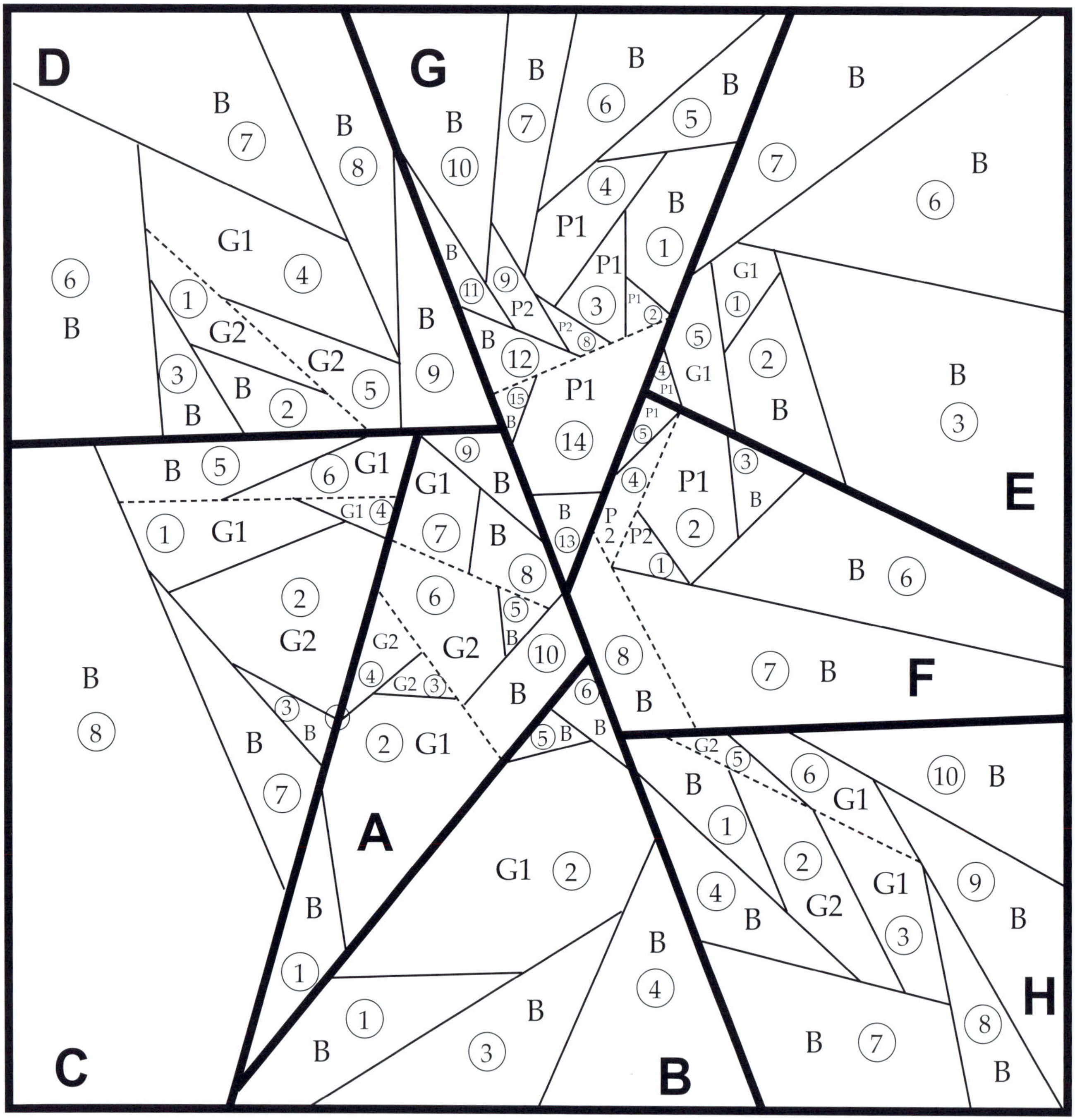

IMPORTANT:
When tracing onto freezer paper ADD 1/4″ extra all around for squaring outer edges.
Note: If you are using pre-printed freezer paper cut on lines. NO EXTRA needed.
After trimming, the block will measure 6 1/2″ X 6 1/2″.

Sewing Sequence

Note: If you have presewn strips you will already have prepped some of the sewn pieces. For instance, 1 and 2 will already be sewn.

Section A: Sew 1 to 2, 5 to 6, 7 to 8. Sew 1/2 to 3, add 4. Sew 7/8 to 9. Sew 5/6 to 7-9. Add 10. Join 1-4 to 5-10.

Section B: Sew 1 to 2, add 3, 4, 5, then 6.

Section C: Sew 1 to 2, 5 to 6. Sew 1/2 to 3, add 4. Sew 1-4 to 5/6. Add 7, then 8.

Section D: Sew 1 to 2, 4 to 5. Sew 1/2 to 3. Join 1-3 to 4/5, add 6, 7, 8, then 9.

Section E: Sew 1 to 2, 4 to 5. Sew 1/2 to 3, add 4/5, 6 then 7.

Section F: Sew 1 to 2, 4 to 5. Sew 1/2 to 3. Sew 1-3 to 4/5, add 6, 7, then 8.

Section G: Sew 1 to 2, 13 to 14. Sew 1/2 to 3, add 4. Sew 13/14 to 15. Sew 1-4 to 5, add 6, 7, 8, 9, 10, 11, then 12. Join 1-12 to 13-15.

Section H: Sew 1 to 2, 5 to 6. Sew 1/2 to 3, add 4. Sew 1-4 to 5/6. Sew 7, 8, 9, then 10.

Sew Section A to B, E to F. Sew A/B to C, E/F to G. Sew A-C to D. Sew E-G to H. Join A-D to E-H.

Piece 4 violet blocks. Trim to 6 1/2" X 6 1/2". When trimming, keep an even amount of background around the flowers. Space between should be around 1/2".

"All of these numbers look scary! But, once you get the hang of it, you won't need them!"

Violet Trim Guide

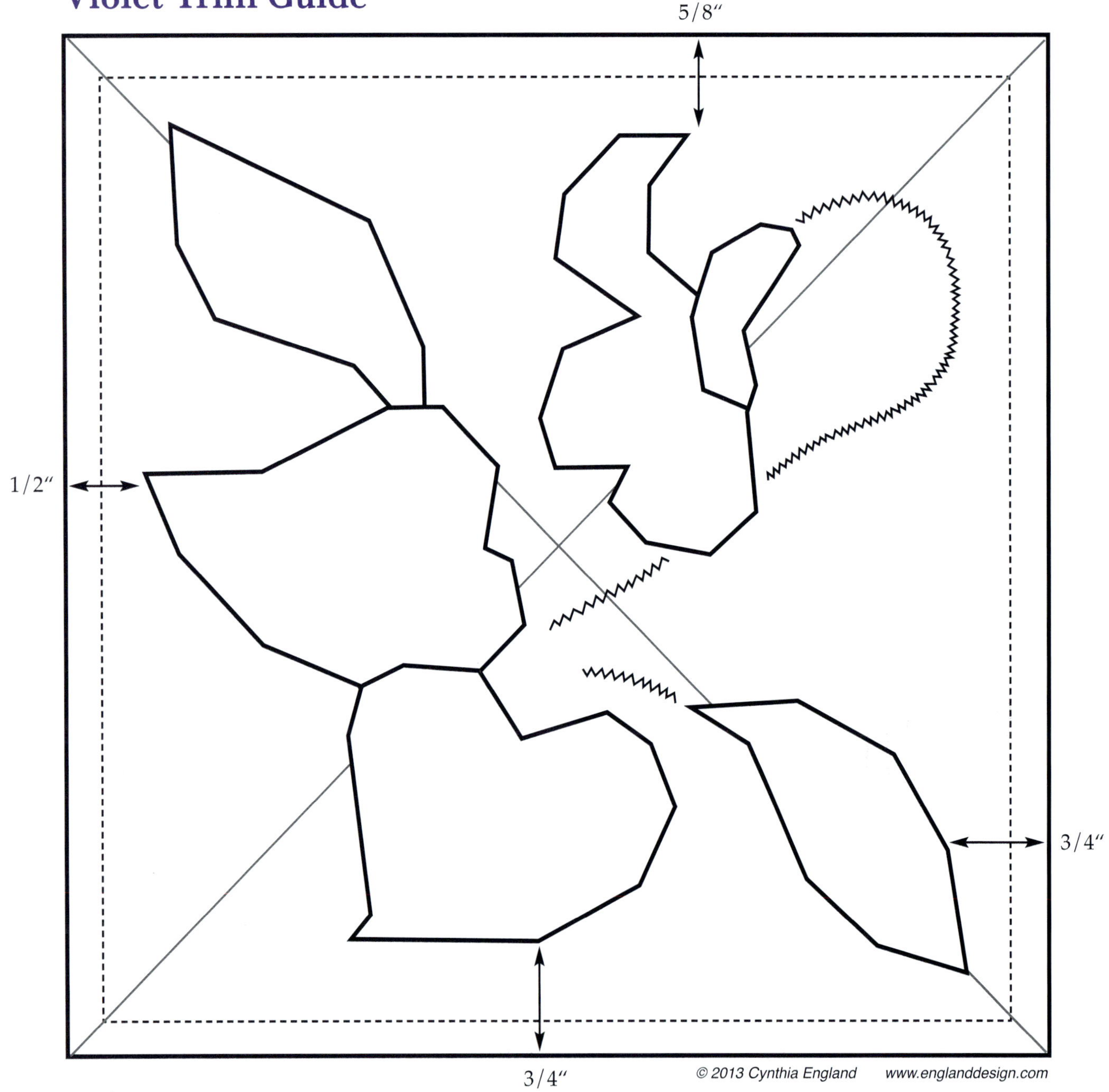

Finished Block size is 6″ X 6″.

Outside solid line is rotary cut trim size 6 1/2″ X 6 1/2″.

- Dashed line is sewing line.
- Diagonal lines for placement reference.
- Larger zig-zag line indicate stems to be embroidered. Use 3 strands of green embroidery floss which match your Light Green fabric.

With a permanent marker, trace the Trim Guide onto template plastic and place over finished Picture Pieced block. Design was intentionally made larger. Trim away excess.

Traditional Quilt Material Requirements

- **A** - Teal...1 yard
  Includes binding
- **B** - Purple................................. 1/4 yard
- **C** - Focus ....1/2 yard
- **D** - Gray.....................................1/4 yard
- **E** - Light gray............................1/4 yard
- **F** - Green...................................1/3 yard
- **G** - Lime green..........................1/4 yard
- Backing - Something pretty!.....1 1/2 yards

Make a color chart for these fabrics as pictured below.

Rotary Cutting

*Before beginning, rotary cut long strips of Fabric A and set aside for borders and binding.

Fabric Color	Size	Shape	Number Needed	Number To Cut
A	2 1/2" X 2 1/2"	square	20	20
	2 7/8" X 2 7/8"	half-square triangles	8	4
	2 1/2" X 34 1/2"	rectangle *borders	4	4
	1 1/2" X 6 1/2"	rectangle strips	16	16
	2 1/4" X WOF	rectangle *binding	162"	5 strips
B	1 1/2" X 1 1/2"	square	16	16
	2 1/2" X 2 1/2"	square	16	16
	2 7/8" X 2 7/8"	half-square triangles	24	12
C	2 1/2" X 2 1/2"	square	8	8
	2 1/2" X 4 1/2"	rectangle	32	32
	2 7/8" X 2 7/8"	half-square triangles	16	8
D	2 1/2" X 2 1/2"	square	32	32
E	2 1/2" X 2 1/2"	square	32	32
F	2 1/2" X 4 1/2"	rectangle	32	32
G	2 1/2" X 4 1/2"	rectangle	16	16

Traditional Block Info

Two traditional blocks were used for this wall hanging. The Violet block was adapted from the Lucky Clover block to accommodate the $6^{1/2}$" X $6^{1/2}$" space needed.

Violet Block
Finished size: 12" X 12"

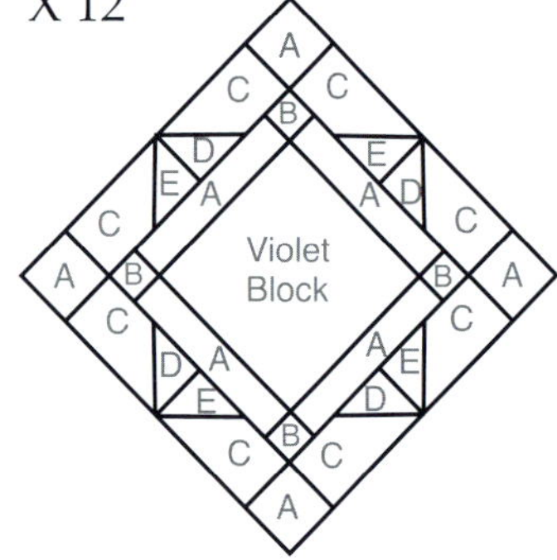

Making the Violet Blocks

Sew right sides together using a scant 1/4" seam allowance.

1 Select one Fabric A $1^{1/2}$" X $6^{1/2}$" strip and sew to each side of the finished $6^{1/2}$" X $6^{1/2}$" Violet Block.

Make 4.

2 Add the cornerstone units:
Select one Fabric B $1^{1/2}$" X $1^{1/2}$" square and sew to each end of one $1^{1/2}$" X $6^{1/2}$" Fabric A strip.

Make 8.

3 Sew one cornerstone strip unit to the top and bottom of each violet block.

Complete 4 Violet blocks with cornerstone sashing.

4 Make the CD rectangle half-square units:
Select sixteen $2^{1/2}$" X $2^{1/2}$" Fabric D squares and sixteen $2^{1/2}$" X $4^{1/2}$" Fabric C rectangles.

- Place one Fabric D square on the ***right*** side of the Fabric C rectangle and draw a diagonal line. Sew along this line. Press and cut away excess.

  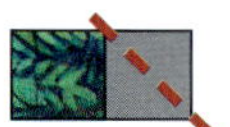 

Make 16 CD rectangle half-square triangle units.

5 Make the CE rectangle half-square triangle units:
Select sixteen $2^{1/2}$" X $2^{1/2}$" Fabric E squares and sixteen $2^{1/2}$" X $4^{1/2}$" Fabric C rectangles.

- Place one Fabric E square on the ***left*** side of the Fabric C rectangle and draw a diagonal line. Sew along this line. Press and cut away excess.

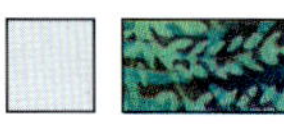  

Make 16 of CE rectangle half-square triangle units.

6 Join the CD and CE units: Match seams where triangle points meet.

Make 16 CDE rectangle half-square triangle units.

7 Sew one CDE rectangle half-square unit to either side of the Violet cornerstone block.

Make 4.

8 Sew one $2^{1/2}$″ X $2^{1/2}$″ Fabric A square to each side of the CDE rectangle half square unit.

Make 8 ACDE units.

9 Sew one ACDE unit to the top and one to the bottom of the Violet block unit. Square to $12^{1/2}$″ X $12^{1/2}$″.

Complete 4 Violet blocks.

Lucky Clover Block

1 Sew two $2^{1/2}$″ X $2^{1/2}$″ Fabric A squares and two $2^{1/2}$″ X $2^{1/2}$″ Fabric B squares and sew together to make a 4-patch. Square to $4^{1/2}$″.

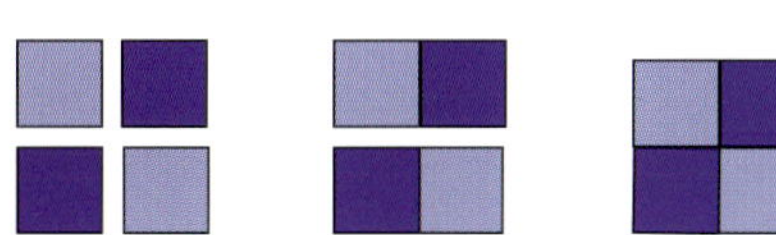

Make 1 four-patch.

2 Sew one $2^{1/2}$″ X $4^{1/2}$″ Fabric G rectangle to each side of the 4-patch unit.

Make 1.

3 Make the CG rectangle square units: Sew one $2^{1/2}$″ X $2^{1/2}$″ Fabric C square to either side of Fabric G rectangle.

Make 2.

4 Sew one CG rectangle square unit to the top and bottom matching seams. Square to $8^{1/2}$″.

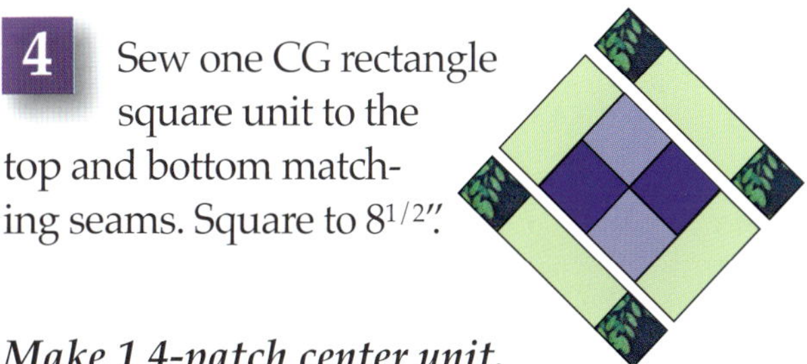

Make 1 4-patch center unit.

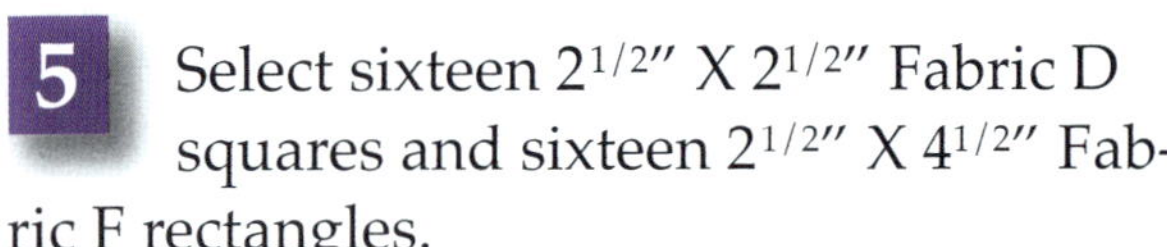

5 Select sixteen 2 1/2" X 2 1/2" Fabric D squares and sixteen 2 1/2" X 4 1/2" Fabric F rectangles.

• Place one Fabric D square on the ***right*** side of the Fabric F rectangle and draw a diagonal line. Sew along this line. Press and cut away excess.

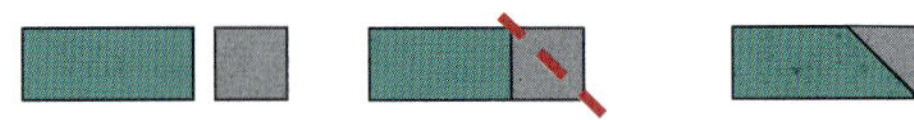

Make 16 DF units.

6 Select sixteen 2 1/2" X 2 1/2" Fabric E squares and sixteen 2 1/2" X 4 1/2" Fabric F rectangles.

• Place one Fabric E square on the ***left*** side of the Fabric F rectangle and draw a diagonal line. Sew along this line. Press and cut away excess.

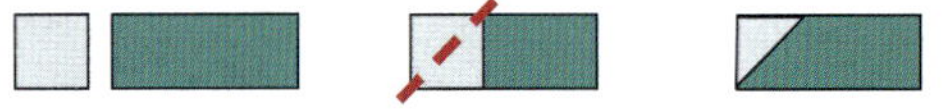

Make 16 EF units.

7 Join the DF and EF units: Match seams where triangles meet.

Make 16 DEF units.

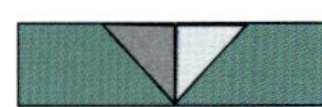

8 Sew one DEF rectangle half-square triangle unit to either side of the 4-patch center unit.

Make 1.

9 Sew one Fabric B 2 1/2" X 2 1/2" square to each side of the DEF rectangle half square units.

Make 2 units.

10 Sew one BDEF unit to the top and one to the bottom of the 4-patch center unit. Square to 12 1/2".

Complete 1 center block.

11 Make the corner edge units: Sew one 2 7/8" Fabric B triangle to either side of DEF rectangle half square unit. *Note position of the triangle.*

Make 4.

12 Make the corner center units: Sew one 2 7/8" Fabric C triangle to either side of one Fabric G rectangle. *Note position of the triangles.*

Make 4.

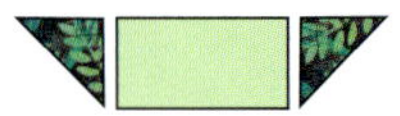

13 Make the corner end units: Sew one 2 7/8" Fabric A and one Fabric B triangle as pictured.

Make 4.

14 Put the corner units together.

Make 4.

15 Make the right side units:
Select four DEF rectangle half square triangle units and sew one Fabric B triangle to the ***right*** side of each. *Note position of triangle.*

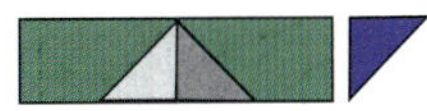

Make 4 right side units.

16 Make the left side units:
Select four DEF rectangle half square triangle units and sew one Fabric B 2 7/8" triangle to the ***left*** side of each. Then add one Fabric B, 2 1/2" X 2 1/2" square to the ***right*** side of each.

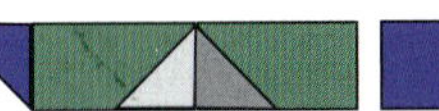

Make 4 left side units.

17 Make the side center units:
Sew one Fabric C, 2 7/8" triangle to the right side of Fabric G rectangle.

Make 4.

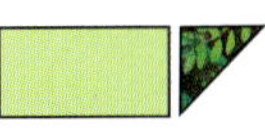

Photo by Cynthia England

18 Make the side center units:
Sew one Fabric C, 2 7/8" triangle to the ***left*** side of Fabric G rectangle. Then sew one Fabric C 2 1/2" X 2 1/2" square to the right side of the Fabric G rectangle

Make 4.

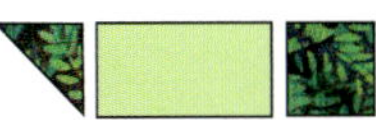

19 Make the end center units:
Sew two Fabric B, 2 7/8" triangles to one Fabric A, 2 1/2" X 2 1/2" square as shown. Repeat, sewing two Fabric A triangles to one Fabric B, 2 1/2" X 2 1/2" square.

Make 2 of each combination.

20 Join the side units together:
Make two as indicated.

Make 2 Fabric A square side units.

Make 2 Fabric B square side units.
Note color difference in lower center square triangle unit colors.

Assembling the Quilt Top

Refer to the illustration below. Work in diagonal rows, pointing the violet blocks facing upright.

- Sew one 2½″ X 34½″ Fabric A border to each side.
- Sew one 2½″ X 2½″ Fabric B corner square to each end of two 2½″ X 34½″ Fabric A border strips.

Sew one to the top and one to the bottom. Finished Size: 38″ square.

Detailed finishing instructions in Traditional Basics beginning on Page 7.

- Bind quilt using 5 strips of Fabric A, cut 2¼″ X WOF.
- Sleeve and label your quilt.

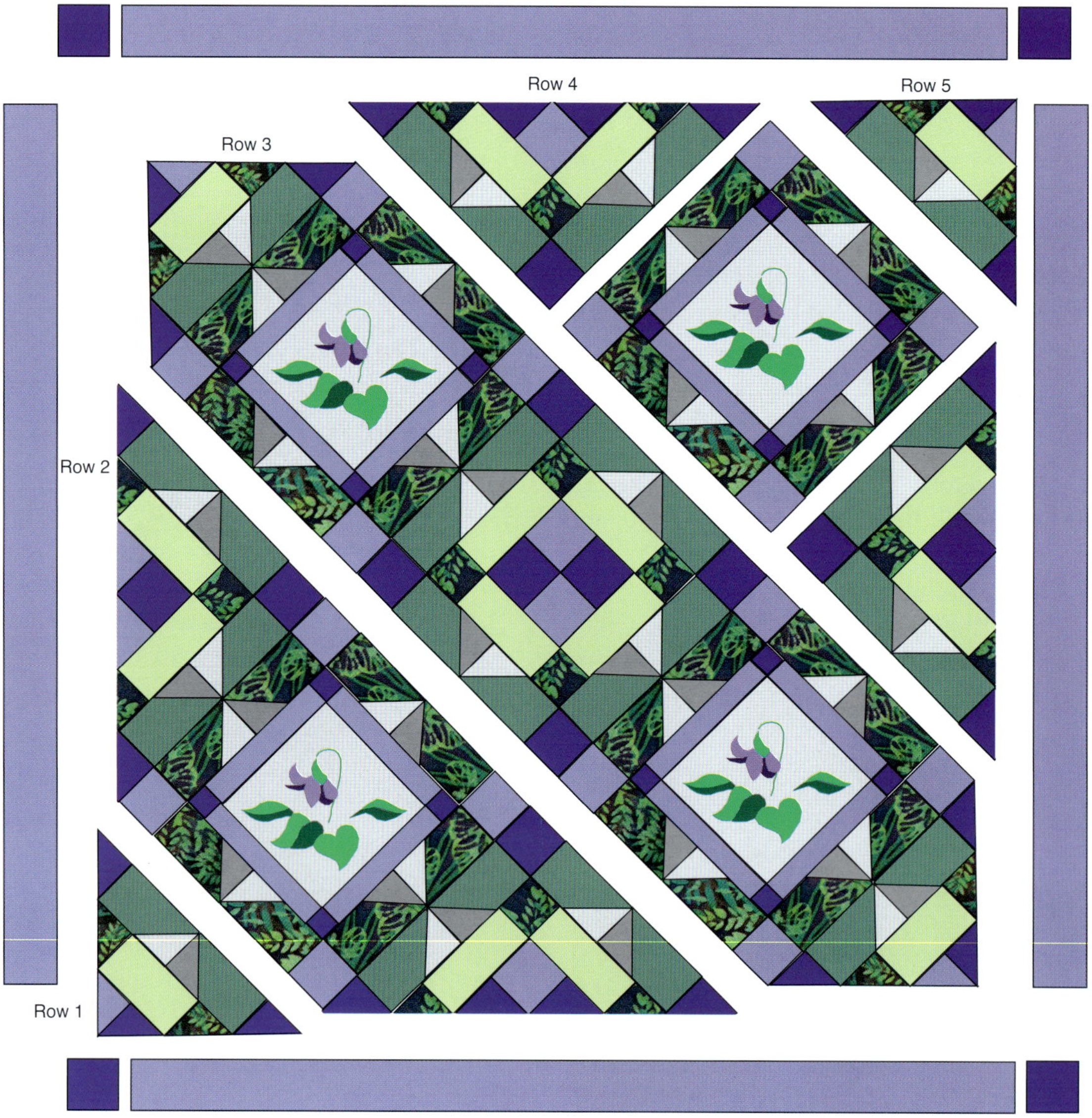

Row 4

Row 5

Row 3

Row 2

Row 1

Field of Violets

Designed and Pieced by Cynthia England Quilted by Richard Larson

Field of Violets

Finished Quilt Size: 67 1/2″ X 90 1/2″
Finished Picture Piecing Block Size: 6″ X 6″
Finished Traditional Block Size: 9″ X 9″

Picture Piecing Material Requirements

For 18 violet blocks you will need:

- **B** - Beige for background............ 2 1/2 yards
  Same color as Fabric A - Traditional yardage
- **P1** - Red violet for flower.............1/2 yard
- **P2** - Dark purple for flower.........1/3 yard
- **G1** - Green for leaves.................... 1/2 yard
  Same color as Fabric C - Traditional yardage
- **G2** - Dark green for leaves......... 1/2 yard
  Same color as Fabric D - Traditional yardage

Make a color chart for the violet fabrics as pictured below.

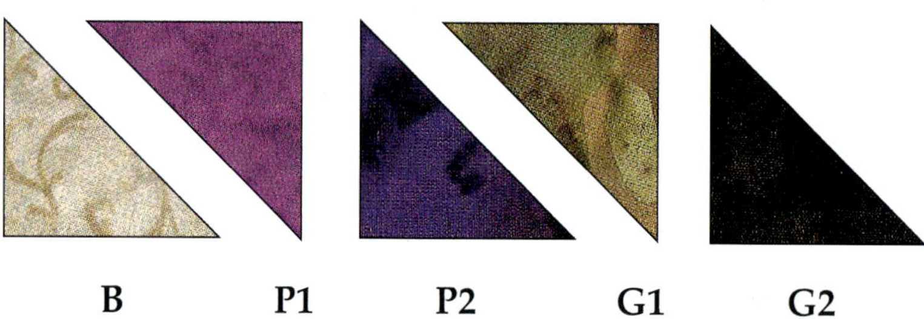

Traditional Quilt Material Requirements

- **A** - Beige ....1 3/8 yards
  Same color as B, Picture Piecing beige
- **B** - Darker beige........................1 3/4 yards
  used for half-squares in dark green sash
- **C** - Green .... 3 1/4 yards
  setting triangles and binding
- **D** - Dark green.........................3 1/4 yards
- **Backing** - Something pretty!.........6 yards

Make a color chart for these fabrics as pictured below.

Rotary Cutting

Before beginning, cut 2 1/2 yards of Fabric C and set aside for Setting Triangles and Binding.

** Note:*
Suggest using half square triangle unit grid papers for the 1″ finished half squares.
For this, use sheets of 8 1/2″ X 11″ paper. See Page 6.
Or.....
Use the 1 7/8″ X 1 7/8″ measurements and cut squares diagonally.

Fabric Color	Size	Shape	Number Needed	Number To Cut
A	1 1/2" X WOF		15 strips	15 strips
	3 1/2" X WOF		68	7 strips
B	*8 1/2" X 11"		768	20 sheets
	or	or		or
	*1 7/8" X 1 7/8"		768	19 strips
	1 1/2" X 1 1/2"		96	4 strips
C	1 1/2" X WOF		18	18 strips
	9 3/4" X 9 3/4"	small set	10	3
	14" X 14"	large set	14	4
	5 1/2" X 5 1/2"	corners	4	2
	2 1/4" X WOF	binding	330"	9 strips
D	4 1/2" X 9 1/2"		48	12 strips
	*8 1/2" X 11"		768	20 sheets
	or	or		or
	*1 7/8" X 1 7/8"		768	19 strips

Picture Piecing Block Info

Finished Block Size: 6″ X 6″

Picture Piecing sewing directions begin on Page 19. See Pages 92-93 for Violet sewing sequence and block pattern.

*Don't forget! There are free videos on the website, **www.englanddesign.com***

Pre-Sewing Recommendations

This makes the little pieces *so* much easier! Cut all strips in half (they will be around 4″ X 22″ long). Eventually you will need to sew more combinations of colors together for pre-sewing.

- Place right sides together and sew a 1/4″ seam. Some of the strips may be different lengths. Just sew along the side to the end. Press open.
- Sew the following strips together:

B to P2 to P1 to B

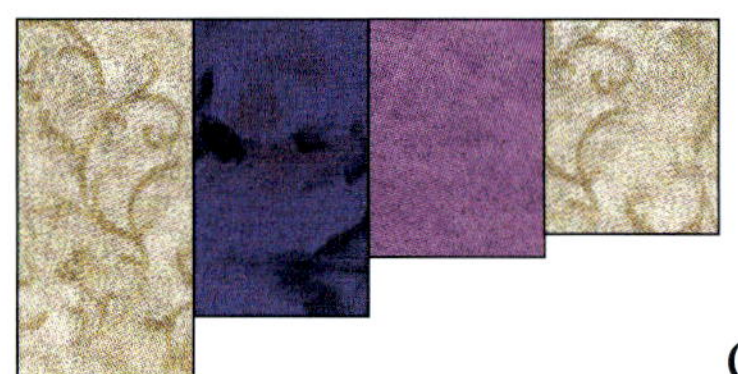

G1 to G2 to B

***Note:** Pre-sewing strips is not recommended for directional fabrics.*

Make 18 Violet blocks. Use 3 strands of green embroidery floss which match your Light Green fabric to stem stitch the lines indicated on the Violet Trim Guide on Page 94.

Traditional Block Info

Sew right sides together using a scant 1/4″ seam allowance.

1 Make the Double Nine Patch block. Start with sewing strips.

Sew one 1 1/2″ X WOF strip of Fabric C on each side of one 1 1/2″ X WOF strip of Fabric A. Press. Make 7 strip sets.

- Crosscut the strip sets into 1 1/2″ X 3 1/2″ units as in diagram.

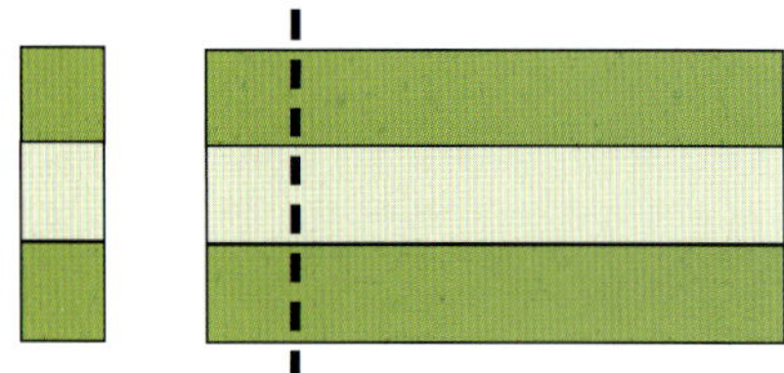

Make a total of 170 CAC units.

2 Sew one 1 1/2″ X WOF strip of Fabric C on each side of one 1 1/2″ X WOF strip of Fabric A. Press. Make 7 strip sets.

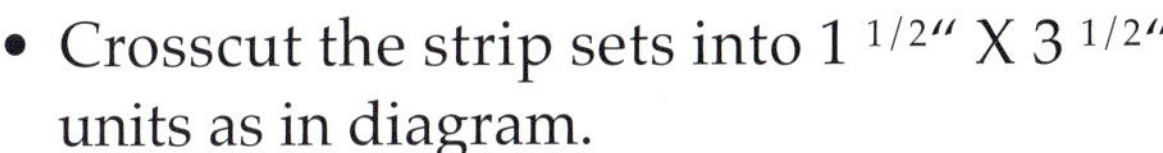

- Crosscut the strip sets into 1 1/2" X 3 1/2" units as in diagram.

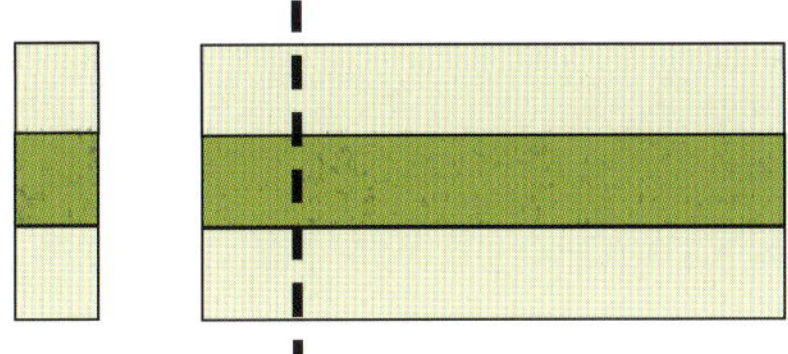

Make a total of 85 ACA units.

3 Sew one CAC unit to each side of one ACA unit to make a nine patch. Square to 3 1/2".

Make a total of 85 nine patches.

4 Select 7 Fabric A 3 1/2"X WOF strips and subcut into 3 1/2"X 3 1/2" squares.

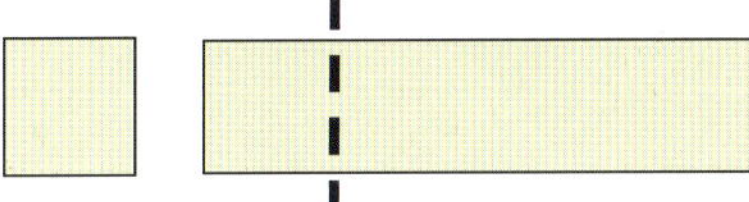

Subcut, for a total of 68 3 1/2"X 3 1/2" squares.

5 Sew one nine patch to each side of a Fabric A square. Make two rows. Sew one Fabric A square to each side of one nine patch. Join as pictured. Square to 9 1/2".

Complete 17 Double Nine Patch blocks.

6 Make the sashing half square units: Using Fabric B and Fabric D make the 1" finished half square triangle units. Either use the triangle unit grid papers as described on Page 6 ... OR...
from 19 strips cut 384 1 7/8" X 1 7/8" squares diagonally to yield 768 triangles. Sew right sides together. Press. Square to 1 1/2".

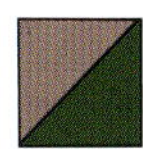

Make a total of 768 BD half square units.

7 Make the sashing row units: Select 8 BD half square units and one 1 1/2" Fabric B square. Sew four to either side of the Fabric B square *reversing directions* in the center.

Make a total of 96 BD sashing row units.

8 Make the sashing row units: Sew one BD sashing row to each side of a 4 1/2" X 9 1/2" Fabric D rectangle. Square to 6 1/2" X 9 1/2".

Note position of the dark green triangles next to dark green on the sash rectangle.

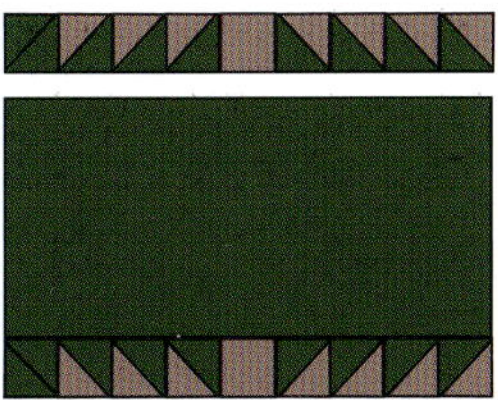

Complete 48 sashing units.

Assembling the Quilt Top

- Refer to the illustration below for the setting. Work in diagonal rows, matching seams.
- Note position of large and small setting triangles on alternate rows.

Finishing

- Bind quilt using 9 strips of Fabric C, cut 2 1/4" X WOF.
- Use a monofilament thread on top and in the bobbin to outline pieced violet designs.

Detailed finishing instructions on Page 7.

Possibilities

Mix and match elements to create your own unique design!

What if the center blocks in Corbin Gold Rush were replaced with cherished family photos? These colors would set off sepia prints! Rosebud blocks would give Corbin Gold Rush (Page 109) a totally different look (below).

Aren't they cute! Pictured are my mother, Christine, and my Aunt Wanda. They are a year apart. Fortunately, they don't dress alike anymore!

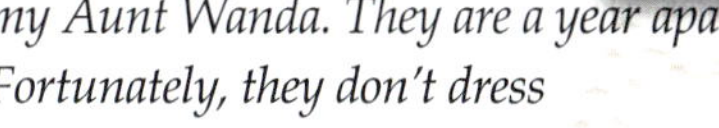

Scarlet Pinwheels (Page 133) would look stunning with a touch of redwork embroidery. Redwork patterns available from Scarlet Today/Redworkplus. See resource listing.
Picture Pieced Red Roses would look beautiful too!

Add 6" finished Picture Pieced blocks to ANY traditional quilt.

Maple Table Runner in shades of green, Page 39.

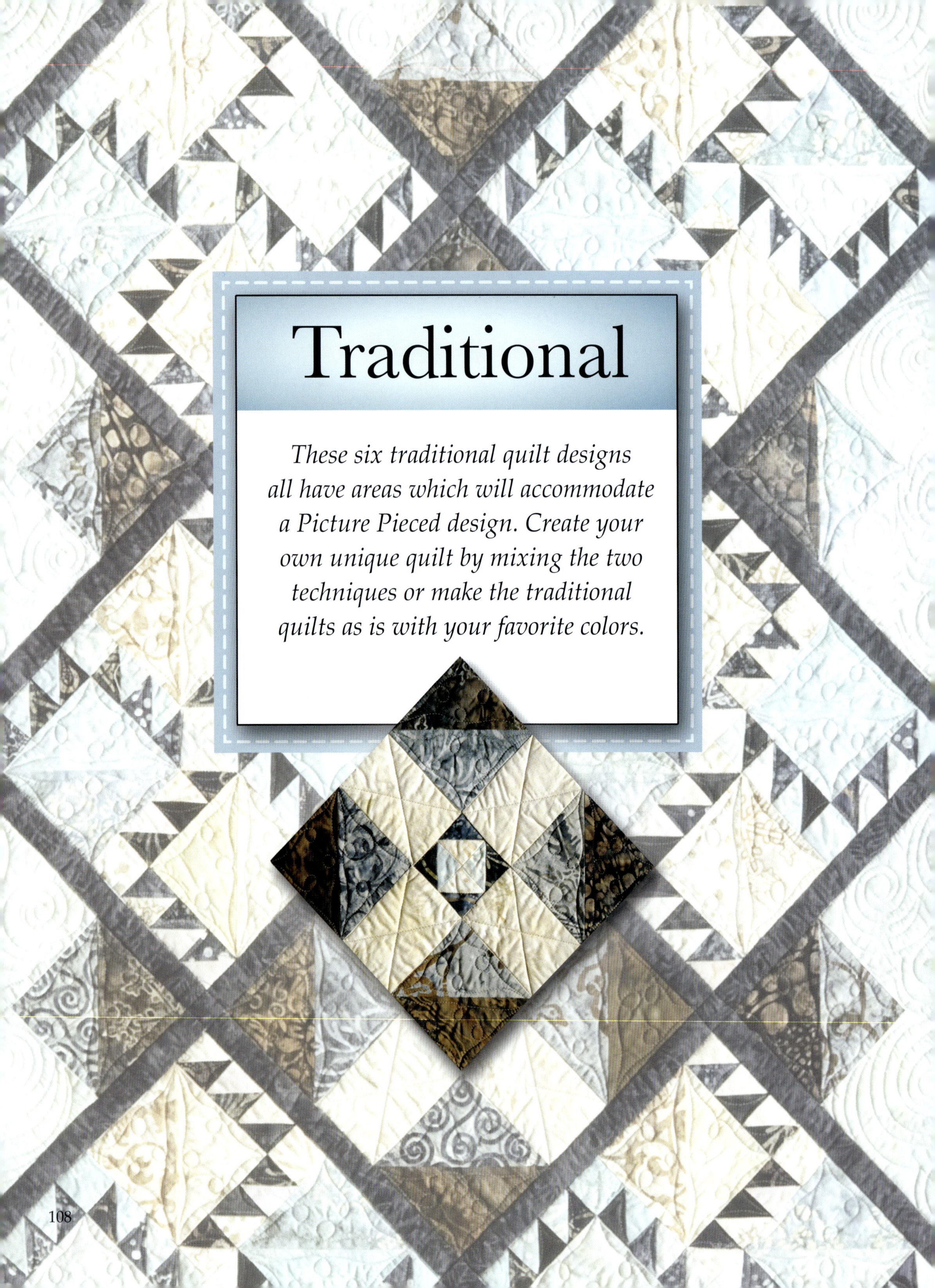

Traditional

These six traditional quilt designs all have areas which will accommodate a Picture Pieced design. Create your own unique quilt by mixing the two techniques or make the traditional quilts as is with your favorite colors.

Corbin Gold Rush

Designed and Pieced by Cynthia England

Quilted by Richard Larson

Corbin Gold Rush

Finished Quilt Size: 62″ X 79″
Finished Traditional Block Size: 12″ X 12″

Traditional Quilt Material Requirements

- **A** - Beige...2 yards
- **B** - Black print.................................... 1 yard

  Inner border
- **C** - Dark pink.................................. 7/8 yard
- **D** - Medium gold...........................1/2 yard
- **E** - Dark gold.................................1/2 yard
- **F** - Light gold print.....................3/4 yard
- **G** - Pink stripe.............................1/2 yard
- **H** - Focus print.............................2 3/4 yards

  Borders and binding
- **Backing** - Something pretty!......... 5 yards

Make a color chart for these fabrics as pictured in the Rotary Cutting Chart.

Rotary Cutting

*Before beginning, cut Fabric A outside setting triangles, Fabric B and Fabric H borders. Set aside.

Fabric F is actually a light gold print in the quilt. For clarification in the illustrations we have used green.

** Note:*
Suggest using half square triangle unit grid papers for the 2″ finished half squares.
For this, use sheets of 8 1/2″ X 11″ paper. See Page 6.
Or.....
Use the 2 7/8″ X 2 7/8″ measurements and cut squares then cut diagonally.

Fabric Color	Size	Shape	Number Needed	Number To Cut
A	2 7/8" X 2 7/8" or *8 1/2" X 11"	or	96 / 96	48 or 8 sheets
	9 3/8" X 9 3/8"	corners	4	2
	18 1/4" X 18 1/4"	*side triangles	10	3
B	2 1/2" X 2 1/2"		96	96
	1 1/2" X WOF	*borders	4	9 strips
C	2 7/8" X 2 7/8" or *8 1/2" X 11"	or	96 / 96	48 or 8 sheets
	2 7/8" X 2 7/8"		48	24
D	2 1/2" X 4 1/2"		48	48
E	4 7/8" X 4 7/8"		48	24
F	4 7/8" X 4 7/8"		24	12
	3 3/4" X 3 3/4"		48	24
G	4 1/2" X 4 1/2"		24	24
H	2 1/2" X 2 1/2"		48	48
	4 1/2" X 4 1/2"		18	18
	5" X LOF	*borders	4	4
	2 1/4" X LOF	binding	300"	3 strips

Album Block

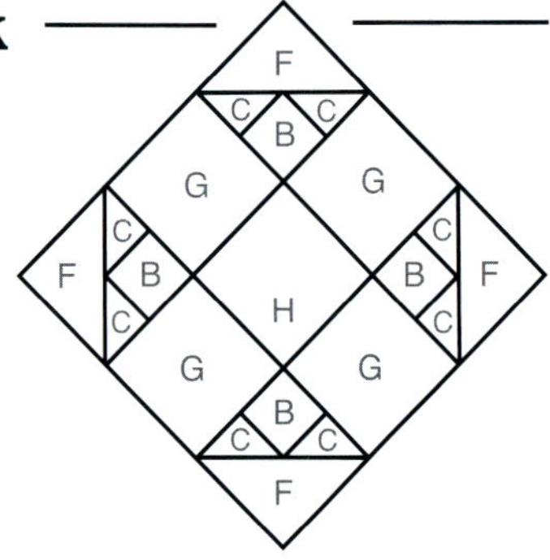

Finished size
12″ X 12″

Sew right sides together using a scant 1/4″ seam allowance.

1 Make the corner units: Select two 2 7/8″ Fabric C (diagonally cut) triangles and sew one to each side of one 2 1/2″ Fabric B square. *Note placement of colors.*

Make 24 CBC triangle units.

2 Sew one 4 7/8″ Fabric F (diagonally cut) triangle to the bottom of one CBC unit.

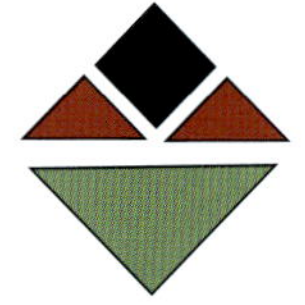

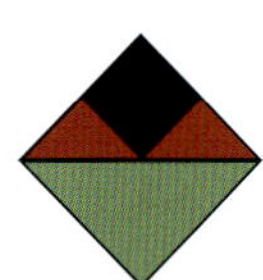

Make 24.

3 Sew one 4 1/2″ X 4 1/2″ Fabric G square to each side of one 4 1/2″ X 4 1/2″ Fabric H square. *Note position of stripe.*

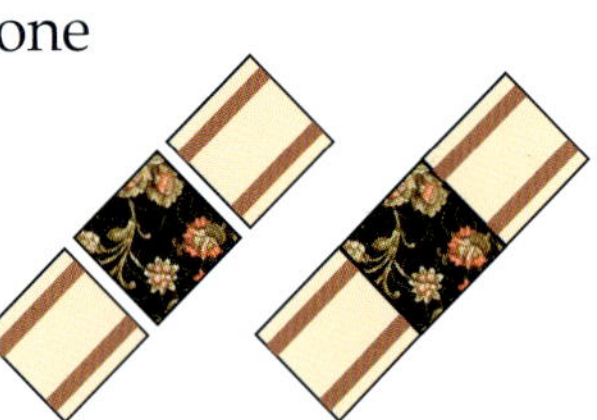

Make 6 HGH rows.

4 Sew one 4 1/2″ X 4 1/2″ Fabric CBC square unit to each side of one 4 1/2″ X 4 1/2″ Fabric G square.

Make 12 CBCG rows.

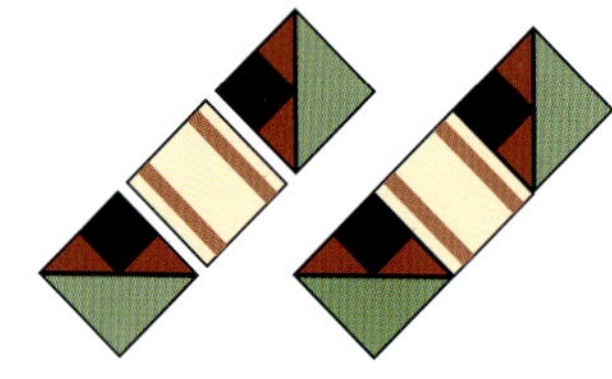

5 Sew one CBCG row to each side of one HGH row. Square to 12 1/2″.

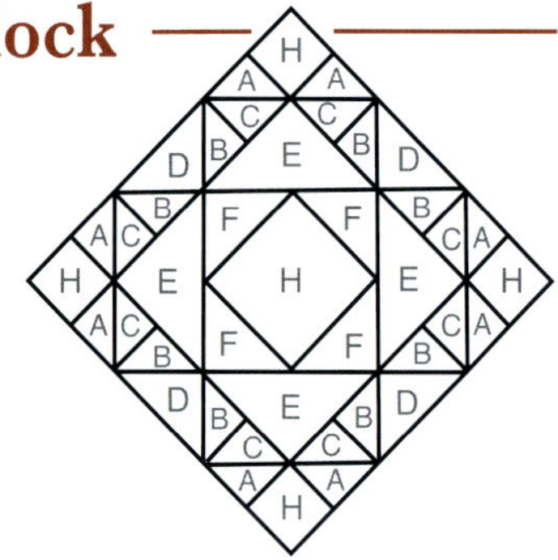

Complete 6 Album blocks.

Double X Block

Finished size
12″ X 12″

1 Sew one Fabric F triangle (cut once on diagonal from 3 3/4″ square) to opposite sides of one 4 1/2″ X 4 1/2″ Fabric H square.

Make 12.

2 Repeat, sewing one Fabric F triangle to remaining sides of Fabric H square. Square to 6 1/4″ X 6 1/4″.

Make 12 HF units

3 Sew one Fabric E triangle (diagonally cut from $4^{7/8}$" square) to opposite sides of one HF unit.

Make 12.

4 Repeat, sewing one Fabric E triangle to remaining sides of the HF unit. Square to $8^{1/2}$" X $8^{1/2}$".

Make 12 focus fabric units.

5 Make the flying geese units: Draw a diagonal line on the back side of one $2^{1/2}$" X $2^{1/2}$" Fabric B square. Place on the right side of a $2^{1/2}$" X $4^{1/2}$" Fabric D rectangle. Sew along the line. Press back and trim away excess fabric from the back.

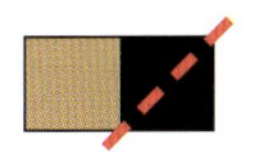

Make 48 BD flying geese.

6 Repeat Step 5, sewing a $2^{1/2}$" X $2^{1/2}$" Fabric B square to the left side of a $2^{1/2}$" X $4^{1/2}$" Fabric F rectangle. Sew along the line. Press back and trim away excess fabric from the back.

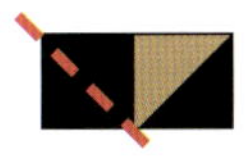

Make 48 BFB flying geese units.

7 Make the AC half-square triangles: Using Fabric A and Fabric C make the 2" finished half square triangle units. Either use the triangle unit grid papers as described on Page 6... OR...
cut 48 ($2^{7/8}$" X $2^{7/8}$" squares) of each color and cut once diagonally. Sew right sides together. Press. Square to $2^{1/2}$".

Make a total of 96 AC half squares.

8 Sew one AC half square to each side of one BDB flying geese unit.

Make 24 short flying geese units.

9 Sew one $2^{1/2}$" X $2^{1/2}$" Fabric H square to each side of one flying geese unit.

Make 24 long flying geese units.

10 Sew one short flying geese unit to each side of one focus fabric unit.

Make 12.

11 Sew one long flying geese unit with squares to the top and one to the bottom of one focus fabric unit.
Square to $12^{1/2}$".

Complete 12 Double X blocks.

Assembling the Quilt Top

Refer to the illustration below for the block setting. Work in diagonal rows. For setting triangles use Fabric A. They will be slightly larger than needed. Trim excess away after sewing rows. Add small setting corner triangles last. Press as you go.

When joining rows match aligning seams.

Adding the Borders

- Sew nine 1 1/2" by WOF Fabric B border strips short end to short end. Press.
- Subcut four 1 1/2" X 90" Fabric B border strips.
- Sew Fabric B border strips to Fabric H border strips right sides together and press towards Fabric H.
- Sew to quilt following mitered corner directions on page 10.

Finishing

Detailed finishing instructions on Page 7.

- Bind quilt using 3 strips of Fabric H 2 1/4" X LOF strips.

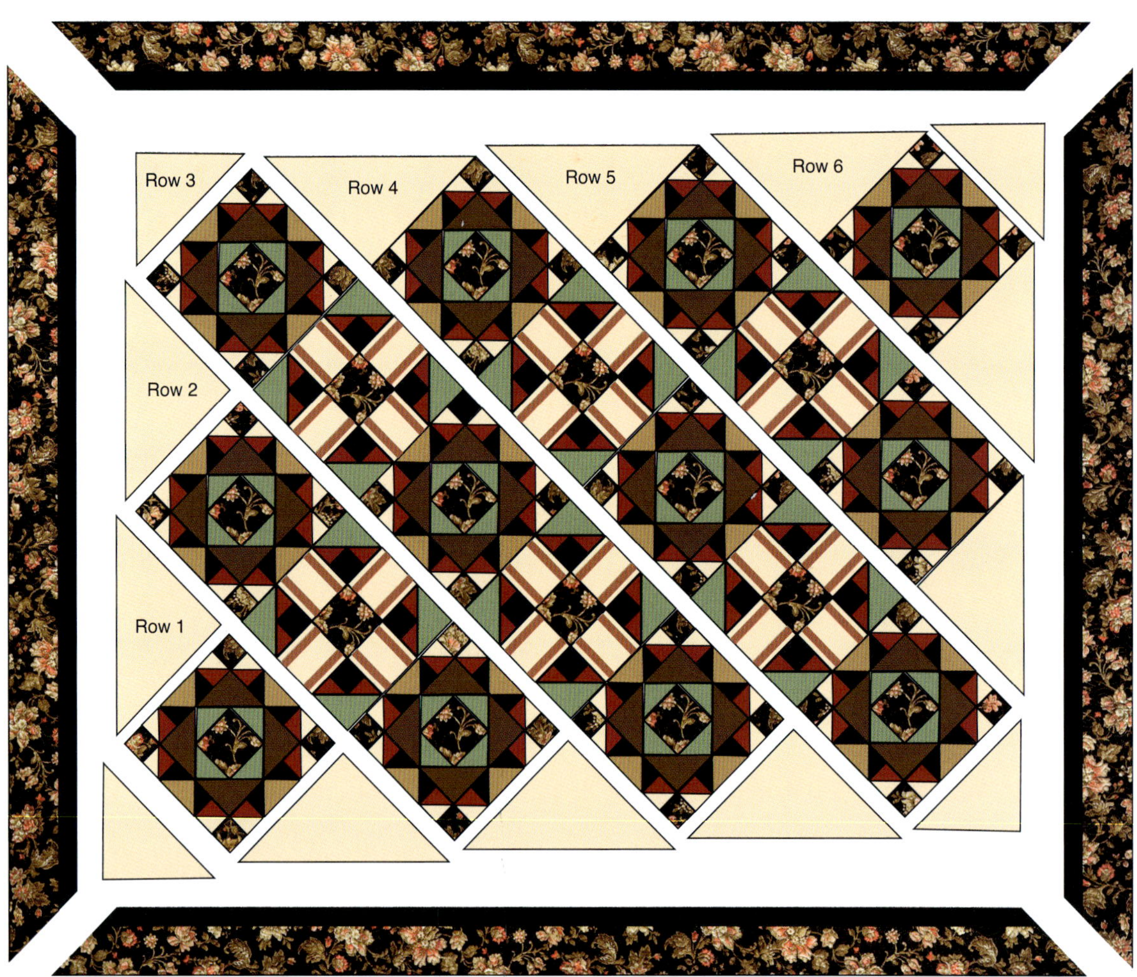

Indigo Lights

Designed and Pieced by Cynthia England

Quilted by Denise Green

Indigo Lights

Finished Quilt Size: 60″ X 75″
Finished Traditional Block Size: 10″ X 10″

Traditional Quilt Material Requirements

- **A** - Light blue....................................2/3 yard
- **B** - Light/medium blue................ 1/3 yard
- **C** - Medium blue plaid....................... 1 yard
- **D** - Med blue w/white...................1/3 yard
- **E** - Medium blue ....1/2 yard
- **F** - Blue with black..........................1/2 yard
- **G** - Dark blue...................................3/8 yard
- **H** - Dark blue centers...................1/4 yard
- **I** - Dark navy..................................$1^{1/4}$ yard
  For sashing
- **Setting Triangles and Binding**
  Medium blue.............................. 2 yards
- **BOR** - Blue border print............ $2^{1/2}$ yards
- **Backing** - Something pretty!....... $4^{1/2}$ yards
  Two lengths

Make a color chart for these fabrics as pictured in the Rotary Cutting Chart.

Rotary Cutting

*Before beginning, cut outside borders (BOR) lengthwise.

Border Print Tip

To determine the width of the border, use border repeat width.

Note:
This quilt is monochromatic. In order for clarification in the illustrations we have used different colors, however, the actual quilt is different shades of blue. Very important to make the color chart with actual fabric swatches!

Fabric Color	Size	Shape	Number Needed	Number To Cut
A	$4^{7/8}$" X $4^{7/8}$" $2^{7/8}$" X $2^{7/8}$"		38 38	19 19
B	$2^{1/2}$" X WOF $1^{1/2}$" X $1^{1/2}$"	cornerstones	36 31	3 strips 31
C	$4^{7/8}$" X $4^{7/8}$" $2^{7/8}$" X $2^{7/8}$"		34 34	17 17
D	$2^{1/2}$" X WOF		36	3 strips
E	$2^{1/2}$" X WOF		72	6 strips
F	$2^{7/8}$" X $2^{7/8}$"		114	57
G	$2^{7/8}$" X $2^{7/8}$"		102	51
H	$2^{1/2}$" X $2^{1/2}$"		18	18
I	$1^{1/2}$" X $10^{1/2}$"	sashing	48	13 strips then subcut $10^{1/2}$" strips
SET	$9^{1/2}$" X $9^{1/2}$" $16^{1/2}$" X $16^{1/2}$" $2^{1/4}$" X WOF	corners setting triangles binding	4 10 290"	2 3 8 strips
BOR	*6" X LOF	*borders	4	4

Traditional Block Info

Finished Block Size: 10″ X 10″
18 Blocks to Make

To create this quilt, **Four** different color variations of the same block were used. They are:

Corner Blocks .... 4 needed
Center Side Blocks.......................... 2 needed
Long Side Blocks............................ 4 needed
Center Dark Blocks......................... 8 needed

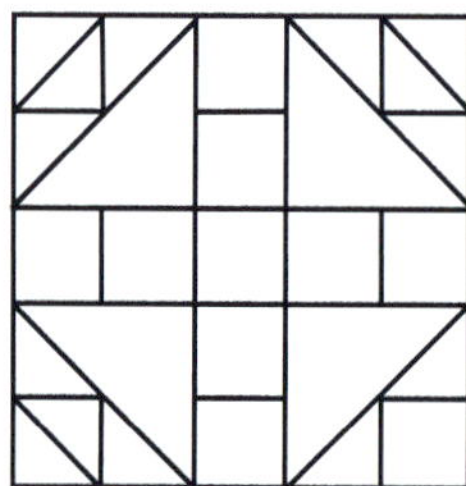

Nine Patch Variation

Sweetheart Roses on Page 75 uses the same Nine Patch Variation block along the outer edges.

Making the Blocks

1 Make the **light** triangle units:
Select one 2 7/8″ triangle of Fabric A
three 2 7/8″ triangles of Fabric F
one 4 7/8″ triangle of Fabric A
Lay out and sew as pictured.

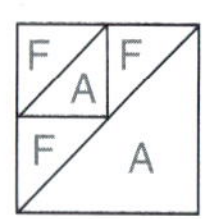

Make 38 light triangle units.

2 Make the **dark** triangle units:
Select one 2 7/8″ triangle of Fabric C
three 2 7/8″ triangles of Fabric G
one 4 7/8″ triangle of Fabric C
Lay out and sew as pictured.

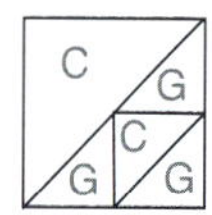

Make 34 dark triangle units.

Making the Strip Sets

1 Select one 2 1/2″ Fabric B strip and one 2 1/2″ Fabric E strip. Place right sides together and sew. Press. Using the rotary cutter, cross-cut the strip set into 2 1/2″X 4 1/2″ units. Make 3 strip sets.

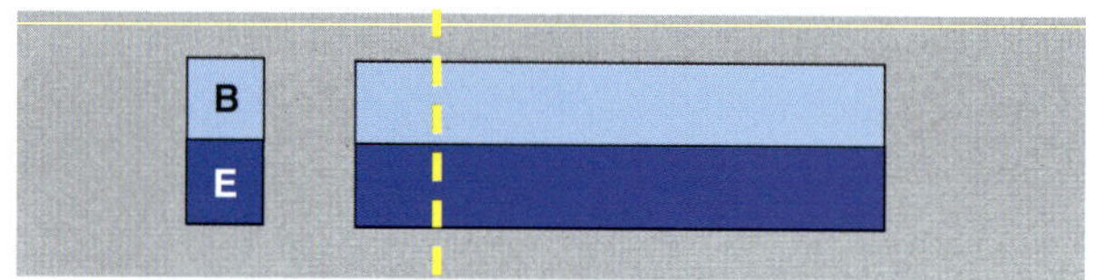

Make 36 of this BE combination.

2 Select one $2^{1/2}$″ Fabric D strip and one $2^{1/2}$″ Fabric E strip. Place right sides together and sew. Press. Using the rotary cutter, cross-cut the strip set into $2^{1/2}$″X $4^{1/2}$″ units. Make 3 strip sets.

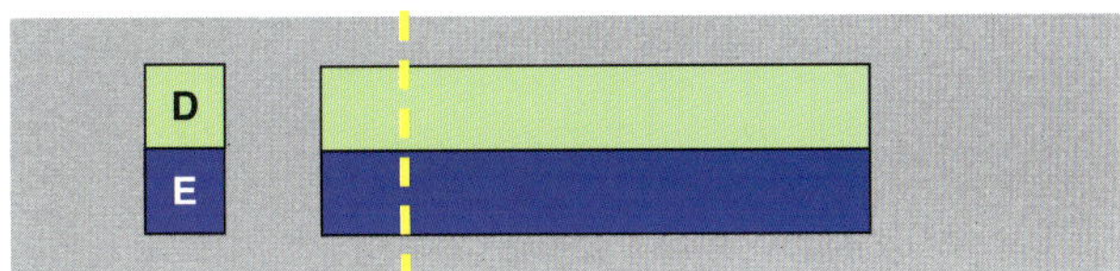

Make 36 DE combination.

Corner Blocks

1 Sew one BE Fabric square unit to one $2^{1/2}$″X $2^{1/2}$″ Fabric H square. Add one Fabric DE square unit to the other side. Square to 10 $^{1/2}$″.

Make 4 BEHED square set rows.

2 Select sixteen light triangle units. Select eight BE square units and four BEHED square sets. Join as pictured. Square to 10 $^{1/2}$″.

Note the yellow box above. This patch is different from the others in the same position in this block.

Complete 4 Corner Blocks.

Center Side Blocks

There are two, located in the top row and the bottom row, center.

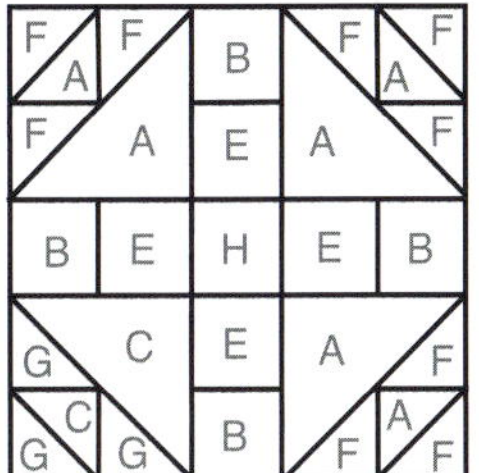

1 Sew two Fabric BE square units to each side of one $2^{1/2}$″X $2^{1/2}$″ Fabric H square.

Make 2 BEHEB square set rows.

2 Sew one light triangle unit to each side of one BE square unit. Sew one dark triangle unit and one light triangle unit to each side of one BE square unit. Square to 10 1/2″.

Note the yellow triangle above. This patch is different from the others in the same position in this block.

Complete 2 Center Side Blocks.

Long Side Blocks

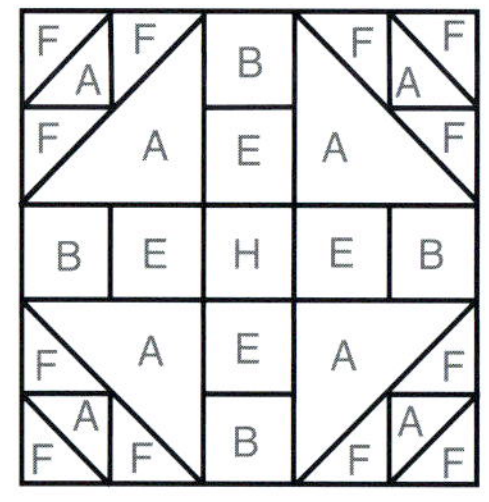

1 Sew one BE square unit to each side of one 2 1/2″X 2 1/2″ Fabric H square.

Make 4 BEHEB rows.

2 Sew one Light triangle unit to each side of one BE square unit. Sew one BEHEB square set row between them. Square to 10 1/2″.

Patches are in the same position in this block.

Make 4 Long Side Blocks.

Center Dark Blocks

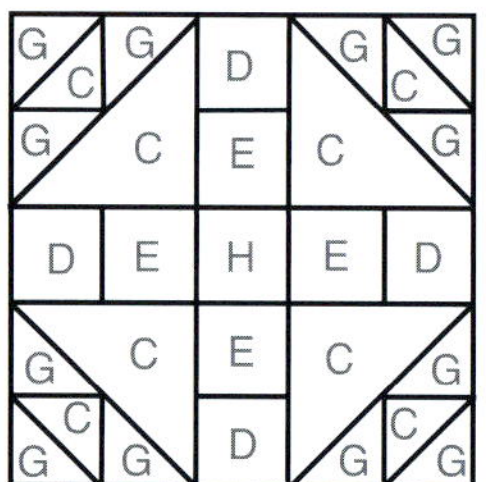

1 Sew one DE square unit to each side of one 2 1/2″X 2 1/2″ Fabric H square.

Make 8 DEHED square rows.

2 Sew one dark triangle unit on each side of a DE square units. Make two rows. Sew one DEHED square set between. Join as pictured. Square to 10 1/2″.

Complete 8 Center Dark Blocks.

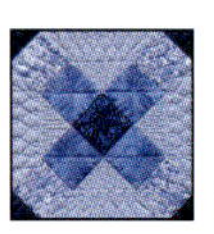

Very important!
Careful! Refer to the illustration on Page 122 when laying out sashing and blocks.

Prepare the Sashing

Sew sashing strips to the sides of the blocks. There are six rows set diagonally.

Rows 1 and 6:
Sew one 1 1/2" X 10 1/2" Fabric I strip to each side of one block for top and bottom rows.

Rows 2 and 5:
Sew four Fabric I strips between and at the end of three blocks to complete the rows.

Rows 3 and 4:
Sew six Fabric I strips between and at the end of five blocks to complete the rows.

Sashing Between Rows

Sew one 1 1/2" X 1 1/2" square of Fabric B to each side of Fabric I strips 1 1/2" X 10 1/2" to create the sashing rows.

Sew two rows with one Fabric B square on each side of one Fabric I strip for rows one and six.

Sew two rows with four Fabric B squares and three Fabric I strips for rows two and five.

Sew two rows with six Fabric B squares and five Fabric I strips for rows three and four.

Sew one row with 7 Fabric B squares and six Fabric I strips for top of Row 4.

Block Layout

Careful color placement creates interesting secondary designs in this quilt. When laying out the rows take extra care to place the blocks accordingly.

Diagonal set row directions are read left to right.

Row 1:
One Corner block with a setting triangle on each side. *Watch placement of the Fabric D square that is unique to this block.*

Row 2:
Setting triangle, Long Side block, Center Dark block, Center Side block and a setting triangle. *Watch placement of the dark unit on the Center Side blocks.*

Row 3:
Setting triangle, Long Side block, three Center Dark blocks and Corner block.

Row 4:
Corner block, three Center Dark blocks, Long Side block and a setting triangle.
Watch placement of the Fabric D square that is unique to this block.

Row 5:
Setting triangle, Center Side block, Center Dark block, Long Side block and a setting triangle. *Watch placement of the dark unit on the Center Side blocks.*

Row 6:
Setting triangle, Corner block and a setting triangle. *Watch placement of the Fabric D square that is unique to this block.*

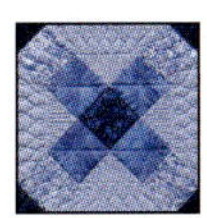

Quilt Top Layout

Use illustration below for block placement. Join rows diagonally. Add small corner SET triangles last. Press as you go.

Detailed finishing instructions on Page 7.

Finishing

- Use BOR, Border Print 6" X LOF and miter corners. Directions begin on Page 9.
- Bind quilt using 8 strips of SET Fabric cut $2^{1/4}$" X WOF.

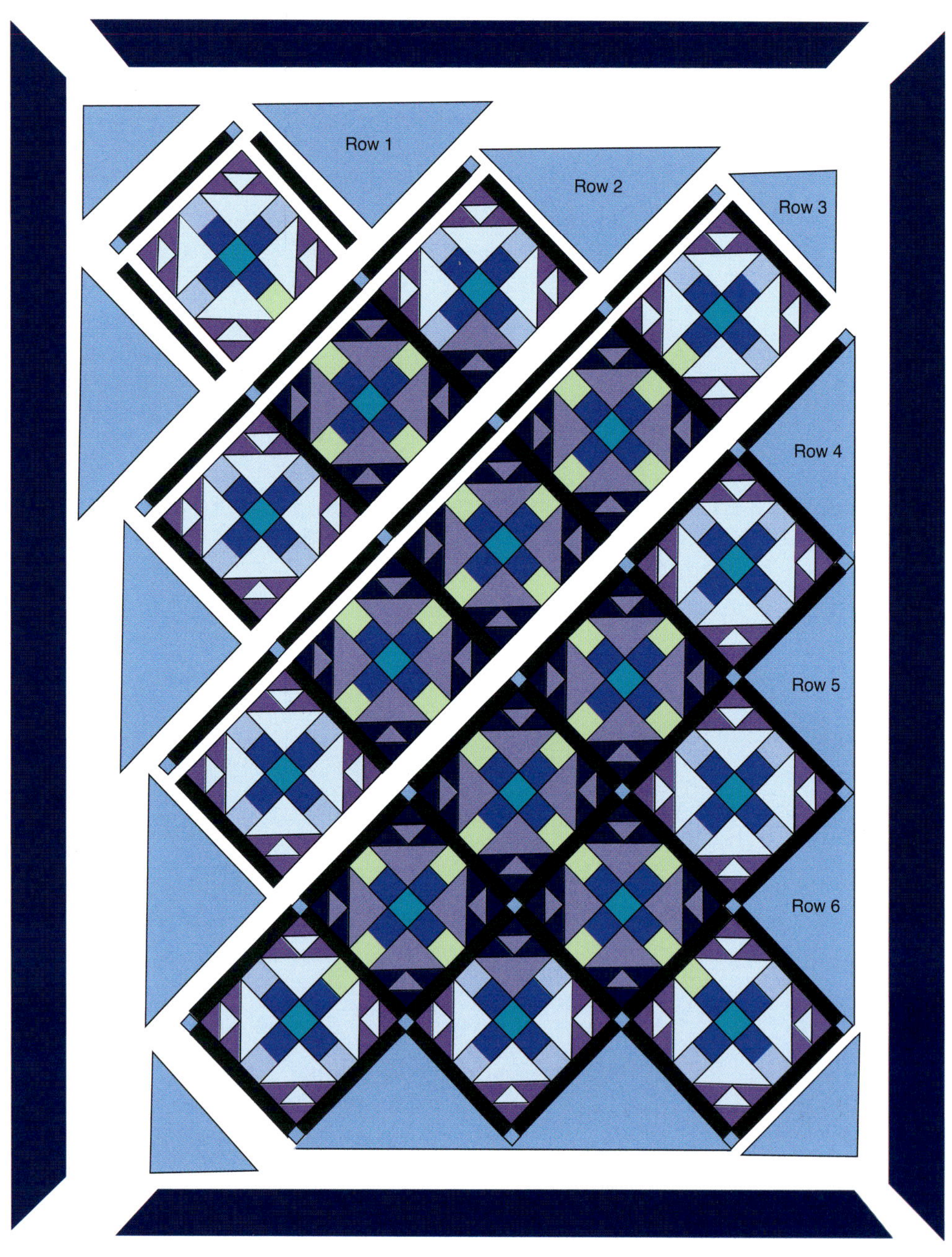

Southern Cross

Designed by Cynthia England | Pieced by Ronda Stockton | Quilted by Denise Green

Southern Cross

Finished Quilt Size: 67″ X 67″
Finished Traditional Block Size: 12″ X 12″

Traditional Quilt Material Requirements

- **A** - Teal....................1/3 yard
- **B** - Medium tan.................... 5/8 yard
- **C** - Light tan.................... 5/8 yard
- **D** - Rust....................2 1/8 yards
  Outside borders, binding
- **E** - Brown....................1/4 yard
- **F** - Orange....................1/3 yard
  Inner border
- **G** - Dark teal....................1 yard
- **H** - Focus print....................1 yard
  Setting triangles
- **I** - Golden brown....................2/3 yard
- **J** - Green ....1/4 yard
- **Backing** - Something pretty!......4 1/4 yards

Make a color chart for these fabrics as pictured in the Rotary Cutting Chart.

Rotary Cutting

*Before beginning, cut Fabric H side triangles and Fabric D, Fabric F and Fabric G borders. Set aside.

Fabric Color	Size	Shape	Number Needed	Number To Cut
A	$2^{1/2}$” X $2^{1/2}$”		52	52
B	$2^{1/2}$” X $2^{1/2}$”		52	52
	$2^{1/2}$” X WOF		36	3 strips
C	$2^{1/2}$” X $2^{1/2}$”		52	52
	$2^{1/2}$” X WOF		36	3 strips
D	$2^{1/2}$” X $4^{1/2}$”		32	32
	$5^{1/2}$” X WOF	*borders	4	8 strips
	$2^{1/4}$” X WOF	binding	280”	8 strips
E	$1^{1/2}$” X $6^{1/2}$”		16	16
F	$1^{1/2}$” X $1^{1/2}$”		16	16
	$1^{1/2}$” X WOF	*borders	4	6 strips
G	$2^{1/2}$” X $2^{1/2}$”		54	54
	$2^{1/2}$” X WOF		18	2 strips
	$2^{1/2}$” X WOF	*borders	4	6 strips
H	$6^{1/2}$” X $6^{1/2}$”		4	4
	$9^{3/8}$” X $9^{3/8}$”	corners	4	2
	$18^{1/2}$” X $18^{1/2}$”	*side triangles	8	2
I	$2^{1/2}$” X $4^{1/2}$”		72	72
J	$2^{1/2}$” X WOF		18	2 strips

Focus Print Block

Two blocks were used for this wall hanging. Minor changes were made to the original to accommodate the focus print block

Lucky Clover Block
Finished size 12″ X 12″

Focus Print Block
Finished size
12″ X 12″

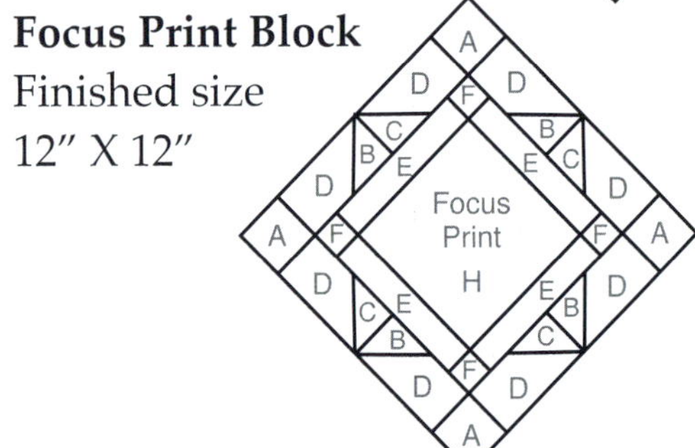

Center block is the same Lucky Clover block as in the African Violet quilt on Page 89.

Making the Blocks

Sew right sides together using a scant 1/4″ seam allowance.

1 Begin with the focus print blocks: Sew one 1 1/2″ X 6 1/2″ Fabric E strip to each side of a 6 1/2″ X 6 1/2″ Fabric H square.

Make 4.

2 Add the cornerstones: Sew one 1 1/2″ X 1 1/2″ Fabric F square to each end of one 1 1/2″ X 6 1/2″ Fabric E strip.

Make 8.

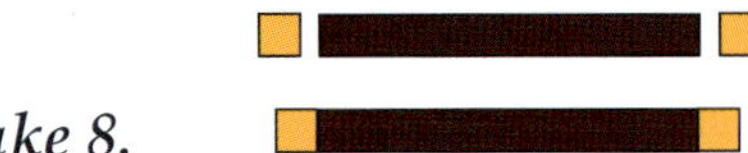

3 Sew one cornerstone strip unit to the top and bottom of each block.

Complete 4 blocks with cornerstone sashing.

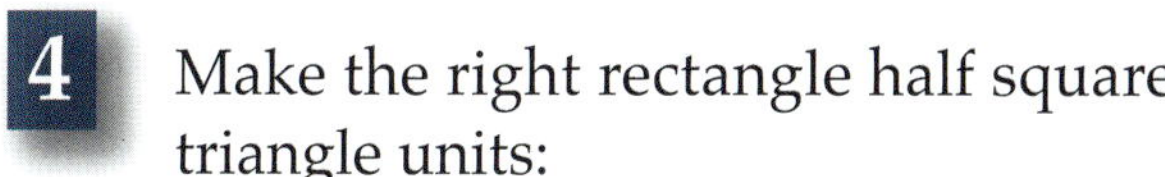

4 Make the right rectangle half square triangle units:

Select sixteen 2$^{1/2}$″ X 2$^{1/2}$″ Fabric B squares and sixteen 2$^{1/2}$″ X 4$^{1/2}$″ Fabric D rectangles.

- Place one Fabric B square on ***right*** side of the Fabric D rectangle and draw a diagonal line. Sew along line. Press back and cut away excess.

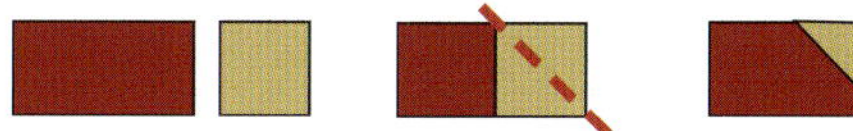

Make 16 of BD rectangle half-square triangle units.

5 Make the left rectangle half-square triangle units:

Select sixteen 2$^{1/2}$″ X 2$^{1/2}$″ Fabric C squares and sixteen 2$^{1/2}$″ X 4$^{1/2}$″ Fabric D rectangles.

- Place one Fabric C square on the ***left*** side of the fabric D rectangle and draw a diagonal line. Sew along line. Press back and cut away excess.

Make 16 of CD rectangle half-square triangle units.

6 Join the units, matching seams where corners meet.

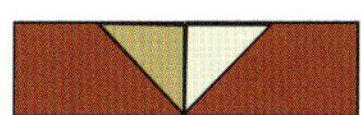

Make 16 joined rectangle half-square triangle units.

7 Select eight of the rectangle half-square triangle units and sew one to each side of the focus print cornerstone block. *Note color placement.*

Make 4.

8 Sew one 2$^{1/2}$″ X 2$^{1/2}$″ Fabric G square to each side of the remaining rectangle half-square units.

Make 8 units.

9 Sew one square unit to the top and one to the bottom of the block unit. *Square to 12$^{1/2}$″.*

Complete 4 focus print blocks.

Lucky Clover Block

1 Make the GJ four patch units:
Sew one 2 1/2"X WOF strip of Fabric G to one 2 1/2"X WOF strip of Fabric J. Press.

Crosscut the strip set into eighteen 2 1/2" units. Sew together, matching seams to make a 4-patch unit.

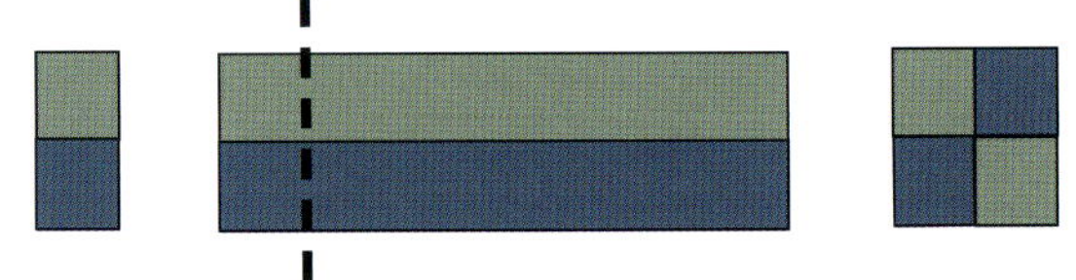

Make 9 GJ 4-patch units.

2 Make BC square units:
Sew one 2 1/2"X WOF Fabric C strip to one 2 1/2"X WOF Fabric B strip. Press. Make 3 strip sets.

Crosscut the strip set into thirty-six 2 1/2"units.

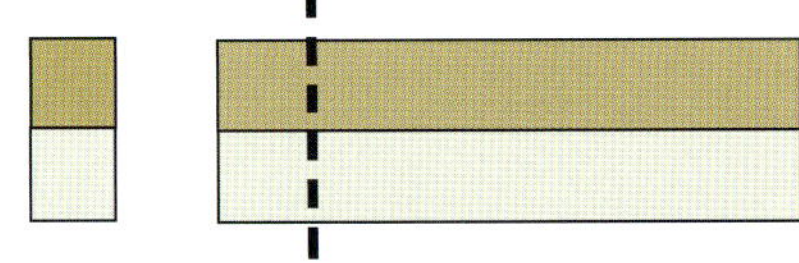

Make 36 BC square units.

3 Add squares to the end of eighteen BC square units:
Sew one 2 1/2"X 2 1/2" Fabric A square to either side of a BC square unit.

Make 18.

4 Select thirty-six 2 1/2" X 2 1/2" Fabric B squares and thirty-six 2 1/2" X 4 1/2" Fabric I rectangles.

- Place one Fabric B square on ***right*** side of the Fabric I rectangle and draw a diagonal line. Sew along line. Press back and cut away excess.

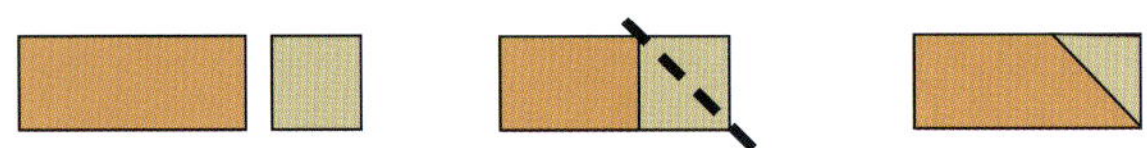

Make 36 IB rectangle units

5 Select thirty-six 2 1/2" X 2 1/2" Fabric C squares and thirty-six 2 1/2" X 4 1/2" Fabric I rectangles.

- Place one Fabric C square on the ***left*** side of the fabric I rectangle and draw a diagonal line. Sew along line. Press back and cut away excess.

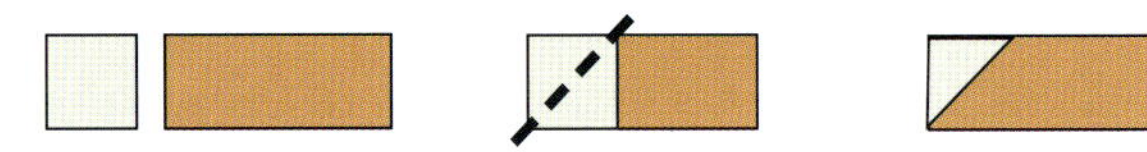

Make 36 of IC units.

6 Join the BI and CI units matching seams where triangle corners meet.

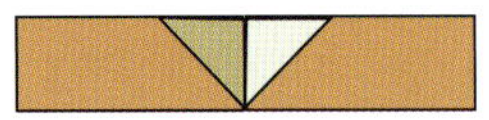

Make 36 BCI units. Set aside 18 BCI units.

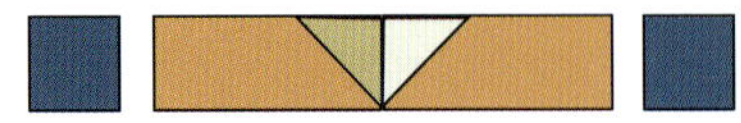

Sew one 2 1/2"X 2 1/2" Fabric G square to either side of 18 BCI units.

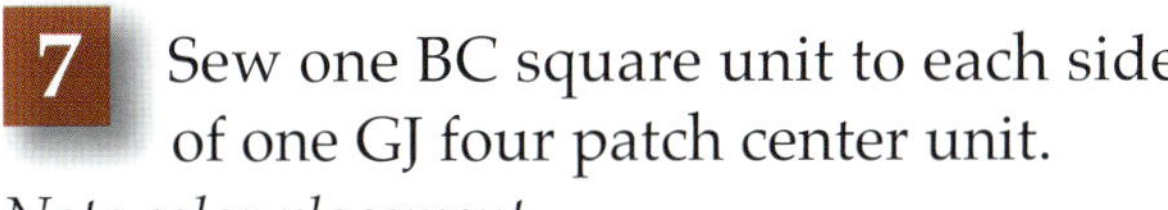

7 Sew one BC square unit to each side of one GJ four patch center unit.
Note color placement.

Make 9 BC-GJ four patch units.

8 Sew one 2½" X 2½" Fabric A square on each side of one BC square unit.
Note color placement.

Make 18 ABCA units.

9 Sew one ACBA square unit to each side of BC-GJ 4-patch units. Square to 8½".

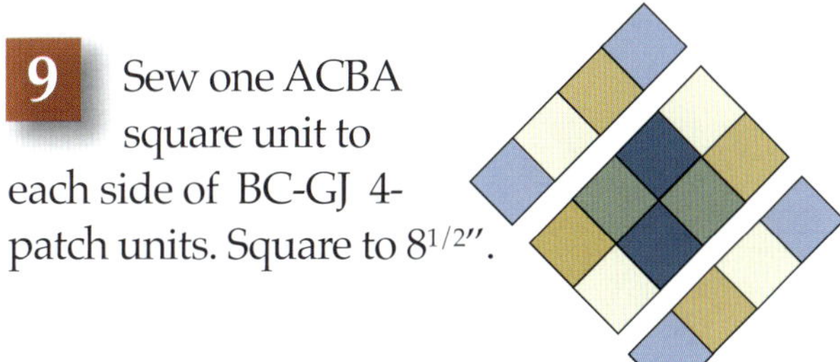

Make 9 for center blocks

10 Add the rectangle / triangle units: Sew one BCI rectangle unit to each side of the center block..

Make 9 units.

11 Sew Fabric G cornerstone rows to each side of the center block unit.

Square to 12½".

Complete 9 blocks

Assembling the Quilt Top

Refer to the illustration on Page 130 for the block setting. Work in diagonal rows.

For setting triangles use Fabric H. They will be slightly larger than needed. Trim excess away after sewing rows.

When joining rows match aligning seams.

Adding the Borders

- Sew one 1 1/2" X 51 1/2", Fabric F border strips to each side. Press. Add one 1 1/2" X 53 1/2" fabric F border strip to the top and bottom. Press.
- Repeat for the 2 1/2" X 53 1/2" Fabric G center borders. Sides first; then add the 2 1/2" X 57 1/2" top and bottom. Press.
- Repeat for the 5 1/2" X 57 1/2", Fabric D outer borders. Sides first; then add the 5 1/2" X 67 1/2" top and bottom. Press.

Finishing

Detailed finishing instructions on Page 7.

- Bind quilt using 8 strips of Fabric D.
- Sleeve and label your quilt.

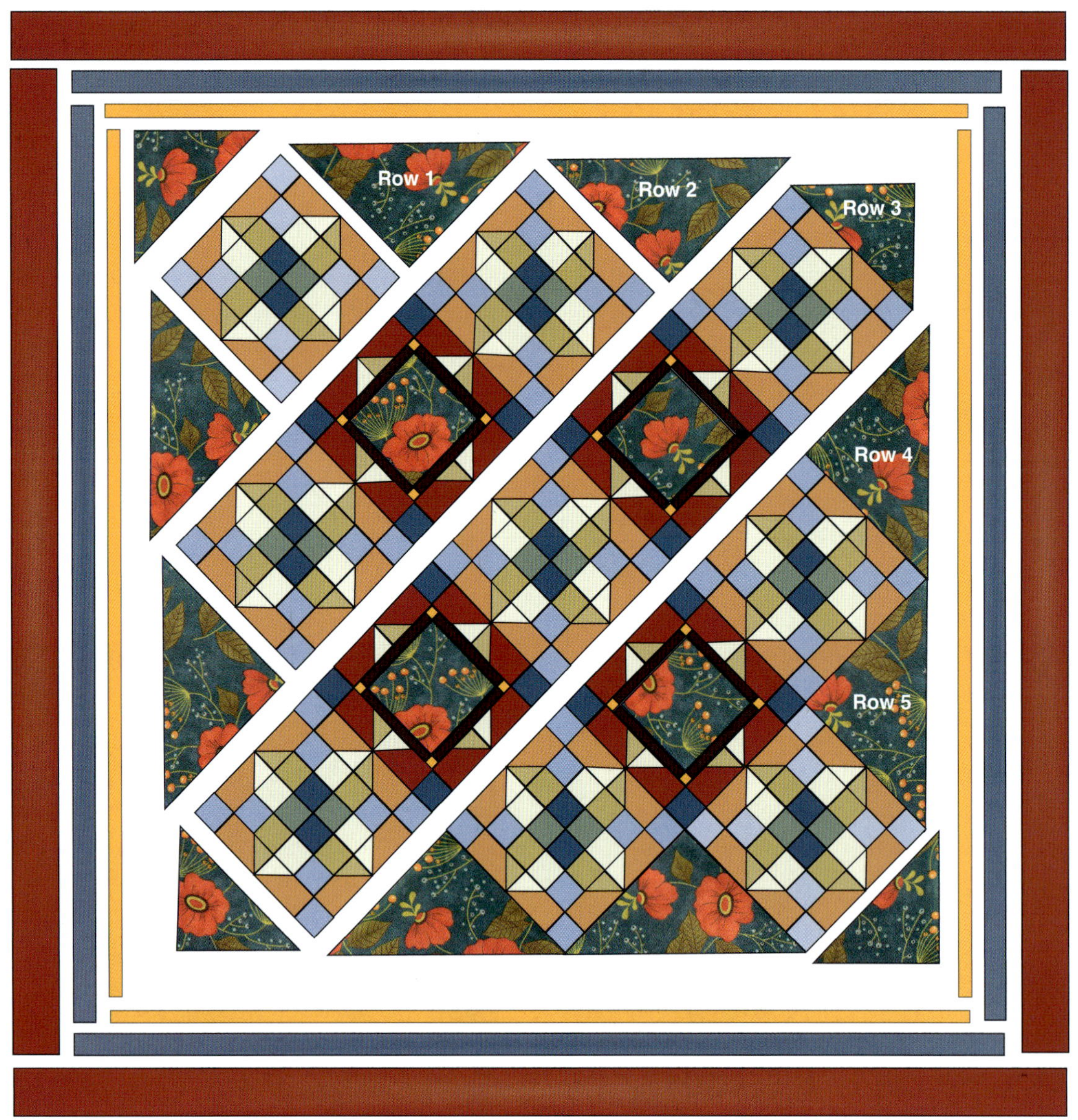

Scarlet Pinwheels

Designed and Pieced by Cynthia England

Quilted by Richard Larson

Scarlet Pinwheels

Finished Quilt Size: 57″ X 72″
Finished Traditional Block Size: $8^{1/2}$" X $8^{1/2}$"

Traditional Quilt Material Requirements

- **A** - Red/cream print for bkg............2 yards
- **B** - Dark red paisley............................1 yard
- **C** - Red..1 1/4 yards
  includes binding
- **D** - Medium red/cream .... 1 7/8 yard
- **E** - Red squiggly stripe...............2 1/2 yards
  includes setting triangles
- **Backing** - Something pretty!...........5 yards

Make a color chart for these fabrics as pictured in the Rotary Cutting Chart.

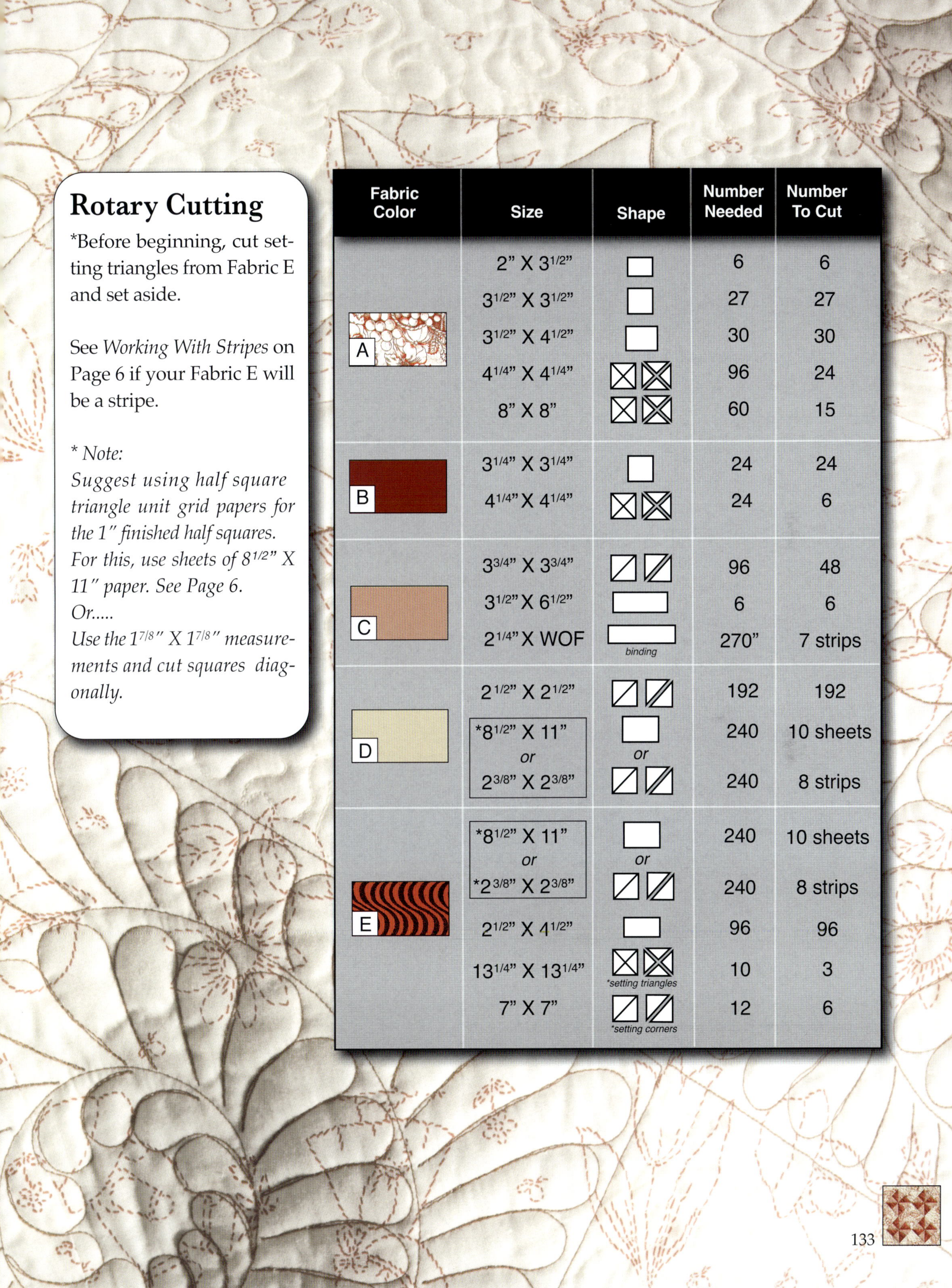

Rotary Cutting

*Before beginning, cut setting triangles from Fabric E and set aside.

See *Working With Stripes* on Page 6 if your Fabric E will be a stripe.

** Note:*
Suggest using half square triangle unit grid papers for the 1″ finished half squares. For this, use sheets of 8 1/2″ X 11″ paper. See Page 6.
Or.....
Use the 1 7/8″ X 1 7/8″ measurements and cut squares diagonally.

Fabric Color	Size	Shape	Number Needed	Number To Cut
A	2" X 3 1/2"	rectangle	6	6
	3 1/2" X 3 1/2"	square	27	27
	3 1/2" X 4 1/2"	rectangle	30	30
	4 1/4" X 4 1/4"	quarter-square triangles	96	24
	8" X 8"	quarter-square triangles	60	15
B	3 1/4" X 3 1/4"	square	24	24
	4 1/4" X 4 1/4"	quarter-square triangles	24	6
C	3 3/4" X 3 3/4"	half-square triangles	96	48
	3 1/2" X 6 1/2"	rectangle	6	6
	2 1/4" X WOF	binding	270"	7 strips
D	2 1/2" X 2 1/2"	half-square triangles	192	192
	*8 1/2" X 11"	rectangle	240	10 sheets
	or	or		
	2 3/8" X 2 3/8"	half-square triangles	240	8 strips
E	*8 1/2" X 11"	rectangle	240	10 sheets
	or	or		
	*2 3/8" X 2 3/8"	half-square triangles	240	8 strips
	2 1/2" X 4 1/2"	rectangle	96	96
	13 1/4" X 13 1/4"	quarter-square triangles (*setting triangles)	10	3
	7" X 7"	half-square triangles (*setting corners)	12	6

Traditional Block Info

At first glance it looks as if this is a two block quilt; not so. One block is in this design: Gentleman's Fancy. Pinwheels in the interior setting corners and the bars between the blocks create the unusual set.

Making the Pinwheels

Sew right sides together using a scant 1/4" seam allowance.

1 Make the half square units:
Using Fabric D and Fabric E make the 1 1/2" finished half square triangle units. Either use the triangle unit grid papers as described on Page 6 ... OR...
from 8 strips of each fabric cut 120 squares (2 3/8" X 2 3/8") once diagonally to yield 240 triangles. Sew right sides together. Press. Square to 2".

Make a total of 240 DE half square units.

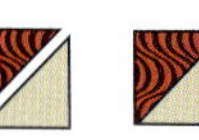

2 Sew two DE half square triangle units together. Match seams where they meet at the bottom. *Note block rotation. Choose half squares with the stripes facing the same direction for the each pinwheel.*

Make 120 DE half square pairs.

3 Sew two DE half square pairs together to create pinwheels. Match points.
Note block rotation.
Square to 3 1/2" X 3 1/2".

Make 60 DE pinwheels.

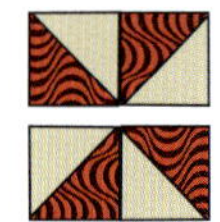
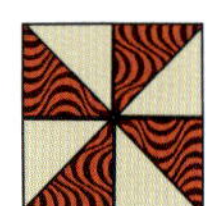

Gentleman's Fancy Blocks

Finished size: 8 1/2" X 8 1/2"

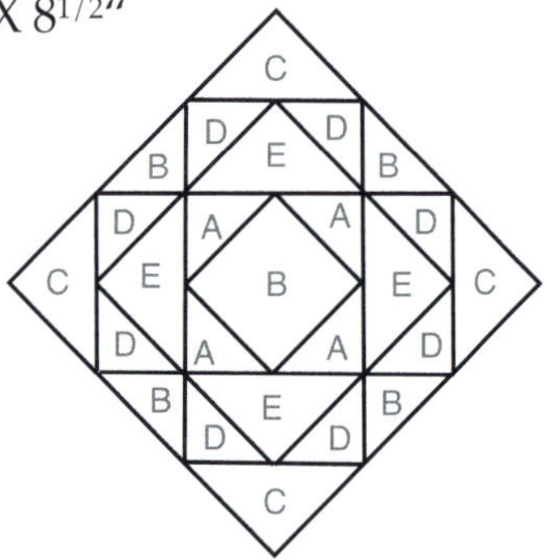

1 Sew one Fabric A triangle (quarter cut from 4 1/4" square) to opposite sides of one 3 1/4" Fabric B square.

Make 24.

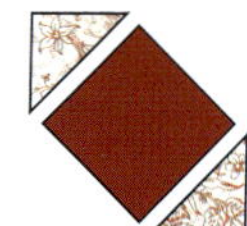
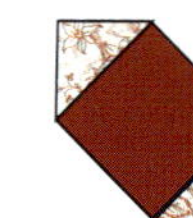

2 Repeat, sewing one Fabric A triangle to remaining sides of Fabric B square.
Square to 4 1/2" X 4 1/2".

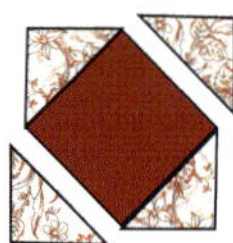
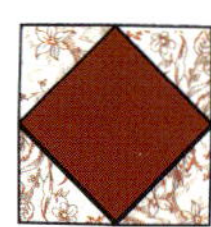

Make 24 AB units.

3 Make the flying geese units:
Draw a diagonal line on the back side of one 2 1/2" X 2 1/2" Fabric D square. Place on the right side of a 2 1/2" X 4 1/2" Fabric E rectangle. Sew along the line. Press back and trim away excess.

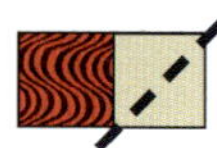

Make 96.

4 Repeat Step 6, sewing a 2 1/2″ X 2 1/2″ Fabric D square to the left side of the same 2 1/2″ X 4 1/2″ Fabric E rectangle. Sew along the line. Press back, trim away excess.

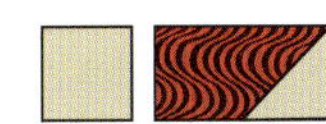
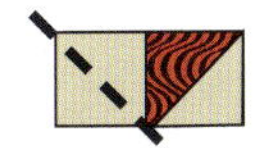

Make 96 DED flying geese units.

5 Sew one Fabric C triangle (from the diagonal cut 3 3/4″ square) to each flying geese unit.

Make 96 DEC units.

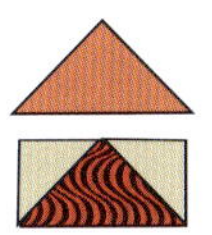

6 Sew one Fabric B triangle (from the diagonal cut 2 7/8″ square) to each flying geese unit.

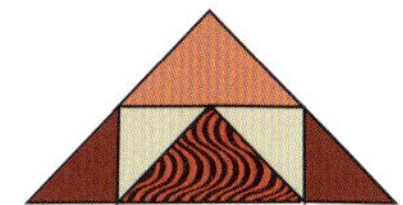

Make 48 corner units.

7 Sew one DEC unit to each side of one AB unit.

Make 24 units.

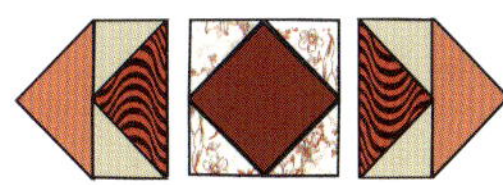

8 Sew one corner unit to the top and to the bottom.
Square to 9″ X 9″.

Complete 24 blocks.

Pinwheel Pieced Units

1 Sew one 3 1/2″ X 4 1/2″ Fabric A rectangle to one pinwheel.

Make 30 pinwheel units.

2 Sew one Fabric A triangle (quarter cut from 8″ square) to each side of one pinwheel unit. After sewing, trim along outside angles to form a point.

Make 30. Note block orientation.

3 Make the pinwheel rows:
Sew one 3 1/2″ X 6 1/2″ Fabric C rectangle to one 2″ X 3 1/2″ Fabric A rectangle.

Make 6 CA rectangle units.

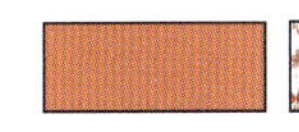

4 Sew one pinwheel to each side of one 3 1/2″ X 3 1/2″ Fabric A square.

Make 15 pinwheel units.

5 Make three pinwheel rows.
Refer to illustration on Page 136 for unit placement.

Assembling the Quilt Top

Use illustration below for block placement. Join Gentleman's Fancy block rows (Row 1, 3, 5 and 7) diagonally as shown. Note placement of setting and corner triangles. Sew one pinwheel row between block rows.

Finishing

- Bind quilt using 7 strips of Fabric C, cut 2 1/4" X WOF.
- Sleeve and label.

Detailed finishing instructions on Page 7.

Longing for the Lake

Designed and Pieced by Cynthia England　　Quilted by Denise Green

Longing for the Lake

Finished Quilt Size: 59″ X 73″
Finished Traditional Block Size: 9″ X 9″

Traditional Quilt Material Requirements

All fabrics in this quilt are batiks.

- **A** - Assorted dark blues.......................1 yard
- **B** - Assorted beiges......................1 1/4 yards
- **C** - Assorted light teal.....................1 yard
- **D** - Assorted medium blues........... 3/4 yard
- **E** - Assorted medium browns........3/4 yard
- **F** - Very light teal................................1 yard
- **G** - Medium dark blue.................1 1/2 yards
  includes sashing and binding
- **H** - Med. dark blue w/tan............1 1/4 yard
  includes setting triangles and corners
- **Backing** - Something pretty!...........5 yards

Make a color chart for these fabrics as pictured in the Rotary Cutting Chart.

Rotary Cutting

** Note:*
Suggest using half square triangle unit grid papers for the 1 1/8″ finished half squares. For this, use sheets of 8 1/2″ X 11″ paper. See Page 7.
Or.....
Use the 2″ X 2″ measurements and cut squares diagonally.

Fabric Color	Size	Shape	Number Needed	Number To Cut
A	*8 1/2" X 11"	rectangle	484	7 sheets
	or	*or*		
	*2" X 2"	half-square triangles	484	242
B	*8 1/2" X 11"	rectangle	242	7 sheets
	or	*or*		
	*2" X 2"	half-square triangles	242	121
	1 5/8" X 1 5/8"	square	40	40
	2 3/4" X 3 7/8"	rectangle	8	8
	4 1/4" X 4 1/4"	half-square triangles	24	12
C	*8 1/2" X 11"	rectangle	242	7 sheets
	or	*or*		
	*2" X 2"	half-square triangles	242	121
	1 5/8" X 1 5/8"	square	40	40
	4 1/4" X 4 1/4"	half-square triangles	24	12
D	4 1/4" X 4 1/4"	half-square triangles	70	35
E	4 1/4" X 4 1/4"	half-square triangles	70	35
F	3 7/8" X 6 1/8"	rectangle	6	6
	6 1/8" X 9 1/2"	rectangle	6	6
	9 1/2" X 9 1/2"	square	4	4
G	1 1/2" X WOF	strip (*sashing)	783"	20 strips
	*2 1/4" X WOF	strip (*binding)	274"	7 strips
H	16 3/4" X 16 3/4"	quarter-square triangles (setting triangles)	14	4
	8 3/4" X 8 3/4"	half-square triangles (corners)	4	2

Traditional Block Info

There are three different blocks in this design.

Center Blocks..2 needed

Alternate Pieced Blocks.........................6 needed

Prickly Pear Blocks..............................20 needed
6 light, 14 dark

Making the Center Blocks

Sew right sides together using a scant 1/4" seam allowance.

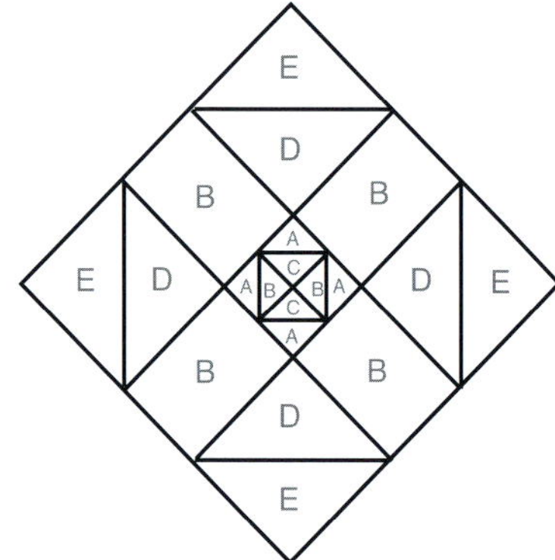

1 Select seventy Fabric E triangles (diagonally cut from the 4 1/4" squares) and seventy Fabric D triangles (diagonally cut from the 4 1/4" squares). Sew together to make 70 half square triangle units. Square to 3 7/8" X 3 7/8".

Make 70 DE half square triangle units. Set aside 56.

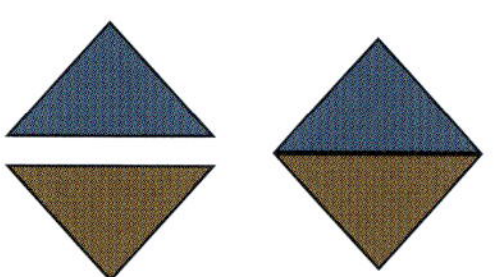

2 Sew 1 DE half square triangle unit to each side of one 2 3/4" X 3 7/8" Fabric B rectangle.

Note color positions.

Make 4 DEB rows.

3 Select one Fabric A triangle (diagonally cut from the 2" square) and one Fabric B triangle (diagonally cut from the 2" square). Sew together to make one half square triangle unit. Square to 1 5/8" X 1 5/8".

Make 4 AB half square triangle units.

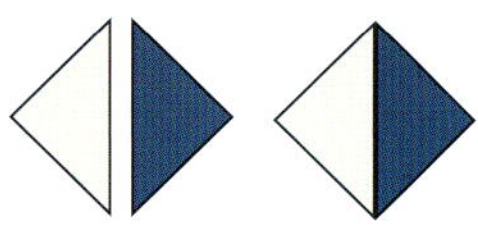

4 Select one Fabric A triangle (diagonally cut from the 2" square) and one Fabric C triangle (diagonally cut from the 2" square). Sew together to make one half square triangle unit. Square to 1 5/8" X 1 5/8".

Make 4 AC half square triangle units.

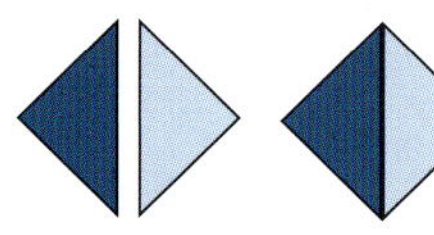

5 Sew two AB units and two AC units together to make one ABC unit.

Square to 2 3/4" X 2 3/4".

Make 2.

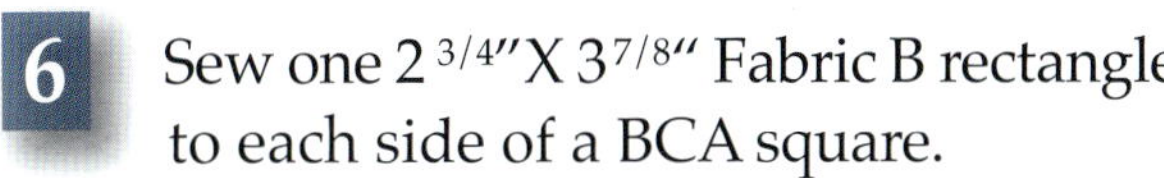

6 Sew one 2 3/4" X 3 7/8" Fabric B rectangle to each side of a BCA square.

Make 2 rows.

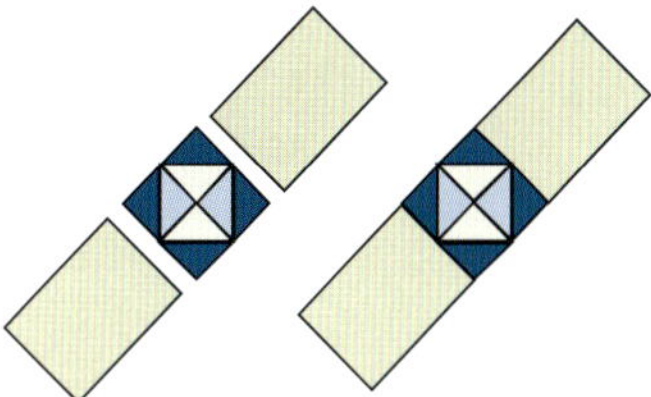

7 Sew one BDE row to each side of a BCA row to complete center blocks. Square to 9 1/2" X 9 1/2".

Complete 2 blocks.

Alternate Pieced Blocks

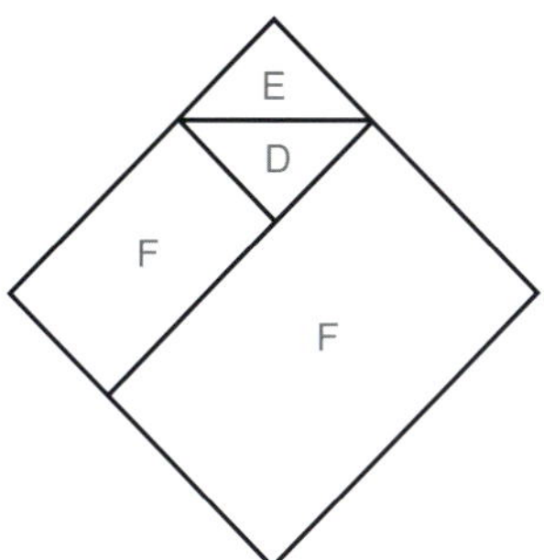

1 Sew one DE half square triangle unit to one 3 7/8" X 6 1/8" Fabric F rectangle.

Make 6 rows.

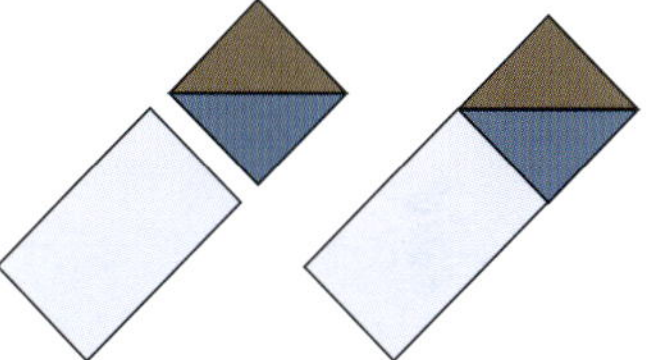

2 Sew one DEF row to one 6 1/8" X 9 1/2" Fabric F rectangle to complete the Alternate Pieced Blocks. Square to 9 1/2" X 9 1/2".

Make 6 blocks.

Canyon Lake, Texas *Photo by Cynthia England*

Light Prickly Pear Blocks

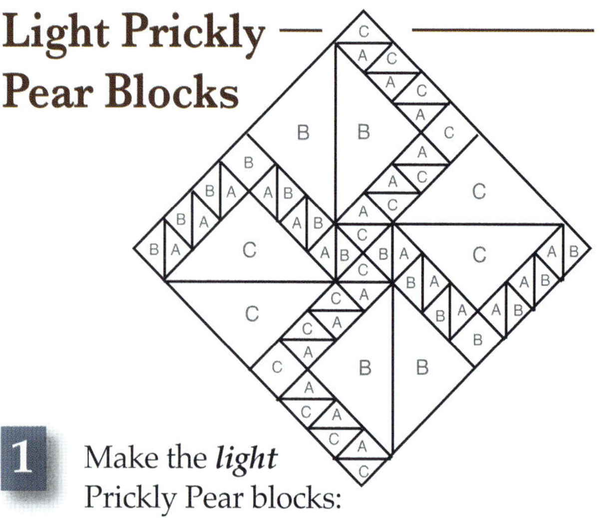

1 Make the ***light*** Prickly Pear blocks:
Select a variety of twenty-four Fabric C triangles (diagonally cut from the 4 1/4″ squares) and sew together to make 12 squares. Vary colors. Square to 3 7/8″ X 3 7/8″.

Make 12 fabric C half square triangle units.

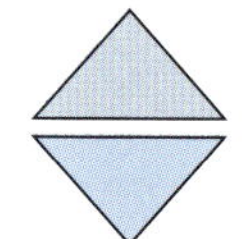 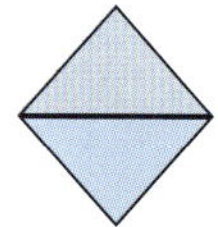

2 Repeat step one. This time, using a variety of twenty-four Fabric B triangles (diagonally cut from the 4 1/4″ squares) and sew together to make 12 squares. Vary colors. Square to 3 7/8″ X 3 7/8″.

Make 12 fabric B half square triangle units.

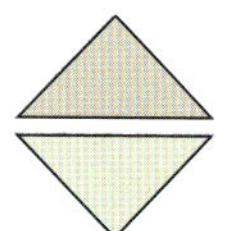 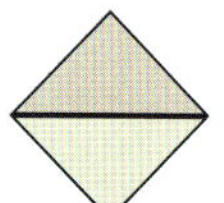

3 Make the half square units:
Using Fabric A, Fabric B and Fabric C make the 1 1/8″ finished half square triangle units. Either use the triangle unit grid papers as described on Page 6, ... OR... cut 120 2″ X 2″ squares of Fabric B and Fabric C once diagonally. Cut 240 2″ X 2″ squares of Fabric A once diagonally. Square to 1 5/8″.

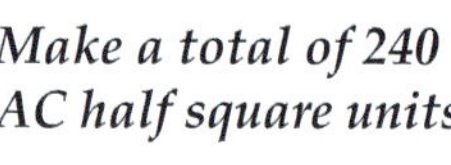

Make a total of 240 AC half square units.

Make a total of 240 AB half square units.

4 Sew three AC half square triangle units in a row. Sew three going in the other direction. *Note diagram for color placement.*

 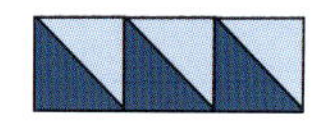

Make 12 AC triangle rows of each.

5 Repeat step four. This time, using Fabric AB half square triangle units. *Note diagram for color placement.*

 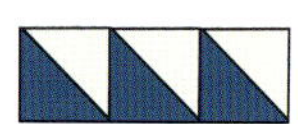

Make 12 AB triangle rows of each.

6 Sew one row of three half square triangles to the side of 12 Fabric B squares.

Make 12 AB units.

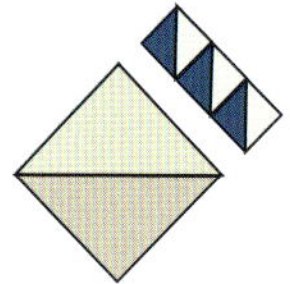 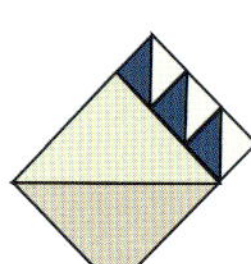

Repeat for AC units.

Make 12 AC units.

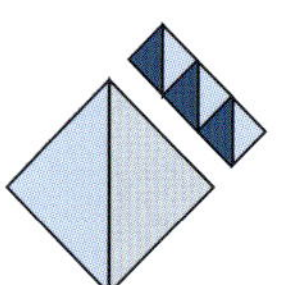 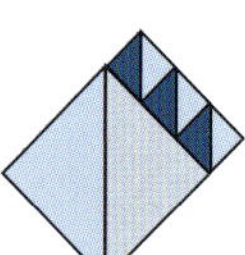

7 Sew one 1 5/8″ X 1 5/8″ Fabric B square to the end of 12 AB sets of three half square triangles. Repeat for AC units, using one Fabric C square.

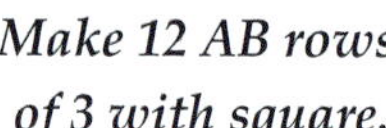

Make 12 AB rows of 3 with square.

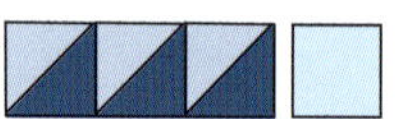

Make 12 AC rows of 3 with square.

8 Sew one AB row with square to AB units. Repeat using AC units. *Follow diagram, note placement.*
Square to 5".
Make 12 of each.

9 Sew one AB unit to one AC unit. *Note color placement and block orientation.*

Make 12 pairs.

10 Sew two AB/AC pair units together to complete the ***Light*** Prickly Pear block.
Square to 9 1/2" X 9 1/2".

Complete 6 blocks.

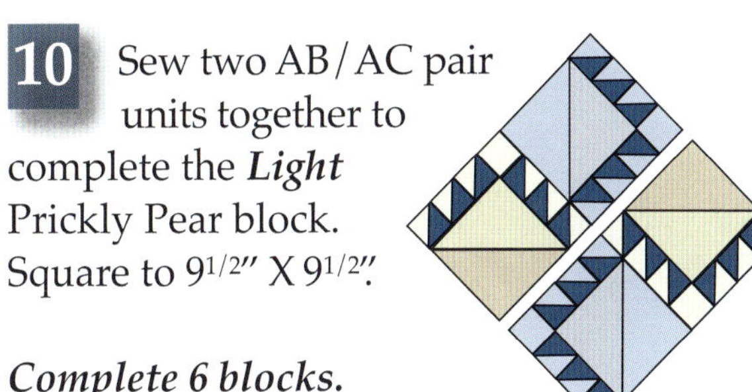

Frame the Maple Leaf blocks (Page 23) with additional background fabric for a totally different look.

Dark Prickly Pear Blocks

This step uses the DE half square units that were set aside in Step 1 on Page 140. Repeat steps 4-10 of the Light Prickly Pear blocks on the previous page to complete the Dark Prickly Pear blocks.
Note color placement and block orientation.

Square to 9 1/2" X 9 1/2".

Complete 14 blocks.

Sashing

Very important!
Place the blocks according to layout on Page 144.

- From ten Fabric G 1 1/2" X WOF strips cut forty 1 1/2" X 9 1/2" sashing strips.
- Using Fabric H large triangles, blocks and Fabric G sashing strips assemble rows 1-8 according to layout on Page 144.
- Sew the remaining ten Fabric G 1 1/2" X WOF strips together short end to short end. Measure each row and cut sashing strips to size.

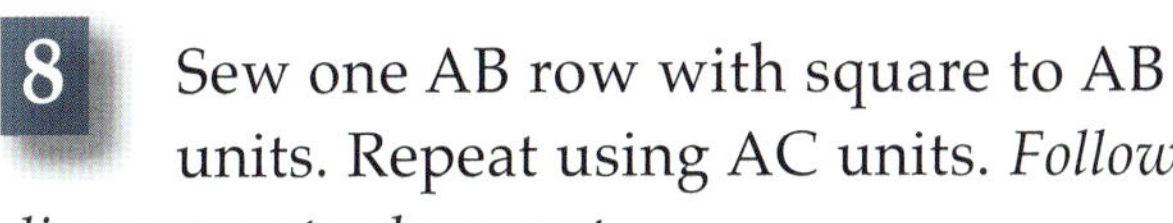

Assembling the Quilt Top

Use illustration below for block placement.

- Join rows diagonally.
- Add small Fabric H triangles to each of the four corners last.
- Press as you go.

Finishing

- Bind quilt using 7 strips of Fabric G, cut 2 1/4" X WOF.
- Sleeve and label.

Detailed finishing instructions on Page 7.

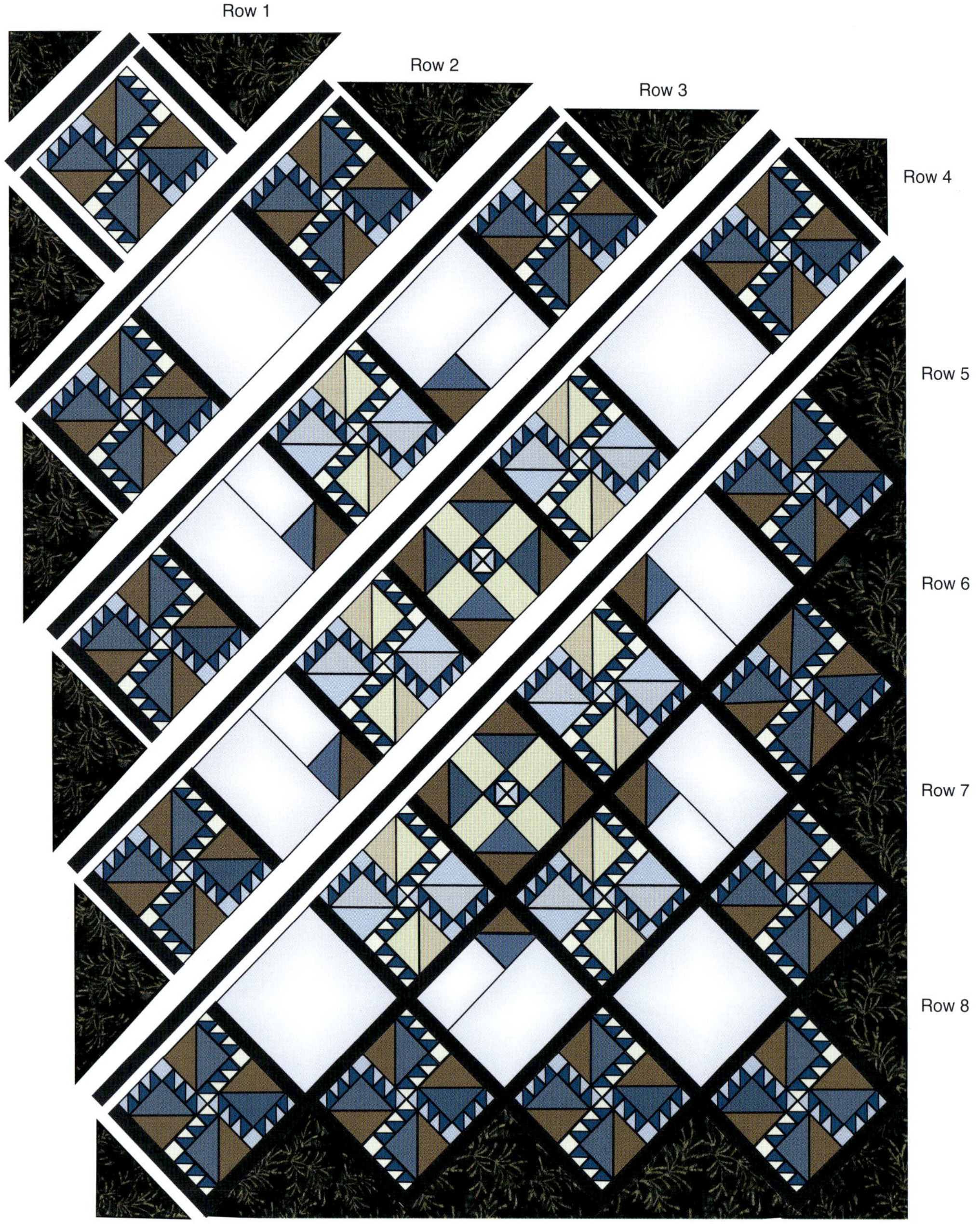

Apple Core

Designed and Pieced by Cynthia England

Quilted by Denise Green

Apple Core

Finished Quilt Size: 51″ X 51″
Finished Traditional Block Size: 6″ X 6″

Traditional Quilt Material Requirements

- **A** - Gold..1 yard
- **B** - Red print.................................... 1 2/3 yard
  Includes borders
- **C** - Dark red.......................................1 1/2 yard
  Includes binding
- **D** - Blue..1 1/3 yard
- **E** - Focus print......................................1 yard
- **Backing** - Something pretty!......3 1/2 yards

Make a color chart for these fabrics as pictured in the Rotary Cutting Chart.

Rotary Cutting

*Before beginning, cut outside setting triangles, borders and binding. Set aside.

** Note:*
Suggest using half square triangle unit grid papers for the 1″ finished half squares. For this, use sheets of $8^{1/2}$″ X 11″ paper with Fabric B facing Fabric D. See Page 6. Or.....
Use the $1^{7/8}$″ X $1^{7/8}$″ measurements and cut squares and cut diagonally.

Fabric Color	Size	Shape	Number Needed	Number To Cut
A	$1^{7/8}$" X $1^{7/8}$"		96	48
	2" X 2"		12	12
	$7^{1/2}$" X $7^{1/2}$"		5	5
	9" X 9"	*side setting	4	2
	$8^{7/8}$" X $8^{7/8}$"	corners	4	1
B	$1^{1/2}$" X $1^{1/2}$"		32	32
	*$8^{1/2}$" X 11" or *$1^{7/8}$" X $1^{7/8}$"	or	256 / 256	7 sheets or 7 strips
	$4^{1/4}$" X WOF	*side setting	12	6 strips
C	$1^{1/2}$" X $7^{1/2}$"		10	10
	$1^{1/2}$" X $9^{1/2}$"		10	10
	1" X WOF	setting	12	6 strips
	$1^{1/4}$" X WOF	setting	12	4 strips
	$1^{1/2}$" X $1^{1/2}$"		96	96
	$1^{7/8}$" X $1^{7/8}$"		48	24
	$2^{1/4}$" X WOF	*binding	220"	6 strips
D	$1^{7/8}$" X $1^{7/8}$"		96	48
	*$8^{1/2}$" X 11" or *$1^{7/8}$" X $1^{7/8}$"	or	256 / 256	7 sheets / 7 strips
E	$5^{1/4}$" X $5^{1/4}$"		48	12
	$4^{1/2}$" X $9^{1/2}$"		16	16

Making the Framed Blocks —

Sew right sides together using a scant 1/4″ seam allowance.

1 Begin with the framed blocks: Select one Fabric A, 7 1/2″ X 7 1/2″ square and two Fabric C, 1 1/2″ X 7 1/2″ strips. Sew one strip to either side of the square.

Make 5.

2 Add the Fabric C 1 1/2″ X 9 1/2″ strips to the top and bottom of the square unit. Square to 9 1/2″ X 9 1/2″.

Complete 5 Framed Gold Blocks.

The Apple Core quilt uses the same setting as the Field of Violets quilt on Page 101. The Violet block was replaced with a traditional block and the green chain block was switched out with a framed block. This timeless diagonal set would also look beautiful with a collection of traditional sampler 6″ finished blocks!

Ruby Chain Blocks

Finished Size: 6″ X 6″

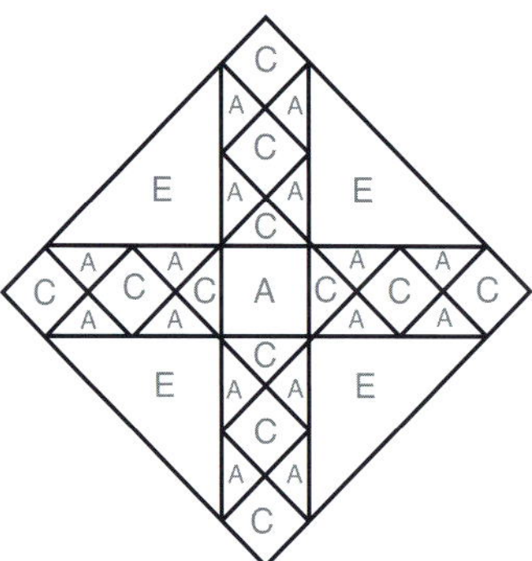

1 Select two 1 1/2″ X 1 1/2″ Fabric C squares, two small triangles of Fabric A and two small triangles of Fabric D and one small triangle of Fabric C (from the 1 7/8″ diagonally cut squares).
Construct unit as pictured.

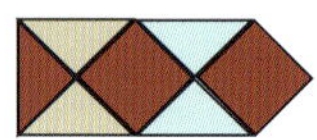

Make 48 CAD units.

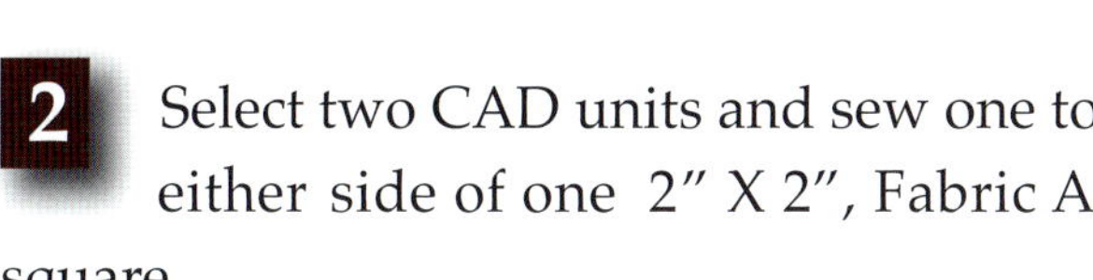

2 Select two CAD units and sew one to either side of one 2" X 2", Fabric A square.

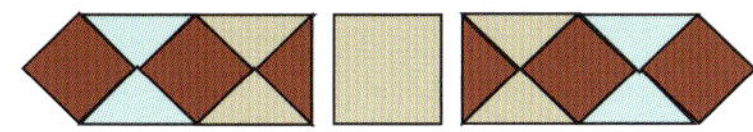

Make 12 units.

3 Select two Focus print triangles (from the 5 1/4" quarter cut squares) and sew one to either side of a CAD unit.

Make 24 units with the triangles on either side.

4 Sew two triangle units to either side of one CAD unit. Square to 6 1/2" X 6 1/2".

Complete 12 Ruby Chain blocks.

Sashing Units

1 Make the sashing half square units: Using Fabric B and Fabric D, make the **1" finished** half square triangle units. Either use the triangle unit grid papers as described on Page 6 ... OR... from 7 strips of each fabric cut 128 squares (1 7/8" X 1 7/8") once diagonally to yield 256 triangles. Sew right sides together. Press. Square to 1 1/2".

Make a total of 256 half square triangle units.

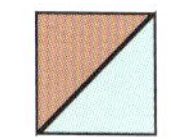

2 Make the sashing row units: Select one Fabric B 1 1/2" X 1 1/2" square and eight 1 1/2" X 1 1/2" BD half square triangles. Sew four on either side of the square. Follow placement in illustration reversing direction in center.

Make a total of 32 sashing row units.

3 Make the sashing row blocks: Select one Fabric E 4 1/2" X 9 1/2" and two of the sashing row units. Sew one to the top and one to the bottom. Make sure to place the Fabric D triangles next to Fabric E rectangle. Fold the rectangle in half and press. Use that center mark to line up the center of the squares in the rows. Square to 6 1/2" X 9 1/2".

Make a total of 16 sashing blocks.

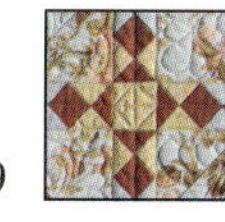

Side Setting Units

1 Make the side setting units: Sew one **1 1/4"** X WOF Fabric C to one 4 1/4" X WOF Fabric B. Press. *Note 1 1/4" width.*

Sew two strips as pictured X WOF.

2 Select one Fabric A triangle (from the 9" diagonally cut squares). Sew strip to long side of triangle and trim following the lines out from the triangle.

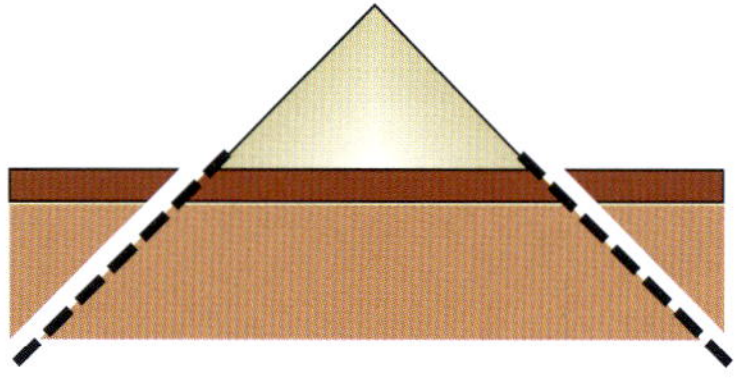

Make 4 side setting units.

3 Sew one **1"** Fabric C strip along right side of triangle matching top edge. Press. Add another 1" Fabric C strip to the left side matching top edge. After pressing, trim off excess along triangle bottom. *Note 1" width.*

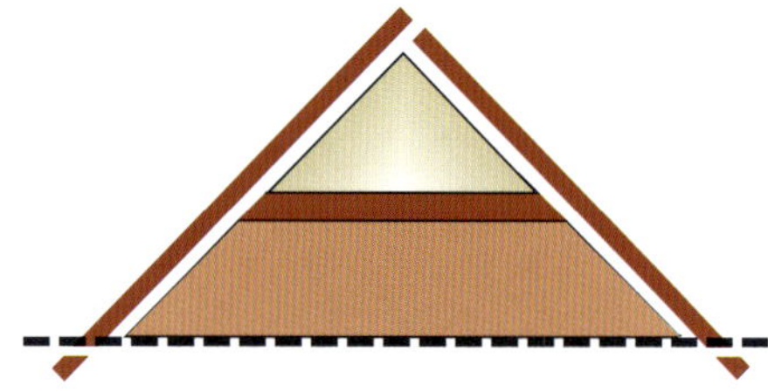

Complete 4 side setting units.

Corner Setting Units

1 Make the corner setting units: Select one 8 7/8" Fabric A quarter cut square and sew one **1 1/4"** Fabric C strip to right side of triangle matching top edge. Press. Add another 1 1/4" Fabric C strip the left side matching top edge. After pressing, trim off excess along triangle bottom. *Note 1 1/4" width.*

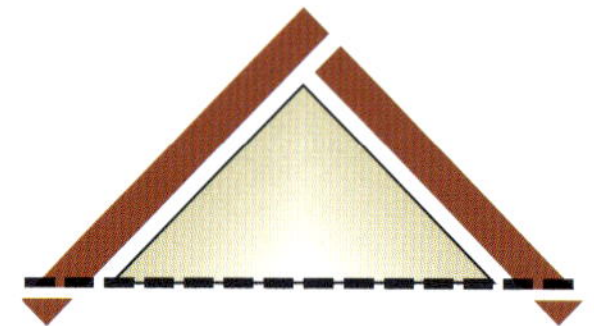

Make 4.

2 Repeat the strip process, using 4 1/4" X WOF Fabric B. Press. Trim away excess Fabric B along bottom.

3 Sew **1"** X WOF Fabric C strip along bottom setting corner unit. Trim away along angle after pressing. *Note 1" width.*

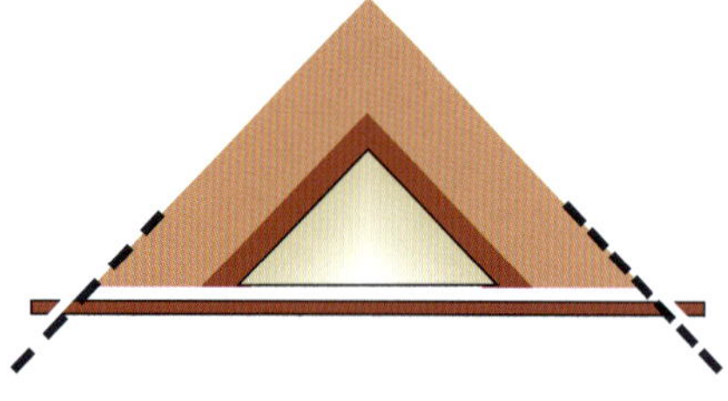

Complete 4 Corner setting units.

Assembling the Quilt Top

Refer to the illustration below for the block setting. Work in diagonal rows.
When joining rows match aligning seams.

Finishing

Detailed finishing instructions in on Page 7.

- Bind quilt using 6 strips of Fabric C, cut $2^{1/4}$" X WOF.
- Sleeve and label your quilt.

Glossary/Index

A listing of terms used in this book.
Page references are in italic.

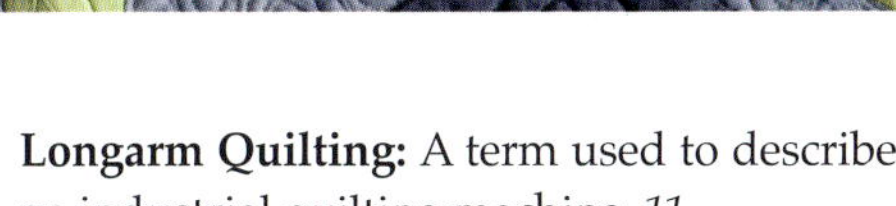

Longarm Quilting: A term used to describe an industrial quilting machine. *11*

M

Master Pattern: Refers to the Picture Piecing pattern that you look at while constructing the block. *23, 24, 57, 92*

Mitering: Joining a seam at a 45 degree angle. Used for borders and binding. *9*

Monofilament Thread: A thin clear thread used for machine quilting. *11*

N

Nine Patch: Nine squares sewn in three rows. *105*

O

On-Point: Taking a square block and turning it 45-degrees in a quilt setting. Associated with a Diagonal set. *8*

P

Pairs: A Picture Piecing term used to describe two pattern pieces which share a common seam. *25*

Paper Piecing: A common quilting technique where you sew through paper while working on the wrong side. Stitch length is reduced. *19*

Pattern Notations, *21*

Picture Piecing: The sewing technique developed by Cynthia England as described in this book. In this technique freezer paper is used as templates. While sewing, fabric faces right sides together. Regular 1/4" stitch length is used. Sew next to paper, not through. No paper to pick out. *19*

Pinwheel, *134*

Pre-sewing: A Picture Piecing term, used as a way of speeding up the sewing process. *22*

Projects:
African Violets, *89, 126*
Apple Core, *145*
Aunt Wanda's Violets, *83*
Autumn Leaves, *49*
Canadian Maple Leaf, *33*
Christine's Rose Garden, *67*
Corbin Gold Rush, *101, 107, 109*
Falling Leaves, *33, 43*
Field of Violets, *101, 148*
Hot Pink Roses, *55*
Indigo Lights, *78, 115*
Longing for the Lake, *108, 137*
Maple Leaf Runner, *39, 101, 107*
Scarlet Pinwheels, *101, 107, 131*
Southern Cross, *123*
Sweetheart Roses, *75, 118*
Windswept Roses, *54, 61*

Q

Quarter Square Triangle: A square that has been cut diagonally twice. When the square is cut you get four triangles with the long edge of the triangle on the straight of grain, not on the bias. *41, 134*

Quilt Artists:
Gabriel, Rhonda, *33, 43*
Green, Denise, *inside back cover, 12, 34, 43, 49, 61, 67, 89, 115, 119, 123, 137, 145*
Larson, Richard, *cover, 12, 75, 83, 101, 104, 109, 131*
Stockton, Ronda, *39, 123*

R

Redwork: An embroidery term for using only one thread color in the design. *107*

Rotary Mat: A surface to cut blocks and quilts on. Used with a Rotary Cutter. *5*

Rotary Cutter: A cutting tool that looks and works similar to a pizza cutter. Allows accurate cutting through more than one layer. *5*

S

Sashing/Spacer Bars: Typically fabric strips sewn between blocks. Can be any width, pieced or in a single strip. *32, 46*

Scant 1/4" Seam: A seam sewn about a pencil line's width smaller than 1/4". *36, 41, 46, 52, 59, 64, 70, 79, 96, 104, 112, 126, 134, 140, 148*

Serrated Scissors: *24*

Sewer's Ham: An ironing surface made to iron sleeves and collars. *5*

Sewing Sequence: A Picture Piecing term. Refers to the order in which the pattern pieces are sewn together. Unlike foundation piecing, chain stitching is encouraged. *5, 22, 56, 93*

Single-hole Needleplate: Refers to the metal plate directly under the needle. Most machines come with a wide needleplate hole which allows zig-zag stitching. This needleplate only allows the needle to go up and down. *5*

Stay Stitching: A single line of stitching through one layer to prevent distortion. *11*

Stem Stitch: An embroidery stitch used to add details to the blocks. *7*

Stitch-in-the Ditch: A quilting term for sewing on top of a seam. Quilting is not visible and doesn't require marking. *13*

Straight Set: A quilt where blocks are joined in rows horizontally. *7*

Strip Sewing: Sewing strips right sides together with a 1/4" seam allowance. Helps speed up the sewing process and is usually more accurate. *22*

Strip Set: A quilt where blocks are joined vertically in long strips. *7*

Strip Stick: A handy pressing stick for ironing seams. *5*

Subcut: After sewing and pressing two or more fabric strips together along the length of the strips, patches are then subcut (cut into smaller patches) from that strip. *65, 79*

Square: After a quilt or block is sewn the outside edges are usually slightly uneven. To straighten, the block is placed on a rotary

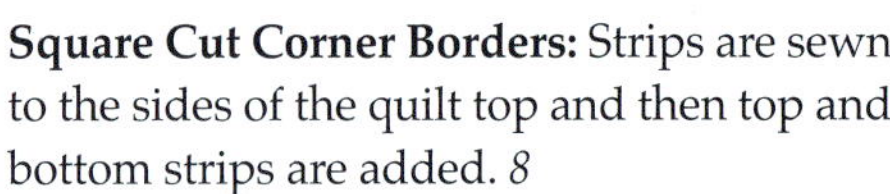

Square Cut Corner Borders: Strips are sewn to the sides of the quilt top and then top and bottom strips are added. *8*

T

Template Plastic: Clear plastic used for making quilt templates. *31, 58, 94*

Tighten Up: A Picture Piecing troubleshooting term which suggests sewing closer so that the paper touches. *32*

Triangle Grid Papers: A technique to speed up sewing half square triangles. A computer disc has the information compiled to print triangles required. Print triangle size needed and cut two fabrics each 8 1/2" X 11" . Fabrics are placed right side together. Printed triangle paper is placed on top. Sew along lines as indicated. Cut on the lines and press. *6*

Triangle Rolls: Works the same way as the triangle grid papers except you work on a purchased roll of thin paper and sew through the lines. *6*

Trim Guide: Picture Piecing blocks are intentionally oversized. Use this Trim Guide for information on how much space to leave around the image when squaring. *31, 58, 94*

Troubleshooting: *30, 32*

W

Walking Foot: A sewing machine foot attachment which helps feed the fabric from the top and bottom evenly. *13*

Wonder Clips: Small gadget similar to a clothes pin used to hold down binding. *13*

WOF: An abbreviation for "width of fabric". Cotton fabric typically comes on bolts which are 42-44" in width. *35, 42, 48, 53, 88, 100, 106, 136, 144, 147, 151*

Z

Zig Zag Lines: A Picture Piecing pattern notion which indicates a stem-stitch embroidery detail. *23, 58, 94*

Resource Listing

Bear Paw Productions / Brenda Henning
P.O. Box 230589
Anchorage, AK 99523-0589
www.bearpawproductions.com

Clover Needlecraft, Inc.
1441 S Carlos Avenue
Ontario, California 91761 USA
www.clover-usa.com

Fairfield Processing Corp.
P.O. Box 1157
Danbury, CT 06813--1157
www.fairfieldworld.com

Hobbs Bonded Fibers
200 South Commerce Drive
Waco, TX 76710
www.hobbsbondedfibers.com

Hoffman California / International Fabrics
25792 Obrero Drive
Mission Viejo, CA 92691-3140
www.hoffmanfabrics.com

Island Batiks
2719B Loker Ave.
Carlesbad, CA 92008
www.islandbatik.com

HollyDee Quilts / Denise Green
hollydeequilts.wordpress.com
Facebook page: HollyDee Quilts
hollydeequilts@gmail.com

Karen K. Buckley - Perfect Scissors
1237 Holly Pike
Carlisle, PA 17013
www.karenkaybuckley.com

Knockout Designs / Peri Gabriel
426 Newport Drive
Naperville, IL 60565
www.knockoutbooks.com

Omnigrid / Prym Consumer USA Inc.
P.O. Box 5028
Spartanburg, SC 29304
www.dritz.com

PCP Group, LLC
2650 Gandy Blvd N.
St. Petersburg, FL 33702
www.PellonProjects.com

Quilting Design Studio / Richard Larson
1939 Sussex Drive
Carrollton, TX 75007
(972) 422-0768
www.qdstudio.com

Quilter's Dream Batting
589 Central Drive
Virginia, Beach, VA 23454
www.quiltersdreambatting.com

Scarlet Today / Redwork*plus*
Rosie deLeon-McCrady
(800) 578-2027
(512) 750-3258
www.redworkplus.com

The Strip Stick
1301 3rd Street
Vidor, TX 77662
(409) 656-3013
www.thestripstick.com

Superior Threads
87 East 2580 South
St. George, UT 84790
www.superiorthreads.com

Timeless Treasures
483 Broadway
New York, NY 1003
www.ttfabrics.com

The Quilters

Awesome! Spectacular! Mindblowing! These are some of the adjectives I would use to describe the work of the two quilters whose quilting grace the pages of this book. Both of these talented quilters use hand guided quilting; no computer programs for them! As you thumb through this book you will be amazed at their exceptional skill.

Denise Green

I am lucky enough to be in the same quilt guild with Denise: The Lakeview Quilt Guild, in Houston, TX. She is the local expert in all things longarm related.

Denise studies a quilt and allows it to "speak" to her. Her goal is to enhance what the quiltmaker has started, while not overpowering it with quilting. She can turn an ordinary quilt into one that is extraordinary!

She began her longarm business called Holly Dee Quilts in 2000. She teaches quilting and is a "Certified Judy Niemeyer Instructor". As a creative and engaging teacher she enjoys traveling to quilt guilds and shops to lecture and give classes.

HollyDee Quilts 281-224-6825
hollydeequilts.wordpress.com
Facebook page: HollyDee Quilts
hollydeequilts@gmail.com

Richard Larson

Ever been to a quilt show and you keep seeing the same name over and over again? That is how I met Richard. At the Dallas Quilt show there must have been at least 30 stunning quilts that he had quilted; each and every one beautifully crafted.

He began sewing at the early age of six. Richard graduated from Wades Fashion Merchandising College and obtained a degree in Fashion Design and Textiles.

Richard got into the longarm profession after making an appliqué quilt top. He sent it off to be quilted and was not satisfied with the results. So, he opened his own quilting studio and has been delighting his customers since 1997.

He was honored as one of the *Top 5 Longarm Quilters of the 21st Century* by American Quilters Society. Richard is proud to point out that he uses no computer *or* stitch regulator. Everything you see is all Richard.
Check his website for classes.

Quilting Design Studio 972-422-0768
1939 Sussex Drive
Carrollton, TX 75007
www.qdstudio.com

About the Author

Cynthia England began quilting at the age of 13 and created her first quilts from a box of her grandmother's stash. Essentially, a self taught quilter, Cynthia soon became obsessed with the craft and has now been creating quilts for more than forty years.

Photo by Mariam Khalili

After Cynthia graduated from the Art Institute of Houston, she applied her artistic background to her quilting. Experimentation with craft and quilting techniques led her to develop her own original technique, known as Picture Piecing.

Cynthia's quilts have been honored with many awards, including two Best of Show wins at the prestigious International Quilt Association. Her quilt, *Piece and Quiet* was distinguished as one of the 100 Best Quilts of the 20th Century. In addition to winning 1st place ribbons at local and national quilting events since 1991, Cynthia's stunning quilts have graced the pages of many quilting publications. Visit the gallery on her website to see more of her work.

After developing her Picture Piecing technique, Cynthia founded her company, England Design, a publishing and pattern company that specializes in Picture Piecing.

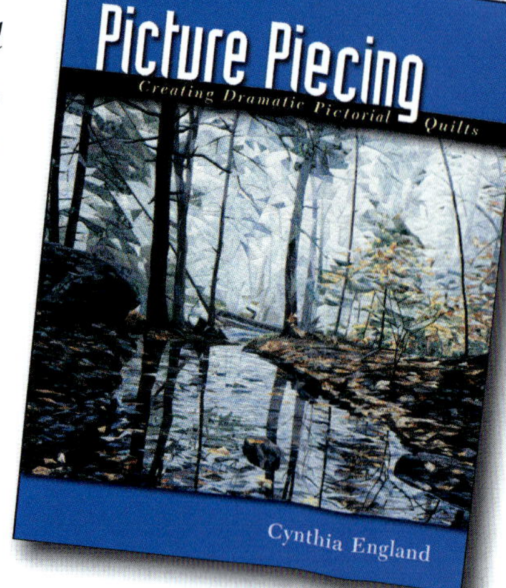

Her book, *Picture Piecing - Creating Pictorial Quilts*, is now in it's third printing. The book explains how to use a captivating photograph to create your own pattern for a realistic quilt.

Although her hallmark is realistically detailed pictorial quilts, Cynthia still loves to make traditional quilts. She frequently combines the traditional with the pictorial, as you will discover in this book, *Picture Piecing Traditional Quilts.*

Cynthia teaches and lectures nationally and internationally. Visit Cynthia's website at www.englanddesign.com to check out her teaching and show schedule. She may be at a show or a guild near you soon.